God's Court and Courtiers in the Book of the Watchers

God's Court and Courtiers in the Book of the Watchers

Re-interpreting Heaven in 1 Enoch 1–36

PHILIP F. ESLER

CASCADE Books • Eugene, Oregon

GOD'S COURT AND COURTIERS IN THE BOOK OF THE WATCHERS
Re-interpreting Heaven in 1 Enoch 1–36

Copyright © 2017 Philip F. Esler. All rights reserved. Except for brief quotations in critical publications or reviews, no part of this book may be reproduced in any manner without prior written permission from the publisher. Write: Permissions, Wipf and Stock Publishers, 199 W. 8th Ave., Suite 3, Eugene, OR 97401.

Cascade Books
An Imprint of Wipf and Stock Publishers
199 W. 8th Ave., Suite 3
Eugene, OR 97401

www.wipfandstock.com

PAPERBACK ISBN: 978-1-62564-908-9
HARDCOVER ISBN: 978-1-4982-8582-7
EBOOK ISBN: 978-1-5326-4449-8

Cataloging-in-Publication data:

Names: Esler, Philip F. (Philip Francis), author.

Title: God's court and courtiers in the Book of the Watchers : re-interpreting heaven in 1 Enoch 1–36 / Philip F. Esler.

Description: Eugene, OR: Cascade Books | Includes bibliographical references and indexes.

Identifiers: ISBN: 978-1-62564-908-9 (PAPERBACK) | ISBN: 978-1-4982-8582-7 (HARD-COVER) | ISBN: 978-1-5326-4449-8 (EBOOK).

Subjects: LCSH: Ethiopic book of Enoch—Criticism, interpretation, etc. | Angels | Heaven—History of doctrines.

Classification: BS1830 E7 E85 2017 (print) | BS1830 E7 (ebook).

Manufactured in the U.S.A.   11/29/17

The cover photo is by Angus Pryor, who retains copyright. Used with permission.

To Angus Pryor

CONTENTS

Acknowledgments | ix
List of Figures | xii
Abbreviations | xiii

Prologue: Raphael the Archangel | 1

1 Interpreting Heaven in 1 Enoch 1–36 | 6

2 Modelling Courts and Courtiers | 35

3 The Nature of the Heavenly Court | 53

4 The Descent of the Watchers: Rebellion in the Heavenly Court | 79

5 The Spatial and Architectural Dimensions of the Enochic Heaven | 109

6 The Enochic Divine Dwelling as a Royal Palace | 136

7 Enoch the Scribe and the Non-Temple Enochic Scribal Group | 153

8 Conclusion: God's Court and Courtiers in the Book of the Watchers | 188

Bibliography | 205
Index of Ancient Documents | 219
Index of Authors | 229

ACKNOWLEDGMENTS

The genesis of this book lies in the early months of 2013 when I was working through the Ethiopic text of 1 Enoch and considering the secondary literature. Much of the scholarship on this text assumes that the presentation of heaven in Chapters 1–36, the Book of the Watchers, is based on the priests and architecture of the temple in Jerusalem. One morning the thought suddenly came to me that the Enochic heaven looked a lot more like a court with its king and courtiers than the Jerusalem temple. I wondered if ancient royal courts had been attracting scholarly attention. To my surprise, an internet search immediately produced Rolf Strootman's splendid 2007 doctoral thesis from the University of Utrecht, *The Hellenistic Royal Court: Court Culture, Ceremonial and Ideology in Greece, Egypt and the Near East*. This alerted me to the existence of a work by Norbert Elias, *The Court Society* (1983), which exercises a major influence on research into royal courts, ancient and modern. From that beginning, a central interest of my own research on 1 Enoch 1–36 has been the extent to which its presentation of heaven draws upon the realities of ancient Persian and Hellenistic courts. This book marks the culmination of this research.

The first public airing of my evolving views came with a paper I gave in the University of Helsinki in early January 2014 at the concluding meeting of the Nordforsk Network devoted to "Social and Cognitive Perspectives on Early Judaism and Early Christianity." I delivered another version to the New Testament Graduate Seminar in Oxford at the end of January 2014. Heaven in 1 Enoch 1–36 formed part of the subject of my Inaugural Lecture as Portland Chair in New Testament Studies in the University of Gloucestershire, in Cheltenham, on 19th March 2014. I also spoke on the subject at the SBL International Meeting in Vienna in July 2014, at the University of Edinburgh early in October 2014 (as the Kennedy Wright Lecture to inaugurate the academic year), and later that month at the University of Bristol. On all of these occasions I profited greatly from the encouragement and feedback received. I am, accordingly, most grateful to my hosts: in Helsinki, Ismo Dunderberg, Jutta Jokiranta, Petri Luomanen, and Risto Uro; in Oxford, Markus Bockmuehl; in Edinburgh, Helen Bond and Paul Foster; and in Bristol, Hilary Carey.

A number of individual scholars have also assisted me at various points. Above all, K. C. Hanson at Wipf and Stock has strongly supported this project from the outset, not only by publishing this book but also by his many helpful and detailed comments and suggestions along the way. The book has benefited greatly from his help. Loren Stuckenbruck, of the Ludwig-Maximilians-Universität in Munich, and Daniel Assefa, of the Capuchin Franciscan Research and Conference Centre in Addis Ababa, have both provided me with valuable references and materials. John Strong, at Missouri State University, alerted me to a number of issues relating to Ezekiel that helped shape my argument. At an early stage, Yoram Cohen of Tel Aviv University kindly communicated with me about the scribes of Emar. Architect Jerry Eccles drew the illustration of heaven that is Figure 5.2, while archaeological illustrator Tessa Rickards is responsible for most of the other drawings in the book. The fact that in 2012 I had written an essay on social-scientific approaches to Israelite apocalyptic literature at the invitation of John Collins for *The Oxford Handbook of Apocalyptic Literature* that he was editing had primed my thinking in a number of ways that later proved useful when it came to writing this book. It probably goes without saying, however, that none of those who are mentioned above bears any responsibility for any defects in this book.

I would also like to thank my colleagues at the University of Gloucestershire in Cheltenham for their support when I was writing the book, in particular Dee Carter, Andrew Lincoln, Adrian Long, Gordon McConville, Pekka Pitkanen, and Melissa Raphael, as well as my Heads of School, Shelley Saguaro, then David Webster, and now Jane Cantwell. University Library staff (especially Deborah Jones-Davis and Kate Rea in relation to interlibrary loans) have efficiently tracked down some of the works I needed.

Angus Pryor, Head of the School of Art and Design at the University of Gloucestershire and himself a painter (in part, of biblical subjects), came along to my Inaugural Lecture at the University and subsequently developed an interest in 1 Enoch as an engrossing subject for practice-based research. This has taken the form of his project to create twenty-one 2 x 2 meter paintings based on 1 Enoch. He is well advanced on this series and the first of the paintings, *God in 1 Enoch 14*, appears on the cover of a collection of essays I have recently edited: *The Blessing of Enoch: 1 Enoch and Contemporary Theology* (Eugene, OR: Cascade Books, 2017). Angus and I have also undertaken two research visits to Ethiopia together, on the second of which he took the photo that appears on the cover of this volume. I have learned a great deal from his fresh vision of the Enochic tradition and of Ethiopia and Ethiopian Christianity, which have bequeathed 1 Enoch to us. As a token of my appreciation, I dedicate this book to him.

FIGURES

5.1	Four-winged genie from the palace of Sargon II at Khorasabad	125
5.2	The wall of heaven and the building within in 1 Enoch 14	129
6.1	Plan of Solomon's temple	138
6.2	Plan of the central area of Pasargadae	144
6.3	Schematic reconstruction of the central area of Pasagardae	145
6.4	A winged genie from Gate R at Pasargadae	146
6.5	Drawing of the winged genie at Pasargadae before removal of the inscription	147
6.6	The floor-plan of Palace S in Pasargadae	148
6.7	Drawing of Palace S in Pasargadae	149

ABBREVIATIONS

1QapGen	*Genesis Apocryphon* (1Q20)
1QSb	*Rule of the Blessing*
4Q203	*Book of Giants*
4Q400–407	*Songs of the Sabbath Sacrifice*
4QMMT	*Miqsat Ma'ase ha-Torah* (4Q394, 4Q395, 4Q396, 4Q397, 4Q398, 4Q399)
11Q17	*Songs of the Sabbath Sacrifice*
ABD	*The Anchor Bible Dictionary*, edited by David Noel Freedman. 6 vols. New York: Doubleday, 1992
b.	Babylonian Talmud (preceding tractates)
BDAG	*A Greek–English Lexicon of the New Testament and Other Early Christian Literature*. 3rd ed. Revised and edited by Frederick W. Danker. Chicago: University of Chicago Press, 2000
BDB	Francis Brown, S. R. Driver, and Charles A. Briggs, *The Brown-Driver-Briggs Hebrew and English Lexicon*. 1906. Reprint, Peabody, MA: Hendrickson, 2001
BTB	*Biblical Theology Bulletin: Journal of Bible and Culture*
CBQ	*The Catholic Biblical Quarterly*
CED	*The Cambridge (online) English Dictionary*
col.	column
ET	English translation
frag.	fragment/s
HUCA	*Hebrew Union College Annual*
JA	Josephus, *Judean Antiquities*

JBL	*The Journal of Biblical Literature*
JSJ	*Journal for the Study of Judaism: In the Persian, Hellenistic and Roman Period*
JSJSup	Journal for the Study of Judaism Supplements
JSOT	*Journal for the Study of the Old Testament*
JSOTSup	Journal for the Study of the Old Testament Supplements
JSP	*Journal for the Study of the Pseudepigrapha*
JW	Josephus, *Judean War*
Leslau	Wolf Leslau, *Comparative Dictionary of Geʿez: Geʿez–English/English–Geʿez*. Wiesbaden: Harrassowitz, 1987
Liddell and Scott	Liddell, Henry George, Robert Scott, and Henry Stuart Jones, *A Greek–English Lexicon*. 7th ed. With a Supplement. Oxford: Clarendon, 1968
m.	Mishnah (preceding tractates)
NTS	New Testament Studies
OED	*The Oxford English Dictionary.* 2nd ed. Oxford: Clarendon, 1989
WUNT	Wissenschaftiliche Untersuchungen zum Neuen Testament

PROLOGUE
Raphael the Archangel

Early in the afternoon of March 17, 2017, I was visiting an ancient Ethiopian Orthodox monastery at Gorgora, on the northern shores of Lake Tana in Ethiopia. Like many Ethiopian monasteries, this one consists of a walled compound, a church and a scattering of other small buildings where the monks live, work, study and eat. The church was erected in the thirteenth century and partly rebuilt in the sixteenth. It is a round building, constructed of baked clay bricks and wooden pillars and beams, with an outer structure and—entirely surrounded by a perambulatory—an inner, higher structure that holds the *tabot* (the box containing the covenant present in every Ethiopian church).[1]

I stood, with a senior monk and a local guide, in the perambulatory facing a doorway into the inner area that was covered by a red curtain. Then the guide drew back the curtain. I was startled by what I saw. In front of me, occupying most of the door leading into the interior, was a large thirteenth century painting of an angel (which is reproduced on the cover this volume). He stood brandishing a sword in his right hand as if he had just drawn it from its scabbard and he was looking directly at me with two piercing eyes. His message was crystal clear: "You shall not enter!" Or at least, not unless you were an Ethiopian Orthodox priest with permitted access to the sanctuary within. The angel is painted in superlative form, line and color; it is a frightening image and a masterpiece of thirteenth century Ethiopian art. He towers over the human viewer and is accessible only by ascending three steps. As he stands with erect wings and raised sword, he produces a very dynamic image, situating the viewer in the very moment when he has sprung into action at your approach. The image brings to mind the "relational aesthetics" of Nicholas Bourriaud in the sense that it exists not just

---

1. On the centrality of the covenant to Ethiopian Orthodoxy, see Antohin 2014.

for the private aesthetic satisfaction of an individual viewer but in a social context where it functions to permit access to the inner sanctuary to some, while denying it to others.[2]

The angel's painted eyelashes, eyelids and double-lined eyebrows indicate elite angelic status. So too do his clothes: his exquisitely patterned tunic, his white under-tunic, scarf-like belt, buttoned leggings in front of the lower part of his cape, and his bare feet firmly planted on the earth and portrayed with close attention to physical form, right down to his toe-nails. Who was this angel? Raphael, explained the guide and the Orthodox priest who was with him.

This identification serves to underline the importance of 1 Enoch in Ethiopian Orthodox tradition, theology and culture across some fifteen centuries,[3] in as much as the only possible ultimate source of Raphael so depicted is the Book of the Watchers (1 Enoch 1–36).[4] It is not uncommon for angels, including Raphael occasionally, to be represented as warriors in the Judean literature of the second temple period.[5] Although Raphael does not appear in the Hebrew Bible, he does have a significant role in the apocryphal Book of Tobit. There he takes human form to guide and advise Tobias through various dangers and experiences, and also offers advice on practical measures to avoid his falling under the power of the demon Asmodeus and to cure the blindness of his father, Tobit. In the latter respect Raphael is acting in accordance with this name, "God has healed" (רפאל; *Rapha'el*). Yet although Raphael is described as binding Asmodeus when he fled off to Egypt (Tobit 8:3), he is not described as having or using a sword. Although a sword is possibly to be implied as providing the force needed successfully to bind Admodeus, the healing role of Raphael has prevailed in depictions of him from the Book of Tobit in Western art (for example the healing of Tobit in 11:10–15). Here the angel is usually portrayed with a staff, not a sword.[6]

Accordingly, the only credible source for the notion of Raphael as a sword-bearing angel is 1 Enoch 1–36. This is not because he is ever described in the text as bearing a sword, since he is not. Rather, it is the decidedly protective and military dimensions to his role in the narrative that make the sword an appropriate, indeed inevitable visual cue. For Raphael "is

2. Bourriaud 2002. I am grateful to Angus Pryor for alerting me to this theorist.

3. Stuckenbruck 2013a:16–20.

4. In this volume 1 Enoch and its constituent parts, and the Book of Jubilees, are cited without italics by virtue of their status as Old Testament scripture in the Tewahedo Orthodox Churches of Ethiopia and Eritrea.

5. See Michalak 2012.

6. As one example, see the painting by Murillo (1617–1682): https://upload.wikimedia.org/wikipedia/commons/9/97/Saint_Raphael.JPG.

in charge of the spirits of human beings" (1 Enoch 20:3); he must not only bind Asael, but also make an opening for him in Dudael and throw him in there (1 Enoch 10:4–5); and he will certainly be at the forefront of God's army when it comes in its myriads of myriads at the End to terminate the sway of evil upon earth (1 Enoch 1:4–9).

A final reason to conclude that 1 Enoch and not the Book of Tobit is the source of Raphael as an angel with a sword is that the latter almost certainly came after and was influenced by the former. Firstly, the postulated date for 1 Enoch (third century BCE) precedes that of the Book of Tobit (early second century BCE).[7] In addition, however, when Raphael declares in Tobit 12:15: "I am Raphael, one of the seven holy angels who present the prayers of the saints and enter into the presence of the glory of the Holy One (RSV)," we have a summary of some (although not all, since the military and protective function of the angels is not mentioned) aspects of the role of the angels in 1 Enoch 1–36, with the seven archangels and their responsibilities actually listed in 20:1–8. The Greek version of 1 Enoch 20:7 (although not the Ethiopic) ends with the words "The names of the seven archangels."[8] Thus in relation to Raphael the Book of Tobit draws on 1 Enoch 1–36 and, in particular, the action of Raphael in binding Asmodeus is probably dependent upon the description of Raphael's divine commission in 1 Enoch 10:4–5 to bind Asael.

So on that day in Gorgora in March 2017 I was looking at a painting of Raphael based on his depiction as an archangel in 1 Enoch 1–36, performing his usual duty to watch and who has charge over the spirits of human beings (1 Enoch 20:1, 3). Yet there was a simple cross on the hilt of his sword and the three steps leading up to the door were, explained the guide and the monk, meant to symbolize the Holy Trinity. A character from 1 Enoch 1–36 had thus been adapted to suit a specifically Christian context where he watches not over heaven and earth below but over the entry to a Christian sanctuary, and thus still exercises his responsibilities over human beings. To pass through the door, his permission would be required.

---

7. For this date for the Book of Tobit, see Fitzmyer 2001:627, who later provided a slightly more nuanced esimate, as somewhere toward the end of the range 225–175 BCE (2003:52).

8. In spite of this summarizing statement, there are only six named archangels listed. But the seventh, Remiel, is included in the Ethiopic version and is probably an accidental omission from the Akhmin Greek manuscript. The Ethiopic version itself fails to include the summarizing statement. Fitzmyer suggests the seven archangels in Tobit derive from the seven eyes of the Lord roaming the earth in Zech 4:10 (2003:296), but he has overlooked "The names of the seven archangels" in 1 Enoch 20:7 which is the actual source.

Here we see Raphael as watcher, charged by God with keeping guard over this particular outpost on earth. He is ready to deal with any threats to it and is armed with a large sword to do so. Like the other archangels, "the angels who watch" (1 Enoch 20:1), he is one of the leaders of God's war-band which in the end-time God, the eternal king, will lead to earth in all their myriads to terminate the power of evil once and for all (1 Enoch 1:4–9). The artist, steeped in the Enochic tradition from the function of 1 Enoch as scripture in Ethiopia, has deployed Raphael in his usual role, but here to watch over and protect the sanctuary of this ancient church. There are other images in Ethiopia of Raphael with a drawn sword and in a protective role, but few of them are as old or as potent as this one.

As I mulled over this image in the days that followed, I realized that my encounter with it had strongly connected with how I was interpreting 1 Enoch 1–36. What struck me most was that the recognition by the artist (and other Ethiopian artists who have produced similar paintings of Raphael) of the military role of the archangel simply could not be ignored. Whereas previously my research into 1 Enoch 1–36 had led me to focus largely on the role of the archangels as senior courtiers at God's heavenly court, the Ethiopian visual tradition forces one to take seriously their role as the embodiment of divine power anywhere in his realm, and that embodiment, here imagined in terms of the raised sword, is inevitably a military one. Accordingly, in addition to recognizing the importance of God's court, it becomes necessary fully to acknowledge the role of his courtiers elsewhere in his realm of which heaven forms, as it were, its capital. Certainly the court around God's throne represents the heart of this capital. But the archangels are not only courtiers, they are also leaders of the divine army poised to go wherever in the spatial reach of God's rule, wherever in his kingdom (although that expression does not occur in the text) they are commissioned to travel in the exercise of his will.

It also struck me that for the Ethiopian tradition to portray Raphael in this way meant that there was little room in its understanding of the Book of the Watchers for interpreting the angels as priests serving in a heavenly equivalent of the temple in Jerusalem. For priests, as priests, have a cultic role and do not bear swords nor have military responsibilities.[9] This image

---

9. This is not to say that priests who were, *in addition*, warriors were unknown. The *Testament of Levi* (discussed in Chapter 1) has a very distinctive passage (2.6—5.4) in which an angel commissions Levi as a priest and then sends him off to take revenge against the Shechemites for the rape of his sister Dinah. Robert Kugler plausibly interprets this passage as legitimation for the Hasmonean combination of princely and priestly rule (1996:218). Mattathias and his son Judah, who led the armed revolt against Antiochus IV Epiphanes, were priests.

underlined the potential of religious art to shape the way we understand religious texts. Yet viewing the Enochic angels as priests is a modern scholarly interpretation that is widely held at the present time. I was already dissatisfied with that view before seeing this painting of Raphael and encountering it brought home to me that here in the indigenous Ethiopian artistic tradition I had discovered an unexpected partner in the dialogue on the meaning of the Book of the Watchers. As I work through my understanding of this text in the chapters that follow, I will at times return to this image of Raphael to show how it can enrich our interpretation.

1

INTERPRETING HEAVEN IN 1 ENOCH 1–36

INTRODUCTION

In one of the most imaginatively charged passages in Israelite literature, 1 Enoch 14 relates how, in a vision, Enoch is summoned to heaven by clouds and mists, hastened along by shooting stars and lightning flashes, and lifted up and brought there by winds. Passing through a wall that is built of hailstones and encircled by tongues of flame, he approaches a large house also built of hailstones with groundworks of snow and upper storeys of shooting stars and lightning flashes among which are fiery cherubim. Entering the first room of the building, he sees, beyond, another door opening onto a larger room that turns out to be the throne-room of God. There he beholds the Great Glory sitting upon his throne. The throne has an appearance like ice but a roundness like the shining sun, while from beneath it issue rivers of burning flame. Myriads of angels stand before God, but not in the throne-room itself (1 Enoch 14:8–23). This passage and the bleak message that God then gives Enoch to convey to the Watchers who have abandoned heaven for women on earth (1 Enoch 14:24—16:4) occupy a central place in the plot and message of 1 Enoch 1–36. They both depend upon, and contribute significantly towards, the prominent role that heaven and those who dwell or, in the case of the Watchers, once dwelled there play in the meaning of the text. The aim of this book is to provide a new explanation of how the original audience of the Book of the Watchers would have understood heaven. Before saying more about heaven, however, it will be helpful to outline the broad nature of the text in which it appears.

THE ORIGINS, CHARACTER, AND INFLUENCE OF 1 ENOCH

First Enoch is an ancient Israelite text, a composite work in five major parts, which presents itself as a series of revelations that God made to Enoch, the sixth patriarch after Adam, who "walked with God" (Gen 5:24). It embraces many subjects, such as the secession of angels from heaven to marry human wives shortly before the time of the Flood, an angel-led tour by Enoch of the cosmos, the history of Israel in the form of *vaticinia ex eventu* and the fact that God will ultimately defeat evil and save the righteous. It was written mostly in Aramaic in stages from the third century BCE to the first century CE, translated into Greek around the turn of the first millennium and then from Greek into Geʿez in the fifth and sixth centuries CE in Ethiopia. Its earliest parts, 1 Enoch 72–82 and 1 Enoch 1–36, constitute the inaugural examples of what we have taken to calling "the apocalyptic genre."[1] 1 Enoch remains scriptural Old Testament for the Ethiopian and Eritrean Tewahedo Orthodox Churches.[2] Although very influential in ancient Israel and the early Christ-movement (it is quoted in the Epistle of Jude),[3] it did not find its way into the Hebrew Bible and is probably the most important Israelite text not to have done so. The work was largely lost to the rest of world, barring some fragments preserved in a ninth century CE work by George Syncellus,[4] until James Bruce brought copies back from Ethiopia to Europe in 1773. The English translation of the Bodleian copy by Richard Laurence in 1821 (the first in a European language) exposed the text to widespread scholarly and popular interest. Editions of the Ethiopic text soon followed from Laurence (1838) and Dillmann (1851). Fresh interest was aroused in 1 Enoch by the discovery of a Greek version of 1:1—32:6a in a monk's grave in Akhmin, Egypt in 1886/87, as evident in works by Charles (1893) and Flemming (1902). Another significant chunk of 1 Enoch in Greek, covering

---

1. See Collins 1979b, and his very recent treatments of the apocalyptic genre (2016:1–53) and the early Enoch literature (2016:53–106).

2. *Tewahedo* is a Geʿez word meaning "unified." It is broadly equivalent to the word "monophysite" that is used in Western theology to refer to the Christology of a number of Eastern Christian Churches that rejected the Chalcedonian formulation of Christ's two natures, one human and one divine, hypostatically joined in one person.

3. Jude 14–15 cites 1 Enoch 1:9, a critical verse for the meaning of the whole work. For possible connections between 1 Enoch and the Synoptic Gospels, now see the essays in Stuckenbruck and Boccaccini 2016.

4. These are: 1 Enoch 6:1–9:4; 8:4–10:14 and 15:8—16:1. A fourth fragment may derive from the Book of the Giants (see Milik 1976:317–319 and Nickelsburg 2001:12–13).

97:6—106:7, turned up in Egypt and was published in 1937.[5] Then, sensationally, came the discovery in Cave 4 at Qumran of Aramaic fragments of 1 Enoch.[6] This ignited a wave of new interest in the historical dimensions of this text and its relationships to other ancient works, Israelite and Christian.[7] Research into 1 Enoch 1–36 depends primarily on the two Greek versions (Akhmin and Syncellus) but supplemented where necessary by attention to the surviving Aramaic text and the versions in Ethiopic.[8] While work has now begun into the theological significance of 1 Enoch,[9] the present volume continues this long-standing historical research with reference to a particular aspect of 1 Enoch 1–36: the original meaning and significance of heaven in the text.

APPROACHES TO THE INTERPRETATION OF 1 ENOCH 1–36

The Book of the Watchers, 1 Enoch 1–36, forms, together with the Book of the Luminaries (1 Enoch 72–82), the oldest stratum in the Enochic corpus. Both works are most probably to be dated to the third century BCE (if not earlier) and such a date of origin makes them the oldest apocalypses extant.[10] As with the Israelite texts that did find their way into the Hebrew Bible, the reason for the composition of 1 Enoch 1–36, which did not, is a matter of great uncertainty. Yet the reason for the exclusion of 1 Enoch from the Hebrew Bible, and from the Christian Bible everywhere except in Ethiopia, is not the focus of the present volume, which is concerned with the more limited question of the presentation of heaven in 1 Enoch 1–36. Nevertheless, I will now set out some of the principal explanations for why this text was written, both to establish a context for my discussion but also because how one understands heaven in the Book of the Watchers bears directly on how one interprets the whole text.

---

5. See Bonner and Youtie 1937.

6. See Milik 1976.

7. A good sense of the flourishing nature of Enochic scholarship can be seen in the 277-page bibliography in Charlesworth and Isaac 2015.

8. For the Greek versions I have used Denis 1970, for the Aramaic fragments Milik 1976, and for the Ethiopic version Flemming 1902. Loren Stuckenbruck is currently leading a project to produce a comprehensive critical Ethiopic text of 1 Enoch (for an early report, see Erho and Stuckenbruck 2013).

9. See the essays in Esler 2017a.

10. For a detailed discussion of the dating of the various parts of 1 Enoch, see VanderKam 1984.

Building on an array of existing scholarship, Archie Wright has offered an explanation for the creation of 1 Enoch 1–36 at a fairly high level of generality (which may indeed be the only level available). This is that the author of the Book of the Watchers "is faced with the problem of affliction that his nation must cope with on a continual basis. Who is responsible for this affliction and why is the God of Israel not coming to deliver the nation?" The Enochic author finds the answer to this question in his understanding of the fallen angels that depends either on his significant reworking of Gen 6:1–4 (in a negative direction) or on a tradition dealing with the fallen angels common to it and 1 Enoch 1–36.[11] This is a fruitful idea. Yet the emphasis placed here on the plight besetting the "nation" (or, to anticipate later discussion, "ethnic group") may, in spite of undoubted references to Israelite tradition in 1 Enoch 1–36, misinterpret the actual object of the author's concern. The author seems to have been concerned not only with the plight of Israelites but with that of all human beings and, indeed, of the earth itself. It is true that as the Enochic tradition developed over time (see Chapter 7) the focus largely narrowed to the fate of Israel. The major stimulus for this was probably the challenges that Judeans began to experience during the latter years of the reign of Antiochus IV Epiphanes (in the period 167–164 BCE). Nevertheless, 1 Enoch 1–36 does not reflect those events and was probably composed well before they occurred.

Wright helpfully considers a number of interpreters who all adjudge the issue prompting the author to write the work as the existence of evil, but who approach the question from different directions. I will mention the three major theories of interpretation, identified by Wright, of the function of the Book of the Watchers in its ancient Israelite context.[12]

George Nickelsburg, firstly (in a proposal that will be found unpersuasive in Chapter 4), relates the text to the wars between Alexander's generals, the Diadochi (to whom some attributed divine ancestry) in the late fourth century BCE that had catastrophic effects on Israel.[13]

The second approach, represented by Paul Hanson—and to a lesser extent by Carol Newsom and John Collins—describes the Book of the Watchers as a work that accounts for the origins of evil in the actions of the Giants and, after their death, their spirits who roam the earth fomenting evil. Paul Hanson argues that the Book of the Watchers aimed to show its audience how the evil they faced originated in the giant offspring of the Watchers. God would intervene at the eschaton to eliminate evil and restore order. Hanson

---

11. Wright 2013:38.
12. Ibid.:37–47.
13. Nickelsburg 1977.

sees in the text the radical mythologization of Israel's perception of history, especially the period of the Flood.[14] Carol Newsom insists on a connection between 1 Enoch 6–16 (concerning the Watchers) and 1 Enoch 17–19 (the beginning of Enoch's journeying through the cosmos accompanied by angelic guides).[15] She connects the journey of Enoch to the practice of Near Eastern diplomacy in showing off the wealth and strength of one's kingdom to visiting courtiers. She argues that the "royal tradition" runs through 1 Enoch 6–19 and this is essential for the life of the audience in the everyday world, in that they can have confidence that God is in control despite the existence of evil spirits, who will eventually be brought under control.[16] For John Collins,[17] distinct strands in the text, such as the Shemihazah and Azazel traditions, could come from the same author, on the basis that evil is a complex phenomenon. He is also sceptical about finding too specific an event in history to explain the work. By keeping the meaning at a general level the author can speak to the current circumstances of his audience. The evident power and wisdom of God (seen in how he deals with the Watchers and in Enoch's journeys) provide reassurance for the righteous. While there is much to agree with in these assessments, my own recent research finds to be flawed any approach arguing that in 1 Enoch 1–36 evil originates with the acts of the Watchers and their offspring, the Giants. In 1 Enoch 1–36 it is Cain's murder of his brother, not the action of the Watchers, that signals the arrival of evil among human beings, even though the activities of the Watchers, the Giants and, above all, of the evil spirits of the Giants who will roam the earth until the final judgment dramatically increase the sway of evil on earth.[18]

Thirdly, David Suter has argued that the explanation of 1 Enoch 6–16 lies in an issue of purity among priests serving the temple of Jerusalem during the third and second centuries BCE: they needed to be careful that they married appropriate wives.[19] George Nickelsburg and Martha Himmelfarb have mounted similar arguments. But these proposals, that the issue concerned marriages with the wrong Israelite wives or with foreign wives, are highly problematic for reasons I will set out in Chapter 4 where they are more directly relevant to my argument. For the present it is enough to note

14. Hanson 1977.
15. Newsom 1980.
16. Ibid.
17. Collins 1978.
18. Esler 2017b.
19. Suter 1979.

that these views derive from the view that the Enochic heaven was modeled on the Jerusalem temple and its priests.

THE PHENOMENON OF HEAVEN IN 1 ENOCH 1-36

As already noted, this book aims to offer a new interpretation of a prominent feature of the Book of the Watchers: the manner in which heaven is presented in the text. By "heaven" I mean: (a) the place; (b) the personal beings to be found there and the interactions between them; and (c) the role that the place and these characters play in the narrative. Because of the central role of heaven in the narrative of the Book of the Watchers, getting to understand it better will also allow a fresh interpretation of many other aspects of this seminal ancient text. While heaven in 1 Enoch 1-36 has frequently been mentioned in Enochic scholarship, this appears to be the first monograph devoted to the subject.

An overview of the data falling within these three aspects of "heaven" will be helpful. *As to place*, in 1 Enoch 1-36 heaven is presented in spatial, indeed in physical and architectural terms. The key passage is Chapter 14, where heaven exists in space and also possesses features such as a wall (v. 9) and buildings (vv. 10-19), in one of which God sits on his throne (v. 20). These buildings constitute God's dwelling that is mentioned earlier (1:3). Throughout the text heaven is presented as another place above but similar in certain ways to the earth. Their comparable nature is underlined by the way characters move from one place to the other. *As to characters*, the personal beings present in heaven are God, the angels (differentiated into named and unnamed, and those who remain in heaven and those who leave) and Enoch. *In relation to the role of this place and these characters in the narrative*, heaven will be the starting-point for God's descent at the time of the final judgment (1:4-9). From heaven the Watchers descend to earth (6:1-7) with catastrophic consequences (1 Enoch 7-8); from there the leading good angels behold the chaos on earth and raise the matter with God (1 Enoch 9); from heaven God sends them to earth to take retributive action (1 Enoch 10-11); Enoch is elevated to heaven, where he converses with God and is sent to the Watcher Asael with word of his divine condemnation (1 Enoch 12:1—13:3); to heaven Enoch is conveyed in a vision where he again converses with God and receives a further message for the Watchers (1 Enoch 14-16); and, finally, various aspects of heaven are mentioned on several occasions during Enoch's journeys through the cosmos (1 Enoch 17-36).

How should we go about interpreting the meaning of heaven in the Book of the Watchers for its original audience? For some scholars, the task would be to plunge immediately into a detailed examination of the various features in the text, no doubt within the context of 1 Enoch 1–36, 1 Enoch generally and the wider literary, religious and political setting of Israel. They would undertake a thorough empirical survey of the available data, no doubt producing valuable results.[20] In accord with my own preference, evident in published work elsewhere, for employing theoretical perspectives, especially social-scientific ones, to inform historical investigations, I will proceed rather differently. In this chapter I will introduce two theoretical areas to assist the enquiry. The first relates to the nature of the social entity within which 1 Enoch was written: putting the matter broadly, was this a religion "Judaism" or a Judean ethnic group. The second relates to the question of how we go about relating a literary construct in 1 Enoch 1–36 to real world phenomena using a theory of metaphor. Following this theoretical discussion, I will discuss various phenomena that have been suggested to explain the meaning of heaven in 1 Enoch, especially the Jerusalem temple and its priests, to pave the way for a new approach set out in Chapter 2.

"JUDAISM" OR THE JUDEAN ETHNIC GROUP

For the majority of scholars today, 1 Enoch and phenomena within it, such as heaven in Chapters 1–36, fall to be considered under the rubric of "Judaism." One only needs to consider the large number of books, articles and essays that appear with Judaism in the title that include a discussion of 1 Enoch to see the truth of this. By and large (there are some exceptions) in using "Judaism" scholars have in mind a religion the adherents of which were "Jews," which is a translation of *Ioudaioi* or *Iudaei* when these people are referred to in Greek and Latin texts respectively. Where relevant, "Christianity" is also posed as a religion, and one that stands alongside Judaism in a symmetrical relationship with it. The common metaphor of "the parting of the ways" reflects this understanding of two entities of the same type, that is, two religions, of "Judaism" and "Christianity" coming to a fork in the road and (sorrowfully, perhaps) parting.[21]

Such an understanding of "Judaism" and "Jews" is, however, becoming increasingly problematic. Recent decades have seen an explosion of

---

20. This type of historical research has been rightly and ably championed by Steve Mason (2016).

21. See the various essays in Dunn 1999 and his 2011 book on the subject (where "parting" gives way to "partings").

research into identity across many disciplines.²² Indeed the word "identity" only came into general use through the writings of the psychoanalytic theorist Erik Erikson, especially with his 1959 work *Identity and the Life-Cycle*.²³ Erikson was interested in personal identity, the identity of an *individual person*, so that identity, or rather 'self-identity', in this sense is closely tied to properties of uniqueness and individuality.²⁴ Yet there is another and quite different meaning of identity that applies to the social and not the personal level. In relation to the social, identity refers to qualities of sameness, where persons associate themselves, or are associated by others, with groups or categories expressed through common salient features.²⁵ These groups take many forms: families, sports teams, scribal groups (in the ancient world), army units, religions, ethnic groups or nation-states, to name a few.

In recent years a branch of social psychology known as social identity theory, which began with the work of Henri Tajfel and John Turner in the University of Bristol in the 1970s and 1980s and which fruitfully probes a wide range of inter- and intra-group phenomena, has probably become the dominant mode of enquiry in this area among social psychologists. From the very beginnings of social identity theory Henri Tajfel included ethnic groups within its ambit. He considered that one of the most important and neglected issues in social psychology was the persistence in our world of differentiation between social groups: the extent to which groups of many types (including national, ethnic and linguistic groups) aimed at preserving their "distinctiveness," their special characteristics and identity in spite of increasing levels of communication and interdependence between groups.²⁶ Indeed, his belief in the early 1980s in the susceptibility of ethnic groups to inter-group tensions proved prescient in the light of the ethnic violence that broke out in Europe and Africa in the 1990s—as Yugoslavia disintegrated into its constituent parts and Hutus killed Tutsis in Rwanda.

The rise of social identity theory roughly coincided with increased interest in the nature of ethnic identity, which had been triggered by the publication of an essay by the Norwegian anthropologist Fredrik Barth in 1969 arguing for a self-ascriptive and process-based approach to ethnic identity, not one tied to the possession of a set of cultural features. He argued that a group's sense of itself as a group came first and that it then chose

22. The founding of the journal *Identity: An International Journal of Theory and Research* in 2001 indicates that interest in the concept had become very lively even by the turn of the millennium.
23. Erikson 1959.
24. Mentioned by Byron 1996:292.
25. Byron 1996:292.
26. Tajfel 1978b:2.

the cultural indicia necessary to express that identity. Moreover, a group could persist for a long time by adopting different cultural features to express its distinctiveness in different periods and thus progressively modify the way it delimited its boundary with other groups.[27] Nevertheless, ethnic identities did tend to reflect certain features and in 1996 John Hutchinson and Anthony Smith published a useful list of such ethnic indicators, which must be regarded as diagnostic and not constitutive of ethnic identity to accord with Barth's self-ascriptive approach:

(a) a common proper name to identify the group;

(b) a myth of common ancestry;

(c) a shared history or shared memories of a common past, including heroes, events and their commemoration;

(d) a common culture, embracing such things as customs, language and religious phenomena;

(e) a link with a homeland, either through actual occupation or by symbolic attachment to the ancestral land, as with diaspora peoples; and

(f) a sense of communal solidarity.[28]

Within this framework, phenomena that we might reasonably label "religious,"[29] in as much as they refer to human activities that are, in various ways, directed toward deities, form but one aspect of the fourth criterion. Indeed, the very act of regarding "religion" as a differentiated province of human action and reflection in the ancient Mediterranean world is increasingly recognized as problematic. As long ago as 1962, William Cantwell Smith had argued that "religion" as we understand it is a construct of the modern world and did not exist in the ancient Mediterranean, with the Latin word *religio* having an entirely different sense.[30] Bruce Malina argued to somewhat similar effect that there was no notion in the ancient world of religion as an entity separate from political or economic issues, but that what we might call "religious" phenomena were embedded in the public cult of the state ("political religion") or in the private rituals of the family ("domestic religion").[31]

---

27. Barth 1969b.

28. Hutchinson and Smith 1996b:6–7, with my phrase "religious phenomena" in the fourth indicator replacing their "religion."

29. Although some scholars are now chary of even using the word "religious."

30. Smith 1962.

31. Malina 1996.

More recently, other scholars have moved in much the same direction as Smith. Thus, in *Before Religion: A History of a Modern Concept* (2015), Brent Nongbri has mounted an argument that the whole idea of religion distinct from politics, economics or science and as a natural and necessary part of our world is a recent development in European history that has been anachronistically projected backwards in time to places and periods where it did not exist.[32] To similar effect is the 2016 work by Carlin Barton and Daniel Boyarin, *Imagine No Religion: How Modern Abstractions Hide Ancient Realities*,[33] where the words *religio* and θρησκεία are analysed in their ancient Roman and Greek settings without reference to the (modern) concept of "religion." All of this research renders problematic the continued use of "Judaism," in the sense of a "religion," as a relevant or even possible entity within which to situate the *Ioudaioi/Iudaei* of the ancient Mediterranean.

"Religious" phenomena—understood (in the sense mentioned above) as interactions between human beings and gods—certainly do occur but they are connected with, or rather embedded in, a wider identity that is best described as "ethnic" in character. More specifically, most ancient states revered particular gods and maintained elaborate cults, situated in temples in their capital cities (and sometimes elsewhere), in their honor. Israel was no exception in this regard, with the temple of its God in Jerusalem. In ancient Near Eastern states, including Israel, there was a strong sense that the proper cultivation of the people's god was essential to their continued well-being. Since failure to maintain allegiance to the god could lead to catastrophe, the leaders of these states generally paid great attention to their peoples' gods. Thus, in the record of his reign carved into rock in Behistun, Darius the Great records on a number of occasions his gratitude to and loyalty towards his god, Ahuramadza.[34] But temples were also central to the economic life of the state, although it would be just as mistaken to regard economics as a differentiated zone of activity as "religion." Temples were repositories for tithes and taxes and sometimes, as with the Herodian temple, for records of debts.

I became interested in both ethnic identity and social identity theory in the mid 1990s and applied these ideas to Israelite and non-Israelite identities in a reading of Galatians in 1998. By the early 2000s I had reached the view, heavily influenced by William Cantwell Smith,[35] that the use of the notion "religion" in relation to the ancient Mediterranean world was anachronistic and that the *Ioudaioi* were best regarded as an ethnic group,

---

32. Nongbri 2015.
33. Barton and Boyarin 2016.
34. See King and Thompson 1907 for a translation of the text.
35. Smith (1991[1962]).

with their name most appropriately translated as "Judeans" to reflect the fact that they, like the other ethnic groups in the Mediterranean world of their time, were named after their ancestral homeland, whether they were actually living there or not.[36] Around 2005 I developed this approach in an essay arguing that in his *Contra Apionem* Josephus presented his people, as one among many in his world, in a manner that was recognizably ethnic, to use our modern conceptual framework. In relation to the Judeans and other ethnic groups mentioned in the text, Josephus frequently referred to features of the sort listed by Hutchinson and Smith.[37] In 2007 Steve Mason, coming at the matter independently but also influenced by William Cantwell Smith, similarly argued for a non-religious and ethnic identity for the *Ioudaioi* and that it was appropriate (but, for him, not inevitable) to translate that word as "Judeans."[38] In the years since 2005 I have sought to show to what extent the meaning of various New Testament texts depends upon their authors seeking to differentiate Judean ethnic identity from the very different Christ-movement identity.[39] One aspect of this research has been my argument that the expression "Judaism," meaning a "religion," is a category error in relation to the ancient Mediterranean. This is not to say that the religious aspect of their ethnic identity was not of great significance to Judeans, especially because they were unique in having a national cult that was monotheistic and they frequently differentiated themselves from other peoples on this account.

There is a passage in Philo that provides remarkable emic confirmation of the accuracy of the etic classification of the identity of the Judeans as ethnic. At one point in *De virtutibus* (102–103), which falls within the section on the virtue of humanity (§§51–174), Philo is dealing with the treatment of the proselyte (προσήλυτος) in relation to Lev 19:33–34. He states as follows:

> When he (Moses) has made laws concerning fellow members of the *ethnos* (περὶ τῶν ὁμοεθνῶν), he considers that incomers (ἐπηλύτας) should be considered worthy of every careful concern because they have left behind their blood-relations (γενεὰν μὲν τὴν ἀφ' αἵματος), their homeland (πατρίδα), their customs (ἔθη), the sacred rites and the temples, gifts and honours of their gods, and they have undertaken a noble migration (ἀποικίαν) from mythical inventions to the clarity of the truth and the

---

36. Esler 2003:12, 62–74.

37. Esler 2009 (the volume in which the essay appeared was several years in preparation).

38. Mason 2007.

39. Esler 2006, 2007, 2011, 2013, 2015a, and 2015b.

worship of the one and truly existent God. He directs those from the (Judean) ἔθνος to love the incomers, not only as friends and relatives (συγγενεῖς), but as themselves, in body and soul, in physical matters acting in common as far as possible, in matters of understanding, grieving and rejoicing over the same things, so that although divided in parts they seem to be a single living being fitted together, and sharing a common nature (συμφυὲς) in fellowship (κοινωνίας) brought perfectly together (102–103).

The transfer being described here is not of a "conversion" to a "religion" but a passage from one ethnic group to another. It is instructive to see that all six of the diagnostic features described by Hutchinson and Smith are found or implied here:

(a) a common proper name to identify the group: this is implied from the references to the *ethnos* and the fellow members thereof, which can only be the Judean *ethnos*; in addition, the name *Ioudaioi* appears a little earlier in the text (*De virtutibus* 65, also in relation to the virtue of humanity);

(b) a myth of common ancestry: this is implied in the use of the word *sungeneis* which refers to a group produced by physical descent (a *genos*),[40] but also in the fact that the proselytes are leaving behind their blood-relations (*genean men tēn aph' haimatos*);

(c) a shared history or shared memories of a common past: Moses and his law-giving are the foundation of the passage;

(d) a common culture, embracing such things as customs, language and religious phenomena: corresponding to this feature are the customs (*ethē*), the sacred rites and the temples, and gifts and honours of their gods being left behind and the worship of the God they are adopting;

(e) a link with a homeland: this is evoked by the express statement that the proselytes are leaving behind their own homeland (*patrida*) and the necessary implication that they are getting another (Judea); and

(f) a sense of communal solidarity: this is powerfully conveyed by the closing statement that they (the Judeans) should love the newcomers like friends and relatives (*sungeneis*), so that they are a single living being fitted together, and sharing a common nature (*sumphues*) in fellowship (*koinonia*) brought perfectly together.

---

40. The related verb is γεννάω, meaning "beget." "Race" is a common but egregiously erroneous translation of *genos*.

When, in the course of social-scientific biblical interpretation, one compares ancient data with a modern perspective from the social sciences, one is not engaged in a pigeon-holing exercise. Often differences will be as interesting as similarities and the social-scientific idea may need to be modified in the process.[41] In spite of this, however, I have never seen a closer match between ancient data and a social-scientific perspective than in this comparison of this passage from Philo's *De virtutibus* and Hutchinson and Smith's indicators of ethnic identity. It is almost incontestable that the Judean identity that Philo has in mind is not religious but ethnic.

Finally, another way to bring out the distinctive ethnic nature of the Judeans is by contrasting them with the Christ-movement and its very different identity. In 2016 Steve Mason published a meticulously evidenced argument to the effect that from the second to the fourth centuries CE many Greco-Roman and Christian authors were unanimously of the view that the Judeans were an ancient and reputable people, an ethnic group in our terms, while the Christ-movement was something very different—to its opponents, a *secta*, *superstitio*, *deisidaimonia*, or *haeresis*.[42] In addition, a number of scholars have recently shown how comparable were the Christ-movement groups to Greco-Roman voluntary associations.[43] Mason and I have co-authored an article integrating his analysis of Greco-Roman and Christian authors with insights from the social sciences and the recent work on Greco-Roman voluntary associations. Our aim is to bring out the distinction between the Judean ethnic group and a Christ-movement more akin to voluntary associations in critique of scholars who believe that early Christian communities show signs of actual "ethnicization."[44] In reality, Christ-movement writers like Paul regularly used ethnic terms but in a fictive sense: they were raiding the collective memory of Israel in the service of mounting particular arguments, not because they understood the Christ-movement as ethnic in character.[45]

None of this, however, is to deny that today's Jews belong to the same group as the ancient Judeans. They do. Jewish people today are the spiritual, cultural, and in many cases biological descendants of the Judeans.[46]

---

41. On the methodology of the social sciences as applied to historical research, see Esler 1987:6–12.

42. Mason 2016.

43. As a sample of this scholarship, see Harland 2013 and Kloppenborg 2006 and 2009.

44. See Mason and Esler 2017, responding mainly to Horrell 2016.

45. For examples of this process see the explanation of Paul's argument in Galatians 3 in Esler 2006 or of Matthew's in Matt 21:43 in Esler 2016.

46. On the biological link between ancient Judeans and today's Jews, see Atzmon

They represent a group who have preserved their sense of group identity for millennia, even as, with the passing of time, they modify the indicators they use to differentiate themselves from other groups, a phenomenon already acknowledged by Fredrik Barth in his explanation of ethnic identity. Translating *Ioudaioi* as "Judeans" is one means of ensuring that we are doing our best to understand them as they understood themselves in the ancient world. And that, moreover, is a way of honoring their memory.

A few years ago I wrote that "In the near future we are likely to see research into the social contexts of apocalyptic texts that takes more seriously the ethnic identity of the *Ioudaioi*."[47] This volume represents an instance of such research. Throughout the pages that follow, therefore, I will be working on the assumption that 1 Enoch 1–36 is best understood within the broad context of its production and reception by members of an ethnic group, the Judeans, and not by adherents to a religion, "Judaism." At various points in the argument I will return to this position, especially in offering critiques of existing scholarship and in highlighting my own proposals.

POSSIBLE MODELS FOR THE ENOCHIC HEAVEN

Conceptual Metaphors and Heaven in 1 Enoch

The detailed presentation of heaven in 1 Enoch 1–36 has attracted interpretations that seek to understand the textual data in the work within a framework familiar to the everyday experience of the author and the original audience. As we will soon see, the currently dominant framework proposed in this context is the Jerusalem temple and its priesthood, whereas this volume will propose a different approach. Before proceeding to a consideration of the options, however, consideration must be given to what is happening when we take such a step, of seeking to understand and interpret one thing in terms of another. In short, this process encapsulates the essence of metaphor, which consists of understanding and experiencing phenomenon A in terms of phenomenon B.

As an aspect of language, metaphor has long been of central interest to specialists in literary criticism, theology, biblical studies and other areas of research and practice.[48] In the last few decades, however, stimulated by the publication by George Lakoff and Mark Johnson of *Metaphors We Live By* in 1980, we have become alert to the cognitive dimension of metaphors, to

---

et al. 2010.
47. Esler 2014a:136.
48. Two milestones are Black 1962 and Soskice 1985.

their role in structuring our conceptual system.[49] Lakoff and Johnson argue that "metaphors allow us to understand one domain of experience in terms of another."[50] Metaphors understood in this way, not as a decorative device in language but as central to language and thought, are called "conceptual metaphors."[51] Such a metaphor entails the systematic application of inference patterns from one conceptual domain to reasoning about another conceptual domain, while the systematic correspondences across the domains are "metaphorical mappings."[52] The first domain is a "source domain" and the second a "target domain."[53]

Lakoff and Johnson first discuss this cognitive dimension in what they call "conventional metaphors," which are those that structure the taken-for-granted conceptual system of our language.[54] Examples include the common metaphors of argument as a war or as a building. This appears to be the main focus of conceptual metaphor theorists because they deal with central issues in life and communication that reflect and shape the thought patterns of a group. Corpus linguistics works by analysing large language data-sets and such analysis can be directed to detecting pervasive metaphors.[55]

But our conceptual system is also structured "by metaphors that are imaginative and creative." One example Lakoff and Johnson offer, created by them for the purpose, is that "love is a collaborative work of art." They suggest that such "metaphors are capable of giving us a new understanding of our experience. Thus, they can give new meaning to our pasts, to our daily activity, and to what we know and believe." They suggest that new metaphors such as these "make sense of our experience in the same way conventional metaphors do: they provide coherent structure, highlighting some things and hiding others."[56]

Even more than this, however, Lakoff and Johnson argue that "new metaphors have the power to create a new reality." They explain the process as follows:

> This can begin to happen when we start to comprehend our experience in terms of a metaphor, and it becomes a deeper reality when we begin to act in terms of it. If a new metaphor enters

---

49. Lakoff and Johnson 1980 (2nd ed. 2003).
50. Lakoff and Johnson 2003:117.
51. See ibid.:245–46.
52. Ibid.:246. Kövecses (2005) makes considerable use of the notion of mapping.
53. Lakoff and Johnson 2003:252.
54. Ibid.:139.
55. Deignan 2005.
56. Lakoff and Johnson 2003:139.

the conceptual system that we base our actions on, it will alter that conceptual system and the perceptions and actions that the system gives rise to. Much of cultural change arises from the introduction of new metaphorical concepts and the loss of old ones. For example, the Westernization of cultures throughout the world is partly a matter of introducing the TIME IS MONEY metaphor into those cultures.

They acknowledge that the idea that metaphors can create realities goes against most traditional ways of understanding metaphors, but argue that this is so because "metaphor has traditionally been viewed as a matter of mere language rather than as a means of structuring our conceptual system and the kinds of everyday activities we perform."[57] In other words, while words alone may not change reality, "changes in our conceptual system do change what is real for us and affect how we perceive the world and act upon those perceptions."[58]

In their afterword to the 2003 reprint of the book Lakoff and Johnson devoted a short section to "Literary Analysis."[59] Here they discuss two works by Mark Turner, *Death is the Mother of Beauty* (1987) in which he shows "how everyday conceptual language can form the basis of allegory when applied to plot structure," and *The Literary Mind* (1996) in which he demonstrates that "metaphoric blends lie behind the construction of fables and of other common products of the literary imagination." These ideas demonstrate the potential usefulness of this approach to metaphor in relation to the creation of narratives in works such as the Book of the Watchers.

The source domain is the conceptual domain from which metaphorical expressions are drawn. The target domain is the conceptual domain that someone is seeking to understand and is typically less concrete and more abstract than the source. Exploring the nature of the conceptual metaphor involved means exposing the systematic set of correspondences (covering phenomena such as physical entities, processes, relationships and attributes) that exist between the elements of the source and the target domains. Conceptual metaphor theorists claim that all metaphors hide and highlight aspects of the target domain.

In seeking to understand the presentation of heaven in 1 Enoch 1–36 existing scholarship has, in effect and probably without realizing it, treated heaven as a target domain that was explicable in terms of a source domain, familiar to the author and his audience from aspects of their actual

57. Ibid.:145.
58. Ibid.:145–46.
59. Ibid.:267–68.

experience, which has been utilized to create it. I fully agree that this is a reasonable approach to interpreting heaven in the Book of the Watchers. Mark Turner's application of the theory to literary works, just mentioned, offers strong warrant for the approach as far as 1 Enoch 1–36 is concerned. I differ, however, in proposing—from within a conceptual metaphor approach—a source domain different from the main one currently in vogue, the Jerusalem temple and its priests, which I will discuss further below.

The Relevance of the Jerusalem Temple?

In Enochic scholarship it has become commonplace, indeed almost universal, to refer to heaven in the Book of the Watchers as a "heavenly temple," usually regarded as modeled on the Jerusalem temple, with the angels as its "priests."[60] At times even Enoch himself is described as a priest.[61] This view at least conforms to the radical difference in nature between God and the angels in the text. A lively focus for this view are the various attempts to explain a central feature of the narrative in 1 Enoch 1–36—the descent of the Watchers from heaven to couple with women and its dreadful consequences for the earth and its inhabitants in 1 Enoch 6–8. Landmarks in this research include essays by David Suter, George Nickelsburg, and Martha Himmelfarb that each relate the behavior of the Watchers to that of priests in the temple in Jerusalem, especially in marrying the wrong women.[62] In Chapter 4, which is focused on the defection of the Watchers from heaven, I will offer a critique of the positions advanced by these scholars and proffer an alternative view. My main issues with the heaven-as-temple theory is that its connection with the textual data is very weak and it is predicated on the error of assuming the relevant social entity is the "religion" of "Judaism," rather than the Judean ethnic group.

---

60. Scholars advocating this position include: Suter 1979 and 2002; Nickelsburg 1981; Black 1985, *passim*; Kvanvig 1988:99–100; Himmelfarb 1993:4, 14–16 and *passim*, and 2007:219–35; Orlov 2005:72–73; Halperin 1988:81–82; Fletcher-Lewis 2002:22–23; Collins 2007a:219; and Kampen 2007:25.

61. See Himmelfarb 1993:25 and 2007:222; Orlov 2005:72–73; Halperin 1988:81–82; and Kvanvig 1988:99–103. Collins, however, specifically rejects the idea that Enoch is a priest (2007a:219).

62. See Suter 1979; Nickelsburg 1981; and Himmelfarb 2007.

Heavenly Temples in Other Israelite Texts

It is not part of my argument that there are no Israelite texts in which heaven is presented in terms of the Jerusalem temple and its priests. There most certainly are, some of them composed not that remotely in time from 1 Enoch 1–36. I will now consider two examples: firstly, the text known as *Angelic Liturgy* or the *Songs of the Sabbath Sacrifice*; and, secondly, the *Testament of Levi*, one of the *Testaments of the Twelve Patriarchs*. My aim is to show that rather than these texts strengthening the case for regarding heaven in 1 Enoch 1–36 as reflecting the Jerusalem temple, they actually exclude that interpretative option.

Songs of the Sabbath Sacrifice

Parts of eight copies of the *Songs of the Sabbath Sacrifice* were found in Cave 4 at Qumran (4Q400–407), one copy from Cave 11 (11Q17) and one from Masada, the latter discovery constituting evidence against this being a text distinctive of or peculiar to the Qumran community.[63] The earliest manuscript witnesses (4Q400 and 4Q407) date to the late Hasmonean period, ca. 75–50 BCE.[64] While Newsom considers it likely that the manuscript was composed no later than 100 BCE, it is extremely difficult to determine the earliest possible date for work. If it was a composition of the Qumran community, a date of 150–100 would be probable, but if the *Sabbath Songs* originated as a non-Qumran composition, the text could be much older.[65]

Consider the following lines from the very opening of the work (4Q400, frag. 1, col. 1):

> [Of the Instructor. Song for the holocaust] of the first [sabbath], the fourth of the first month. Praise [the God of . . . ,] you, the gods, among the holy of holies; and in the divinity [of his kingdom, rejoice, because he has established] the holy of holies among the eternal holy ones, so that for him they can be priests [who approach the temple of his kingship,] the servants of the Presence in the sanctuary of his glory.[66]

The picture here is unambiguously one of a sanctuary, with a holy of holies, and with "gods" or "eternal holy ones," angels in short, serving as his priests.

---

63. Falk 1998:126; for a critical edition of this document, see Newsom 1985.
64. Newsom and Charlesworth 1999:4–5.
65. Ibid.
66. ET García Martínez 1994:419.

Later in the text (4Q403 I, 40–45) we learn something of the architecture of heaven, with foundations, supporting [columns] of the highest vault and corners being mentioned. There are also (4Q403, frags. 14–15) lobbies with entrances and embroidered work.[67] Later in the text (4Q405, frags. 20–22) we encounter the throne of (God's) kingship and a throne-chariot that is above the shining vault of the cherubim.[68] There are also gates through which the holy angels enter and depart (4Q405, frag. 23, col. 1).[69] The temple model is even stretched so far that the text mentions sacrifices conducted by angels in heaven: "the sacrifices of the holy ones [. . .] the aroma of their offerings [. . .] and the aroma of the libations" (4Q405, col. 4).[70]

Yet rather than the existence of a text such as this pushing us in the direction of interpreting heaven in 1 Enoch 1–36 in terms of the Jerusalem temple and the priests who maintained its cult, as if finding a phenomenon in one text were warrant for finding it in another (which, as we will see in Chapter 4, is a step taken by Martha Himmelfarb), the converse is the case. The *Songs of the Sabbath Sacrifice* show us precisely what would happen if an Israelite author elected to take the step of envisioning heaven in terms of the temple. He would, in no uncertain terms, mention the sanctuary and the holy of holies. He would directly equate the angels with priests and he would, perhaps most remarkably of all, describe these angelic priests as offering sacrifices, producing an aroma from their offerings and libations. On the other hand, there is nothing whatever like this in 1 Enoch. Yet if the Enochic author was intent on making the temple comparison, why not? What was there to stop him?

The *Testament of Levi*

Even more revealing is the *Testament of Levi* because of its connection with the Enochic tradition. It forms one of the *Testaments of the Twelve Patriarchs*, probably a Judean text written in the second century BCE that has some (possibly second century CE) Christian interpolations.[71] Important for dating is that the *Testament of Levi* refers to the "book" or "writing"

---

67. See ibid.:427–28.
68. See ibid.:428–29.
69. See ibid.:429.
70. ET ibid.:431.
71. Kee 1983:777–778. An alternative view is that it is a Christian text based on Judean material (so de Jonge 1991). For a discussion of the *Testaments of the Twelve Patriarchs*, see Kugler 2001. For the Greek versions of the text, see Charles 1908.

of Enoch on two occasions (10.5 and 14.1).[72] Similarly, the *Testament of Simeon* at one point mentions "the copy of the writing of Enoch."[73] It is more likely that these references are to the text of 1 Enoch itself and not to the report of that work in Jubilees 4:16-26.[74] This result flows from the references to "writing" and "book" and also to some very specific details from the *Testament of Levi* not found in Jubilees, such as the fact that God is described as "the Great Glory" (3.4), as he is in 1 Enoch 14:20 (and in 102:3). As we will see in Chapter 7 of this volume, four of the main parts of 1 Enoch were completed by the 160s BCE, so that date represents a *terminus a quo* for the Enochic features in the *Testament of Levi*.[75]

I will now briefly mention the broad similarities between the two texts.[76] Like Enoch in 1 Enoch 14, Levi has a dream in which he is shown heaven and enters it (2.5-7). Also like Enoch, he observes there various phenomena or has them explained to him by an angel (2.7-8; 3.1-8). They both see God sitting on a throne (1 Enoch 14:18-20; *Testament of Levi* 5.1). God sends both Enoch and Levi back to earth with a mission (1 Enoch 15:1—16:4; *Testament of Levi* 5.2). Both texts contain prophecies of future punishment for the wicked and reward for the righteous (1 Enoch 1:4-9; *Testament of Levi* 18).

There are, however, differences in the way that heaven is presented in the *Testament of Levi*, especially in the elaboration of seven levels of heaven, which need not detain us here, and, most notably, the addition of explicit references to the cult and priesthood. The latter are to be expected in a text which functions in large part as an aetiology for, and defence of, the

---

72. *Testament of Levi* 10.5 states: "For the house which the Lord will choose will be called Jerusalem, as the Book of Enoch (ἡ βίβλος Ἐνώχ) the Righteous maintains." In fact, 1 Enoch does not say this, yet the "house" mentioned in the Animal Apocalypse (1 Enoch 89:39, 50, 54, 66, and 72) refers to Jerusalem (see Hollander and de Jonge 1985:160). At 14:1 the text has this: "And now, my children, I know from the writing of Enoch (ἀπὸ γραφῆς Ἐνώχ) that in the end-time you will act impiously against the Lord, setting your hands to every evil deed" (ET Kee 1983:793). Three of the five Greek manuscripts used by Charles (1908) have this reading).

73. "For I have seen in the copy of the writing of Enoch (ἐν χαρακτῆρι γραφῆς Ἐνώχ) that your sons will be ruined by sexual immorality" (5.4). For the Greek, see Charles 1908:22.

74. See ET by Wintermute 1985:62-63. Jubilees is not italicized in this volume by virtue of its status as Old Testament scripture in the Orthodox Tewahedo Churches of Ethiopia and Eritrea.

75. It is unclear to me why Kugler, in discussing the origin of the *Testament of Levi* in relation to *Aramaic Levi* (1996:196-98 and *passim*), does not mention 1 Enoch, while devoting some attention to Jubilees (although not 4:16-26).

76. For a more detailed account see Nickelsburg 1981:588-90.

Levitical priesthood.[77] A central feature of this narrative is that God gives Levi the blessing of priesthood until the end-time (5.2). Later seven "men" in white clothing dress Levi with the vestments of priesthood (8.2–10) and Isaac teaches him the law of the priesthood (9.7).

Yet the point of critical importance is that such features did indeed need to be added: *the author of the Testament of Levi most certainly was not of the view that they were already present in his Enochic source.* Major reverse engineering was required! Let us consider the main cultic features. God is located in "the holy of holies" (ἐν ἁγίῳ ἁγίων; 3.4). At one point (5.1), after the angel has opened the gates of heaven for Levi, three of the five Greek manuscripts used by Charles have the reading: "And I saw the holy temple (τὸν ναὸν τὸν ἅγιον) and the Most High upon a throne of glory."[78] The heavenly temple is also mentioned later in the text:

> The heavens will be opened,
> and from the temple of glory (ἐκ τοῦ ναοῦ τῆς δόξης)
> sanctification will come upon him. (18.6)

In a text that clearly portrays a heavenly temple with a holy of holies, we are not surprised by the following description of God's companions:

> There with him are the archangels,[79] who serve and offer propitiatory sacrifices to the Lord in behalf of all the sins of ignorance of the righteous ones. They present to the Lord a pleasing odor (ὀσμὴ εὐωδίας), a rational and bloodless oblation. (3.5–6)[80]

These features, including the odor of sacrifice, are similar to those found in the *Songs of the Sabbath Sacrifice*. And if the text of 1 Enoch 1–36 already contained a warning against priests marrying the wrong women, that message was lost on the author of the *Testament of Levi*. For at one point Isaac gives Levi the following instruction:

> Therefore take for yourself a wife while you are still young, a wife who is free of blame and profanation, who is not descended from foreign peoples (μὴ ἐκ γένους ἀλλοφύλων ἐθνῶν). (9.10)

---

77. See Kugler 1996.

78. Charles 1908:37.

79. ET Kee 1983:789. "Archangels" is the reading in Charles' Greek manuscript α, while three others have "the angels of the presence." The fifth of Charles' Greek versions has "The powers of the angels are serving." See Charles 1908:34.

80. ET Kee 1983:789. The material about sacrifices appears in four of Charles' five Greek manuscripts (1908:34).

This analysis suggests that one of the earliest writers who responded to 1 Enoch 1-36, someone almost contemporaneous with the composition of later parts of the Enochic corpus in the second century BCE, did not regard the text as presenting heaven as a temple with the angels as priests. Those features had to be added to it. This consideration provides further reason for caution in relation to modern scholarship which does take such a view.

To conclude on this issue, therefore, the existence of these two Israelite texts, the *Songs of the Sabbath Sacrifice* and the *Testament of Levi*, expressly delineating heaven in terms of the Jerusalem temple, and the openness with which they do so count as strong factors against such a comparison existing in 1 Enoch 1-36.

TOWARDS AN ALTERNATIVE EXPLANATION FOR THE ENOCHIC HEAVEN

The Divine Council and the Heavenly Bureaucracy as Subject Domain?

The Divine Council

One possible candidate for the subject domain is the divine council, given that it "is not uncommon for Bronze Age texts from Mesopotamia and Syria to refer to the general collectivity of deities as a 'council' or 'assembly.'"[81] To an extent, this means interpreting the target domain (heaven in 1 Enoch 1-36) not so much in terms of terrestrial reality but using another literary and religious construct, namely, ancient Near Eastern modes of understanding gods and goddesses and the relationships between them in their divine abode. The literature of Ugarit, for example, provides rich data about the heavenly council from a region only a little to the north of Israel from about 1450 to 1200 BCE. On one view of Ugaritic beliefs, moreover, ably proposed by Lowell Handy, the portrayal of the gods in their abode itself represents a target domain that arises from mapping against a source domain in the form of the bureaucracies of cities like Ugarit.[82] For aspects of the Ugaritic pantheon to have exerted a direct influence on 1 Enoch 1-36, however, one must assume that knowledge of such matters persisted for many centuries right down to the period of composition of 1 Enoch 1-36 in the third (or

---

81. M. Smith 2001:41.

82. Handy 1994. Handy does not, however, use the ideas of "subject domain" and "target domain." Handy's ideas are discussed below.

maybe fourth) century BCE.[83] Nevertheless, in spite of these issues, consideration of the Ugaritic picture will prove useful, even if it will not provide the solution.

At first sight the notion of the divine council, a term used by commentators on ancient Near Eastern, including Israelite, texts to refer to the heavenly host, the pantheon of gods and goddesses who administer the affairs of the cosmos, does indeed appear promising as a source domain.[84] Interest in this area, and its relevance to the understanding of God in the Hebrew Bible, was fired by the discovery of the cuneiform tablets from Ugarit containing mythological texts that in a number of places refer to collectivities of gods using a variety of expressions, such as "the assembly of the gods" (*pḥr 'lm*), "the assembly of the divine sons" (*pḥr bn 'lm*), and "the assembly of the council" (*pḥr m'd*).[85] Although Mullen considers that these expressions generally refer to the whole pantheon, they may refer to gatherings of a subgroup of gods.[86] Arguably similar notions of a divine council appear in various parts of the Hebrew Bible, including 1 Kgs 22:19–23 and Pss 82 and 89:6–7. The gods and goddesses of Ugarit met on a cosmic mountain, where El dwelt, for which parallels can also be found in descriptions of Yahweh's locations on Sinai and Zion. The material concerning God and his angels in heaven in 1 Enoch 1–36 inevitably prompts comparison with the divine council scenes in the Ugaritic texts and in the Hebrew Bible. Psalm 82 evokes a situation rather similar to that of 1 Enoch 9 and 10.

Nevertheless, on closer inspection the presentation of such a divine council differs in very significant respects from the representation of heaven in 1 Enoch 1–36. The primary difference lies in the complete lack of any notion of council or assembly. Certainly God exists in heaven where there are other beings, the angels, but he is presented as spatially separate from angels and human beings (1 Enoch 14:21). Moreover, although there is sometimes conversation between God and one or other of the angels and, indeed, with Enoch, there is nothing like the discussions between the gods preparatory to a decision such as we find in the Ugaritic documents and also in 1 Kgs 22:19–23 and Job 1:6–12 and 2:1–6.[87] The only time we see anything even

---

83. On the persistence of some attributes of the Ugaritic deities in relation to the Hebrew Bible, see M. Smith 2002:202–7. It is also possible that aspects of Ugarit-type beliefs persisted among the Phoenicians who could have been a source of information concerning them for any Israelites who were interested.

84. See Clifford 1972; Mullen 1980; Handy 1994; Day 1994; Kee 2007; and M. Smith 2001 and 2002 for discussion of the divine council.

85. See M. Smith 2001:41; for the Ugaritic texts, see Gibson 1978.

86. Mullen 1980:113–20; and Mark Smith 2001:42. Also see Kee 2007.

87. See, for example, El's questioning of the gods in *Keret* as to which of them would

remotely like this comes when four leading angels complain to God about his inaction over the violence affecting the earth (9:1–11) and God responds with instructions in turn for each of them (10:1—11:2). There is no sense that a genuine discussion, prior to a decision being made, is occurring. Part of the reason for this is that, unlike the position at Ugarit where the heavenly beings described were all of divine status—all gods or goddesses of the family of El—the angels in 1 Enoch are of a rank and status far below God; they are, indeed, of a different order of being. This is a strongly monotheistic text. Yet even in 1 Kgs 22:19–23, where God sits on his throne with "all the heavenly host" standing on his right and left hands, who are clearly lower in status than God, to and fro discussion takes place between them as to whom should go to Ahab to persuade him to travel to Ramoth-Gilead and die there: "And one said, 'In this manner,' and another said, 'In this manner'" (1 Kgs 22:20). Not so in 1 Enoch 1–36.

The Ugaritic Pantheon as Heavenly Bureaucracy

A significant contribution to the discussion of the portrayal of Near Eastern divine beings in a heavenly setting is found in Lowell Handy's *Among the Host of Heaven: The Syro-Palestinian Pantheon as Bureaucracy*. Handy argues that the pantheon that was worshiped in Syria-Palestine reflected the social structure of the city-states in that region, with the divine beings functioning as a "bureaucracy."[88] The Ugaritic gods exhibited a hierarchical and differentiated arrangement. Thus, there were gods who exercised the highest authority, especially in relation to the possession of wisdom and the maintenance of order (El and Asherah), gods under El and Asherah who had active roles in maintaining the universe (especially Baal, Anat, Mot and Shapshu), gods who were artisans (Kothar-wa-Hasis), and (at the lowest level of the hierarchy) gods who were messengers (*mlakm*, such as *gpn w ugr*; cf. Hebrew מלאכים, *ml'kym*) and repeated verbatim the messages they were entrusted to convey from one deity to another.[89]

Similar to the divine level was the social and political organisation among human beings, where there was a central city-state like Ugarit, with

---

banish the illness from Keret, followed by his announcing he would resolve the problem himself (Gibson 1978:99–100).

88. For the main references to the divine council in this work, see 1994:43, 81, 91, 117–19, 122.

89. Handy 1994, *passim*. In similar vein, Mark Smith (2001:45) has identified four tiers of the Ugaritic pantheon: (a) El and Athirat as king and queen; (b) the royal family, that is, the seventy sons of Athirat; (c) The servants of the royal family, especially Kothar-wa-Hasis; and (d) the minor deities who serve other deities.

a king (*mlk*), under whom was the mayor of a daughter-city, and under him a leader of each profession, and under them the people and then the slaves. Although he does not himself make the point, in developing this proposal Handy was reflecting the central insight of the sociology of knowledge, going back as far as Emile Durkheim and further, that theoretical bodies of knowledge (including mythologies) can have social origins and, indeed, social impacts.[90] In terms of conceptual metaphor theory, Handy views civic bureaucracies as providing the subject domain that is mapped onto the target domain, the picture of the assembly of the gods. When one comes upon textual material depicting the pantheon in the Ugaritic works (and God and his angels in heaven in 1 Enoch 1–36 for that matter), it is entirely reasonable to look for some aspect of the social, civic or political realms that could have stimulated and provided a metaphor for such a representation and Handy has shown a fine exegetical imagination in taking this step. The fact that in 1 Enoch 1–36 the leading angels are reported to have differentiated roles (20:1–8) does resonate with Handy's picture.

Whether Handy's notion of "bureaucracy," however, with its very particular connotations, is the right model is another matter. Max Weber, it will be recalled, developed a three-part typology of authority: traditional, charismatic and rational/legal, with the latter characteristic of modern bureaucracies, where decisions are (in principle at least!) based on rational grounds rooted in impersonal rules enacted by statute or contractually agreed.[91] The "traditional" type of authority, which predominated in premodern societies such as the agrarian ones of the ancient Mediterranean world, was based on the sanctity of tradition (to which patrilinear descent was integral), especially in the sense that it was vested in particular persons who had inherited it or had been given it by a higher authority. At one point Handy summarizes Weber's understanding of "bureaucracy" yet without appreciating that this type is not appropriate to an ancient agrarian society where kinship was a dominant institution—a society that was actually far more readily capable of analysis as manifesting "traditional" authority.[92] Yet even in examples of traditional authority, like ancient Near Eastern and Hellenistic monarchies, there was a differentiation of military, administrative, and artisanal functions and their allocation to functionaries in a hierarchical fashion under the sovereign, such as Handy has described for the pantheon and city-state of Ugarit—albeit within a "bureaucratic" rather than

---

90. Berger 1969:48.

91. Max Weber set out his typology of authority in his essay, "The Social Psychology of World Religions," in Gerth and Mills, eds. 1991:267–301, at 295–301.

92. Handy 1994:10–11.

the more appropriate "traditional" mode of authority. Accordingly, we will see that some of his astute observations concerning the functioning of the pantheon and city-state of Ugarit are capable of redeployment in relation to aspects of 1 Enoch 1–36, a work from a context also characterized by "traditional" authority.

Rather surprisingly, the notion of the divine council as a way into understanding heaven in the Book of the Watchers has not found much favour with Enochic scholars. Thus neither Theodore Mullen's important 1980 monograph on the subject, *The Divine Council in Canaanite and Early Hebrew Literature*, nor Lowell Handy's *Among the Host of Heaven*, are cited by Nickelsburg in his commentary on 1 Enoch.[93] One might speculate that commentators on 1 Enoch would have taken more cognisance of the heavenly council and weighed up the sort of factors, mentioned above, which differentiate divine council scenes in Ugaritic and Israelite texts from what he find in 1 Enoch 1–36, were it not for the fact that most scholars have been beguiled by another underlying model, or source metaphor, found to be more appealing, that of the temple in Jerusalem.

The Royal Court and Courtiers as the Source Domain

In Chapter 4 we will see how, in the space of four years, George Nickelsburg proposed the war of the Diadochi as the context for the secession of the Watchers from heaven in 1 Enoch 6–11 and the Jerusalem temple as the source for heaven in 1 Enoch 12–16. Presumably, he considered that it was possible to find what we are referring to here as different source domains for different parts of a text. But what if we seek a more economical explanation that looks for just one source domain? In particular, pushing the fact of the Watchers' departure from heaven in 1 Enoch a little farther brings us inevitably to the monarch whom they abandoned: God himself. Is it not reasonable to begin with a working hypothesis that when we see God in his heavenly realm, including in his throne-room, in 1 Enoch 12–16, there is a continuation of the imagery from the previous chapters, especially as this is a God who is still concerned with rebuking the Watchers for their defection from heaven (1 Enoch 15–16)? In other words, should we not be thinking about a king in his court, surrounded by his courtiers, in 1 Enoch 12–16, and in the rest of the Book of the Watchers, rather than a God in the Jerusalem temple attended by priests?

---

93. Nickelsburg 2001. Himmelfarb (1993) does refer to Mullen (1980); see her discussion of the Divine Council in 1993:13–14.

It is intriguing to note that commentators who employ the temple model occasionally also mention a royal court dimension to 1 Enoch 1–36. Yet they do not develop that idea, nor show much appreciation of just how very different are these two proposals for the underlying model for heaven in the text. Thus Black notes, "The idea of a House of God in heaven, a Palace or Temple (according as he is conceived as object of worship or as King) is a familiar one in the Old Testament."[94] He mainly fixes on the temple alternative, however. Similarly, Martha Himmelfarb makes the following observations:

> In biblical Hebrew *hekhal* serves for both the king's palace and the temple. In relation to a god, temple and palace are two aspects of the same dwelling place. Thus even in those texts where the idea of temple dominates, the imagery associated with the royal palace never disappears. The purpose of Enoch's ascent is still participation in the deliberations of the heavenly court, but a shift in emphasis in the description of the heavenly council and its setting has begun.[95]

By this "shift in emphasis" she means to the temple and its priesthood (including Enoch) as the dominant model for the heaven in 1 Enoch 1–36, as she then proceeds to explain.[96] To anticipate the conclusions of the argument to come, views such as these of Black and Himmelfarb both understate the difference between a palace and a temple, given the different functions and functionaries associated respectively with each, and also run foul of the extent to which an analysis of 1 Enoch 1–36 indicates that the model unambiguously in view is that of a court and courtiers and not a temple and priests.

During the course of the argument, it will be submitted that there is a close correlation between advocacy of the heaven-as-temple view of 1 Enoch 1–36 and a belief that the relevant group entity in play is "Judaism," understood as a religious identity. In other words, scholars who believe that the focus of their work is the "religion" of "Judaism" seem naturally to construe the phenomenon of heaven in the Book of the Watchers in terms of the Jerusalem temple that they consider played a central role in that "religion." They also attribute much the same understanding to whatever ancient writer was responsible for 1 Enoch 1–36.

---

94. Black 1985:148, citing Isa 6:1–2; 2 Sam 22:7; Pss 18:6 and 29:9; Mic 1:2; and Hab 2:20.

95. Himmelfarb 1993:14.

96. Ibid.:14–28.

On the other hand, if the Enochic heaven is actually depicted in terms of a royal court, we will probably need to be thinking of another identity (or even other identities) as the context for the creation of the text, *an ethnic one for example*. This means that Lowell Handy's attempt to find the model for the Syro-Palestinian pantheon in the organisation of Syro-Palestinian cities bears some similarities to what is proposed here. This question of the social context and group identity that are reflected in the Book of the Watchers will, however, be deferred until later in this volume (see Chapter 7). For the moment, we must lay the foundations for an analysis of heaven in 1 Enoch 1–36 based on the model of a royal court. This will involve an account of Achaemenid and Hellenistic royal courts that utilizes sociological research into the French courts of the *ancien régime*.

For here I will propose a very different model as underlying the presentation of heaven, namely, that of the royal court and palace of ancient Near Eastern kings, especially those of the Achaemenid and Hellenistic multi-nation states. Here "court" is not used in the judicial sense but in relation to the household, courtiers, retinue and administration of a monarch. Time and again we will see that not only is evidence urged in support of the temple/angels-as-priests model not probative of that position, but that it actually points in another direction—to the royal court.

As well as connecting my argument with the current debate about the best way to interpret the identity of the ancient Judeans, the proposal that a court and courtiers model forms the source domain for the representation of heaven in the Book of the Watchers also brings this volume into dialogue with the current view that in apocalyptic texts such as 1 Enoch 1–36 we have discourses against "empire" and "imperial oppression." Eminent representatives of this view include Richard Horsley in *Revolt of the Scribes: Resistance and Apocalyptic Origins* and Anathea Portier-Young in *Apocalypse against Empire: Theologies of Resistance in Early Judaism*.[97] In an essay published in 2014 I have lodged some caveats against this approach: it depends on under-theorized notions of "empire;" it allows scholars to find in biblical texts support for moral positions they hold in the contemporary world which might get in the road of the accurate examination of ancient historical data; and it neglects the question of ethnic versus religious identity as far as the Judeans were concerned.[98] The main thesis now proposed in this volume, however, represents a new and additional reason to doubt the wisdom of the "apocalypse against empire" proposal as far as 1 Enoch 1–36 is concerned. This reason is that far from attempting to criticize or subvert "empire," this

---

97. See Horsley 2010; and Portier-Young 2011.
98. See Esler 2014a:132–37.

text accepts the complex of king, court and courtiers existing at the heart of multi-state monarchies, with which its author must have been familiar, as a model, regarded in a positive light, for the representation of God in his heaven with the angels and Enoch.

Here, then, is how I will develop this thesis in this volume. In Chapter 2 I will model the royal court using sociological research on the court of Louis XIV. In the four chapters after this I will investigate heaven in 1 Enoch in the light of this model. This will entail, firstly, a presentation of the nature of the heavenly court in the Book of the Watchers in the light of the model (Chapter 3). Next I will offer a new interpretation of the defection of the Watchers and its aftermath in 1 Enoch 6–8 as inspired by the rebellions that frequently shook Achaemenid and Hellenistic royal courts (Chapter 4). After that I will explore the spatial and architectural dimensions of the Enochic heaven, especially God's house in 1 Enoch 14 (Chapter 5) and then argue that the Achaemenid palace at Pasargadae might have served as a model for the Enochic divine dwelling (Chapter 6). Having thus shown how heaven in 1 Enoch 1–36 is plausibly interpreted as a "target domain" of which the "source domain" is the royal court, my final substantive argument will be to show how this result bears upon the authorship of the text (Chapter 7). This will involve focusing upon the portrayal of Enoch as a scribe in this text and in other constituent parts of 1 Enoch, and exploring how this relates to the social location of the author or authors. This process will situate the author or authors of the Book of the Watchers as scribes operating in the wider social, ethnic and political context of Judea, but not in the Jerusalem temple. These were scribes who saw in Enoch a prototype of their social identity. This conclusion will provide further evidence against the view that the Enochic heaven was based on the Temple, while explaining the composition of 1 Enoch in a new way. In Chapter 8 I will bring the various threads of this volume together in a summarising conclusion.

2

MODELLING COURTS AND COURTIERS

NORBERT ELIAS, ROYAL COURTS, AND HEAVEN IN 1 ENOCH 1-36

As mentioned at the end of the previous chapter, a prominent theme in recent research into Judean apocalyptic texts has been the extent to which they represent forms of resistance to "imperial" oppression. While the idea of "empire" itself attracts surprisingly little close investigation, let alone modelling, in much of this work, hence the inverted commas, the patterns of oppression practised by hereditary monarchies in the Eastern Mediterranean, especially that of the Seleucid dynasty (312–64 BCE), and responses to them by subject peoples receive close attention. Research frameworks largely borrowed from post-colonial studies have proved fruitful in this work.

A subject that has hitherto received very little attention in research into apocalyptic texts, however, has been that of the royal court and royal palace at the heart of these monarchies. Until recently, this area had also been neglected by specialists in the history of the Hellenistic period, perhaps because they tended to be more interested in the autonomous Greek citystate, the *polis*, than in eastern kingdoms.[1] Previously, the limited literature on the court mainly focused on the institutional, prosopographical and literary patronage dimensions of Hellenistic courts.[2] We are now, however,

1. Strootman 2011:64.
2. Ibid.:65.

witnessing a sharp uptake of interest in court studies in historiography and this has begun to flow into ancient Greco-Roman and Near Eastern studies in Germany, the UK and the Netherlands.[3]

This research has been inspired largely by a sociological investigation into the French courts of the *ancien régime* by German social historian Norbert Elias (1897–1990). This work formed his *Habilitation* thesis, which was completed in 1933, when, being Jewish, he fled from Germany to Paris, before moving to the UK, where he settled, in 1935. It was not until 1969 that it was published (with a new introduction by Elias valuably tracking the use of sociology in historical enquiry) under the title *Die höfische Gesellschaft* ("The Court Society"). A French translation appeared in 1974 and an English translation, *The Court Society*, in 1983.[4] In the last two decades Elias' work, focused on the French courts but feeding into research into the early modern European court and state formation generally, has had a powerful influence on research by classical scholars into the courts of ancient Mediterranean kingdoms. In addition, palace architecture, with its obvious relevance to understanding the court and easily integrated into perspectives derived from Elias, has become a lively sub-field of Hellenistic archaeology.[5]

In spite of criticisms leveled at *The Court Society*, for example, that the absolutism of the French monarch was not so untrammelled as Elias claimed,[6] it has been extremely influential. Gabriel Herman has provided the following explanation for this influence:

> Elias' main achievement in this book is the discovery of the court as a subject for investigation. Studies of courts have been published before, but they have all been marred by a tendency to concentrate on curiosities, on the "pomp and circumstance" of courtly life. Elias proposed that the court should be studied as a system of power relations given its structure by unwritten rules prescribing specific behaviour, both to the ruler wishing to master that system and to the courtier wishing to be part of it.[7]

---

3. See the essays in Winterling, ed. 1997; and Spawforth, ed. 2007a; as well as Herman 1997; and Strootman 2007 and 2011.

4. For an explanation of the circumstances of the publication of the book in 1969, see Smith 2009. For the place of Elias in modern social theory, see D. Smith 2001.

5. See Heermann 1986; Nielsen 1994 and 1998; Brands and Hoepfner 1996; Kutbay 1998; Netzer 1999; and Nielsen 2001.

6. Strootman 2014:33–34.

7. Herman 1997:201–2.

In addition, Herman notes, Elias' general framework transcends the particulars of French courts and has the capacity to promote understanding of court societies other than those of the *ancien régime*.[8]

Accordingly, the time has now come to apply Elias' views and their recent use by classicists, together with work on the archaeology of ancient Near Eastern palaces, to the presentation of heaven in 1 Enoch 1–36 (the Book of the Watchers). The use of a model derived from early modern French courts, yet enriched with data from ancient Near Eastern courts, holds the promise of providing fresh insights into the meaning of heaven 1 Enoch 1–36 and will also assist a critical appraisal of the currently dominant temple and angels-as-priests model. Although beyond the scope of this volume, other texts such as Daniel and Esther are likely to repay investigation from these perspectives.

MODELLING ROYAL COURTS

In this chapter I will summarize important aspects of Elias' *Court Society* and also indicate how they find responsive data in evidence concerning ancient Near Eastern and Hellenistic courts prior to or roughly contemporaneous with the composition of 1 Enoch 1–36. I will include the Achaemenid and Hellenistic kingdoms, while acknowledging that there are differences between them that would profit from closer attention at a more granular level of analysis than is possible here.[9] Similar patterns were also evident in the Neo-Assyrian kingdom.[10] It is worth noting, however, that the three main Hellenistic courts (Antigonid, Seleucid and Ptolemaic) had identical origins (all three arising from Alexander's court) and evolved in a way whereby they had very similar structural features.[11] In subsequent chapters of this volume I will apply the picture that emerges to heaven as it is depicted in the Book of the Watchers.

---

8. Ibid.:202.
9. On continuities and discontinuities, see Strootman 2014:3.
10. See Parker 2011:376, who argues that "an analysis of how Neo-Assyrian kingship is operationalized suggests that the performance of kingship is produced and staged by the inner and provincial elite. Whether we call them courtiers, followers, stakeholders, beneficiaries, or agents, they are the essential ingredient in the institution of kingship."
11. So Herman 1997:207.

The Social Constitution, Functions, and Persistence of the Court

The Raison d'Être of the Court

Elias noted that in countries ruled in an absolutist way, that is without the involvement of assemblies of the people—and it is submitted that this was the case with the ancient Egyptian, Achaemenid, and Hellenistic monarchies as well as with the *ancien régime*—the court existed for two primary functions. First, it served as the household for the extended royal family and, secondly, it provided the "central organ of the entire state administration, the government."[12] A closely related way of encapsulating the main functions of the court, proposed by Spawforth, is to regard it as embracing the ruler's dwelling, the αὐλή (orginal meaning "court" or "courtyard") and people there, those περὶ τὴν αὐλήν ("the courtiers"; Polybius 5.36.1). This means that it is "both the spatial framework for the ruler's existence and also the social configuration with which he shares that space."[13] A slightly different perspective distinguishes between the court as a social grouping (the king and the people around him) and as an institution (the extent to which it is the center of the king's power and authority).[14] This approach, however, may understate the spatial, especially the architectural component of the nature and operations of the court.

The fundamental reality of such an arrangement was that the king ruled "the whole country from his house and through his household."[15] Or, as Gabriel Herman has put it while discussing the Hellenistic kingdoms, "Within the court were taken the decisions which shaped the destiny of the kingdom."[16] In focusing on the court we must not forget the kingdom over which the king ruled; without a kingdom there can be no court, nor, except in very special circumstances (of an exiled king, for example), any court without a kingdom. To explain how royal power was exercised in such a context it is first necessary to consider the various individuals and groups who constituted the court and then to set out how they interacted with one another and with other people and entities in the kingdom beyond the court.

---

12. Elias 1983:1.
13. Spawforth 2007b:3.
14. Butz and Dannenberg 2004:4; followed by Brosius 2007:18.
15. Elias 1983:42.
16. Herman 1997:200.

The Members of the Court

At the center of everything was the king himself, and his family. For the monarchs of the *ancien régime* this meant the king's wife and children, and his other relatives, but also his mistresses. In the ancient kingdoms in view here the court contained the king and his wife or wives, their children, his concubines and other relatives. All courts also required numerous household servants, including domestic attendants and bodyguards. Yet, since the court was the center of government, there were also other personnel with significant administrative and military positions. These latter were principally those whom we call "courtiers," who frequently had their own staff. In Hellenistic courts these people were designated as "friends" (*philoi*) of the king and more will be said on them below.[17] Very often the court also hosted people who were temporarily visiting it for some purpose or another, subjects of the king or not. In ancient courts these included sages or "intellectuals" (about whom more will be said below), very often from abroad, and other foreigners, such as politicians from Greek cities, exiles or envoys of foreign powers.[18]

The courtiers, however, were not an undifferentiated group. In the courts of the French kings there were different ranks among the nobility. Louis XIV deliberately fostered distinctions of rank among the high nobility at court, especially by restricting access to his person. He did this, for example, during the ceremony that occurred every morning when he awoke and dressed. On these occasions there were six different groups permitted to enter his bed-chamber, strictly in turn. First of all came his family, while later entrants included "the ministers and secretaries of state, the *conseillers d'État*, the officers of the bodyguard, the Marshall of France and others."[19] In short, the "king used his most private acts to establish differences of rank and to distribute distinctions, favours or proofs of displeasure."[20]

Such a pattern was also evident in ancient courts, in the distinction between courtiers of the "inner" and "outer" court and in the differentiation present in the former.[21] The inner court comprised "the ruler and those whom service or kinship kept more or less permanently in his vicinity," while the latter "were a more intermittent presence, in part by virtue of the

---

17. Ibid.:213.

18. See Herman (1997:213–14) and Spawforth (2007b:3) for the various people at court.

19. Elias 1983:83.

20. Ibid.:84.

21. Spawforth (2007b:4) notes that most chapters in Spawforth, ed. 2007a distinguish between an inner and an outer court.

coming-and-going between center and periphery imposed on them by the delegated power with which the ruler entrusted them."[22] Maria Brosius finds this pattern in the Achaemenid court, with the inner court representing the king's "permanent entourage" and the outer court the rest.[23] She also notes the existence of complexities within the inner court, where "Different hierarchies of tribe, rank and high office were interwoven to create a court organisation," while the flexibility of the system allowed changes within and between these hierarchies (as would later occur in the courts of the French kings).[24] Xenophon records that when Cyrus invited people to a dinner, a careful gradation of guests was arranged, so that the most esteemed sat on the king's left, the next most esteemed on his right, third again on the left, the fourth on the right and so on.[25]

At each of the courts in view certain courtiers were charged with specific responsibilities. Important roles in the Persian court included: "the king's spear-bearer, his bow- and axe-bearer, the heads of the king's bodyguard (*hazarapatiš*), palace administration and royal treasury, the chief scribe, the keeper of the gate, and the priest(s), along with the Persian nobles serving as the King's Councillors, as Royal Judges, and as the King's Eye. In a separate category were the royal physicians . . ."[26] Those forming the penultimate category—the Councillors, Judges, and the King's Eye—no doubt advised the king on important matters of state. Herodotus tells a story concerning the Persian king Cambyses, who fell in love with his sister and wished to marry her, although it was not a custom in Persia for brothers and sisters to marry. To obtain advice on the matter, Cambyses summoned all the royal judges; they advised him that he could: there was no Persian law legitimating such marriage but there was one saying that the king of Persia could do whatever he wanted![27] It is probably the case that the Persian kings were fonder of seeking advice than some monarchs, because otherwise there would be little point in the delightful parody of the process in the book of Esther when King Ahasuerus seeks advice from his royal courtiers on how to respond to his queen Vashti's refusal to come to his banquet when he summoned her:

> Then the king said to the wise men who knew the times—for this was the king's procedure toward all who were versed in law

22. Spawforth 2007b:4.
23. Brosius 2007:18.
24. Ibid.:53.
25. Xenphon, *Cyropaedia* 8.4.3–5.
26. Brosius 2007:27.
27. Herodotus 3.31.

and judgment, the men next to him being Carshena, Shethar, Admatha, Tarshish, Meres, Marsena, and Memucan, the seven princes of Persia and Media, who saw the king's face, and sat first in the kingdom. "According to the law, what is to be done to Queen Vashti, because she has not performed the command of the King Ahasuerus conveyed to her by the eunuchs?" (Esth 1:13–15, RSV)

Memucan provides the advice, to the effect that Vashti must be replaced since she has wronged not just the King but all the other husbands in Persia who might follow her precedent and hold them in contempt (Esth 1:16–20)! This advice pleased the king and he acted upon it (Esth 1:21–22). Another feature of this passage is worthy of note here: that these seven were clearly part of the "inner court" and "saw the king's face," meaning that they had direct access to him.

The ultimate means by which the king exercised power was through his army. Louis XIV created the French Royal Army and in so doing took away the power of the nobles to raise their own forces.[28] The king appointed his generals from among his nobility—from the "princes, peers, marshals of France and other less exalted nobles."[29] Such appointments would have required the frequent attendance at court by those seeking such commissions. The King gave his generals commissions only for a limited period, usually a campaign season.[30] Sometimes, however, Louis XIV appointed provincial governors, who were less likely to be at court, to lead armies.[31] The Persian kings also used courtiers to lead armies (but sometimes, like Louis, satraps of provinces). In the remarkable Behistun inscription, Darius I ("the Great") recounts the nineteen rebellions he put down at the start of his reign, in 522–521 BCE. The first was led by a magus called Gautama, whom Darius says he slew "with a few men" (line 13).[32] Towards the end of the inscription (line 68) he lists their names, stating that all of them are Persians: Intaphrenes, Otanes, Gobryas, Hydarnes, Megabyzus, and Ardumaniš. These men must certainly have formed the inmost part of the Darius' inner court, and among his various "servants" whom he sent to quell the rebellions were Intaphrenes (lines 49–50) and Hydarnes (lines 24–25). On occasion, Darius sent a satrap to lead an army.[33]

28. See Lynn 1997.
29. Rowlands 2002:269.
30. Ibid.
31. Ibid.:310–12.
32. See King and Thompson 1907.
33. Here is an example from line 38: "A certain Margian named Frâda they made

Sages and Foreigners at Court

It will be useful to explore the question of sages and foreigners at court, mentioned above, a little more closely, noting, however, that very often these two categories overlapped. There is a reasonably long-standing scholarly interest in the presence and role of sages in ancient Near Eastern courts.[34] Sages were important figures in Egyptian royal courts, and fulfilled functions such as magician and sorcerer, interpreter of dreams, adviser, counsellor, diplomat, problem solver, physician, eloquent entertainer, architect and government official.[35] As for Mesopotamia, Sweet has summarized the position as follows: "The record is clear that the palace provided patronage for science and technology of all kinds throughout Mesopotamian history, and the sage, both in the narrower and the broader senses, was always a familiar and welcome figure in Mesopotamian royal palaces."[36]

There even exist almost 350 letters on cuneiform tablets addressed to the Neo-Assyrian kings Esarhaddon and Ashurbanipal from scribes (*tupšarru*) who were experts in celestial and terrestrial portents, diviners, exorcists, physicians, and singers of laments.[37] Sages and scribes also featured in the courts of Iranian kings, encompassing the Achaemenid (ca. 550–333 BCE), the Parthian (250 BCE—224 CE) and Sassanid (224–651 CE) periods.[38]

The presence of sages at Hellenistic courts had begun to attract attention before the work of Norbert Elias began to permeate into classical studies.[39] More recently, however, Rolf Strootman, as part of his project to situate Hellenistic courts within this new framework of investigation, has highlighted two important contexts in which learned men and skilled professionals were to be found in the courts of Hellenistic kings: as tutors and as the recipients of royal patronage. First, they served as tutors to train princes and young nobles, with the most notable instance being that of Aristotle who was invited to the court of Philip II of Macedon as tutor for Alexander. Other examples include: Aristotle's pupil Callisthenes at Alexander's court;

---

their leader. Then sent I against him a Persian named Dâdarši, my servant, who was satrap of Bactria, and I said unto him: 'Go, smite that host which does not acknowledge me.' Then Dâdarši went forth with the army, and gave battle to the Margians" (ET, slightly modified, from King and Thompson 1907).

34. See the essays in Gammie and Perdue, eds. 1990.
35. Williams 1990.
36. Sweet 1990:107.
37. Ibid.:106; for the letters, see Parpola 1970–1983.
38. Russell 1990.
39. For example, Gammie 1990.

Strato at the court of Ptolemy Soter; Aristarchos, Apollonius of Rhodes and perhaps Callimachos at the court of Ptolemy Philadelphus; and the Stoic philosopher Persaios at the court of Antigonus Gonatas.[40] Secondly, they were the recipients of patronage by kings, queens and other elite courtiers determined to see "literature, technology, philosophy, and visual arts" flourish: "The Ptolemaic court at Alexandria was the greatest center of art and learning in the Hellenistic east, followed, at some distance, by the peripatetic courts of the first three Antigonids and early Seleukids, and later also for a short while at the Attalid court at Pergamon."[41] With Hellenistic court patronage, Aristarchos argued that the sun and not the earth was the center of the universe, Eratosthenes calculated the circumference of the earth, Hero built a steam engine, Euclid and Archimedes developed mathematics, Herophilus and Erasistratus charted the human vascular and nervous system and Callimachus, Theocritus and Apollonius pushed on with literary innovations.[42] The great library at Alexandria, as well as other libraries at Pergamum, Tarsus and Antioch, were important in attracting philosophers to the court, leading Gammie to comment: "Included among the sages, then, at the Hellenistic royal courts were intelligentsia of a variety of sorts, lured to the courts not only for the remuneration but also for access to other intellectuals and a sizeable research library."[43]

As noted above, another type of individual found in royal courts was the foreigner, whether a sage or not. Particularly relevant for 1 Enoch are the stories from Israelite literature of Judeans, often presented as wise and skilful courtiers rather than full-time "sages," in the courts of foreign kings.[44] These include Joseph, Daniel and Ahiqar. Although a version of the Ahiqar story is known from an Aramaic papyrus from Elephantine, in which he is a scribe and counselor in the court of the Assyrian kings Senanacherib and Esarhaddon, his character finds its way into the Book of Tobit (which is also set in Assyria) and there Ahiqar is a Judean related to Tobit. While the Ahiqar story is not a diaspora one, the Judean examples, and similar cases where we find wise Ionians (Greeks) in Lydian courts and wise Lydians in the Persian court, are. In all these cases, according to the highly plausible view of Lawrence Wills, "the ruled ethnic perspective court legend is used

40. Strootman 2007:185–87.
41. Ibid.:189.
42. Ibid.:189–90.
43. Gammie 1990:148.
44. On this subject, see Wills 1990.

to the same effect: to assert the wisdom and statecraft of the cultural hero of the ruled ethnic group," thus asserting the value and identity of the latter.[45]

Identity and Prestige from Court Membership

Membership of the court was itself a significant social attribute. Elias argued that in the court of the French king the courtiers, by distinguishing themselves—individually and as a group—from non-members, confirmed their whole existence as a value in itself:

> The courtier had no possibility of changing place, leaving Paris or Versailles and continuing his life elsewhere without loss of prestige or self-respect. Only in this one court society could its members preserve what gave them direction and purpose in their own eyes, their social existence as court people, their aloofness from all else, their prestige—the centre of their self-image and of their personal identity. *They went to court not only because they were dependent on the king; they remained dependent on the king because it was only by going to court and living within court society that they could preserve the distance from everything else on which their spiritual salvation, their prestige as court aristocrats, in short, their social existence and their personal identity depended.*[46]

While the situation may not have been quite so extreme in the ancient courts of the Egyptian, Persian, and Seleucid kings, with the courtiers not quite so constrained to remain at court, their access to power and to honour was probably most secure if they did, unless the ruler sent them elsewhere on specific missions.

Court Relationships, Functioning, and Continuance

Yet the French court was not a static system, since the order of rank among the courtiers was constantly fluctuating: "The balance within this society was . . . very precarious. Now small, almost imperceptible tremors, now large-scale convulsions incessantly changed the positions of people and the distance between them."[47] One's individual standing was always fragile.

---

45. Wills 1990:68.
46. Elias 1983:99 (italics original).
47. Ibid.:91.

Writing of Hellenistic courts in the late second century BCE, Polybius describes much the same situation as follows:

> The truism that a fleeting opportunity raises a man up or lays him low is nowhere more true than in the courts of kings. Courtiers are indeed just like the counters on an abacus, which according to the will of the person doing the calculating are worth now a fraction of an obol, and a moment later a talent. Just so, courtiers become objects of envy and then of pity at the whim of the king.[48]

The Persian court provides evidence for a small group of courtiers having particularly distinguished positions and being publicly honored by the king, but also suffering dramatic falls. The Behistun Inscription, mentioned above, names a number of men who helped Darius defeat Gaumata and to two of whom he delegated the quelling of various revolts against his rule. Yet one of these, the first mentioned in fact, Intaphrenes, later fell out of favour with Darius for alleged treason and he and the male members of his family were executed.[49]

It is important to bear in mind the significance of Elias's statement that a court society was "a formation consisting of many individual people."[50] It was not an anonymous group of people.[51] People knew one another and were very interested in knowing where, at any given time, they each stood in the pronounced social hierarchy of the court. To describe the court in this perspective Elias coined the phrase "social figuration." He was attracted to the fact that "figuration" was neutral: "It can refer to harmonious, peaceful and friendly relationships between people, as well as to tense and hostile relationships."[52] Each of the individuals making up the court as a social figuration "is unique and unrepeatable" but the "figuration itself can be preserved relatively unchanged over many generations."[53] Brosius reasonably summarises this dimension of Elias's approach as asking "how the social position of monarch was perpetuated over numerous generations and dynasties and over considerable time periods."[54]

How was it that a court could persist for generations? Elias addresses this question by asking: "What distribution of power, which socially instilled

---

48. Polybius, *The Histories* 5.26; ET Waterfield 2010:310.
49. Herodotus, *Histories* 3.119.2.
50. Elias 1983:141.
51. Brosius 2007:54.
52. Elias 1983:141.
53. Ibid.:13.
54. Brosius 2007:17.

needs, which relationships of dependence brought it about that people in this social field constantly converged over generations in this figuration, as a court, as court society?"[55] His primary answer, and one that has proved very influential among researchers on the ancient Near Eastern and Greco-Roman kingdoms in the last two decades, focuses on the condition of interdependence that existed between king and courtiers. Even a king like Louis XIV, whom many take as the supreme example of an absolute monarch, "proves on closer scrutiny to be an individual who was enmeshed in his position as king in a specific network of interdependences."[56] In brief, the courtiers were dependent upon the king and the king upon the courtiers in "a mutual dependence embodied in the court."[57] On the one hand, "A courtier's position in this depended on the favour he enjoyed with the king, his power and importance within the field of court tensions."[58] On the other hand, since the court was the French king's "primary and most direct sphere of activity," with the country being "only a secondary and indirect one," he exercised power through the court.[59] Elias notes that this was more the case for kings like Louis XIV than for kings who fought their enemies personally at the head of an army, or (he could have added), for kings who continually moved their courts around, as did the Achaemenid and Seleucid kings. Nevertheless, whether the court was mobile or remained in one place, Elias was certainly correct in the view that "Everything that came from the king's wider possessions, from the realm, had to pass through the filter of the court before it could reach him; through the same filter everything from the king had to pass before it reached the country. Even the most absolute monarch could exert an influence on his country only through the mediation of people living at the court."[60]

Access to the Achaemenid and Hellenistic kings, for example, was overseen by the members of the court elites.[61] The fact that the Achaemenid kings followed in the tradition of extreme isolation from their subjects established by Deioces, the (possible) first king of the Medes, a people whose kingdom they conquered, necessarily increased the power of those with a gate-keeping function in relation to them. Brosius explains that the Medes, like the Persians after them, were an Iranian people. Their political order

55. Elias 1983:35.
56. Ibid.:3.
57. Ibid.:157.
58. Ibid.:90.
59. Elias 1983:42.
60. Ibid.:42.
61. Spawforth 2007b:4.

Modelling Courts and Courtiers 47

appears to have been a loose federation of kings based in different cities. From this arrangement emerged "a dominating dynasty under Deioces of Ecbatana. Herodotus credited him with the introduction of court etiquette and court procedures." She then quotes Herodotus 1.99:

> It was Deioces first who established the rule that no-one should come into the presence of the king, but all should be dealt with by means of messengers; that the king should be seen by no man; and that it should be in particular a disgrace for any to laugh or to spit in his presence.

He did this, says Herodotus, so that his contemporaries with whom he had been brought up, and who were as noble as he, would not be vexed by seeing him and plot against him, and by not seeing him they would consider he was changed from what he had been.[62] Brosius continues by noting that: "Even if the historicity of Herodotus's Median *logos* must be regarded with caution, the portrayal of the king's recognition of his unique position, which set him apart from people who had been formerly his peers, reflects a credible historical development from tribal or military leader to kingship. The idea that the king had to distance himself from his subjects is echoed in Xenophon's description of Cyrus' court."[63]

At this point she quotes Xenophon's *The Education of Cyrus* 7.5.37–41, which ends with this statement: "So Cyrus stationed a large circle of Persian lancers about him and gave orders that no-one should be admitted except his friends and the officers of the Persians and their allies." To similar effect is what Aristotle says of the Persian king in *De Mundo*:

> The king himself, so the story goes, established himself at Susa or Ecbatana, invisible to all, dwelling in a wondrous palace inside a fence gleaming with gold and amber and ivory. And it had many gateways, one after another, and porches many furlongs apart from one another, secured by bronze doors and mighty walls. Outside them, the foremost and most distinguished had their appointed place. Some were the king's bodyguard and attendants; others were the guardians of each enclosing wall, the so-called doorkeepers and listeners, so that the king himself, called their lord and god, might thus see and hear all things. (398a)[64]

---

62. Brosius 2007:22.
63. Ibid.:22.
64. ET in Kuhrt 2007:581.

Not all members of the Persian court had direct access to the king. "Information was filtered through to the chief officials who were entitled to approach the king."[65] Those who had access could probably only speak with the king's express permission, as was the case with Nehemiah in Neh 2:2.[66]

The King's Need for Knowledge

This question of the provision of information to a king needs further exploration. Elias mounted a useful distinction between a "conquering ruler" and a "conserving ruler." The former was actively involved in military campaigns and the loyalty of his inner group was secured by their sharing in common military action within the wider dominion. The latter, however, could not count on the same degree of loyalty, "For the pressure he must exert to maintain his rule finds no relief in communal outwardly directed actions, at least as long as there are no wars."[67] For a "conserving ruler" "the observation and supervision of people is (sic) indispensable in defending his rule."[68] This applied *a fortiori* in the case of a king who had decided to sequester himself from his subjects at court and to rely only on a small group of intermediaries. Louis XIV addressed this problem by engaging a number of Swiss guards and secretly commissioning them to frequent the various parts of the Palace of Versailles and report on everything that they heard and saw to the king's first valet and Governor of Versailles.[69] Herodotus reports something similar in relation to Deioces, mentioned above, when he had gained the kingship:

> Once his sovereign power was firmly established, he continued his strict administration of justice. All suits were conveyed to him in the form of written documents, which he would send back after recording upon them his decisions. In addition to this there were other practices he introduced: if he heard of any act of arrogance or ostentation, he would send for the offender and punish him as the offence deserved, and his spies were busy watching (οἱ κατάσκοποι) and listening (κατήκοοι) in every corner of his dominion.[70]

---

65. Brosius 2007:39.
66. Ibid.:40.
67. Elias 1983:128.
68. Ibid.
69. Elias 1983:129.
70. Herodotus, *Histories* 1.100; ET from de Selincourt 1954:55.

Bradley Parker has described in relation to the Neo-Assyrian kingdom a somewhat different notion of "watching" related to the role of scholars at the court: the role of the Assyrian scholars (*ummânī*) was, to use the words of the scholars themselves, to "keep the king's watch"—that is, to protect, guide, and advise the king. The Assyrian scholars did so by interpreting omens, conducting extispicy, protecting the king from evil, and maintaining the king's ritual purity."[71] Another aspect worth noting is that in this passage Herodotus attributes to Deioces the introduction of written petitions of grievance to the ruler, an important subject to which we will return below. The Persian kings sought to professionalize the receipt of intelligence by creating a position at court known as "the King's Eye" or "Eyes."[72] This role may have been a development of Deioces' κατάσκοποι just mentioned.[73]

While no Old Persian document refers to the Eye, there are numerous Greek references suggesting that the role of the person or persons holding this office was "to supervise the imperial territories and to prevent rebellion, and to supervise the local governments."[74] The Persian kings further developed their intelligence gathering capacity by the construction of a system of royal roads and the establishment of a type of royal post.[75] They also set up a telegraph system of fire signals that stretched from the furthest bounds of the empire to Susa and Ecbatana.[76] Even before the Persian kings, the neo-Assyrian kingdom ran a sophisticated spying operation, for which startlingly detailed and direct evidence exists in the form of cuneiform tablets containing both reports from operatives in the field and instructions to local commanders from the king and other palace officials.[77] The passage from Aristotle's *De Mundo* just cited also mentions royal listeners in the palace itself, like Louis XIV's Swiss guards.

The Mediating Role of Courtiers

We have noted above Elias' view that "Even the most absolute monarch could exert an influence on his country only through the mediation of people living at the court."[78] One particular area that clearly reveals the ex-

71. Parker 2011:370.
72. See the discussion by Balcer 1977:255–61.
73. Balcer 1977:256.
74. Ibid.:260, 261.
75. Dvornik 1974:26–31.
76. Ibid:31–32.
77. See Dubovsky 2006:32–158.
78. Elias 1983:42.

tent to which Seleucid kings and those outside the court relied on courtiers with access to the king to facilitate his rule was in the relationship between ruler and cities. According to Strootman, like many large empires the Seleucid state was "basically a tribute-taking military organisation, offering protection and benefactions to city states and local princes. To finance its military strength, the empire depended on tribute, paid overwhelmingly by cities." Accordingly, maintaining good relations between itself and the cities was a principal concern of the Seleucid administration.[79] Traditional Greek patterns of aristocratic guest friendship, known as *xenia* or *philoxenia*, linked members of the royal household with members of the city elites. At the heart of *xenia* was *philia*, ritualised friendship between two people of roughly equal status involving mutual loyalty and gift exchange.[80] Relationships of *xenia* allowed the Seleucid court to wield influence in the cities, but also "offered the cities the opportunity to exert influence on political matters at court and *to obtain privileges*."[81]

Philia also played an important role in men attaching themselves to the royal household (*oikos*) and becoming courtiers there, in which capacity they were involved in "serving the king as court officials, ambassadors or military commanders."[82] Hellenistic courtiers were known as *philoi tou basileôs*, "Friends of the King."[83] Strootman summarizes their mediating role as follows:

> The royal friends played a crucial role in the negotiations between city and king both directly and indirectly. Directly, they could act as negotiators on behalf of their own cities of origin. They represented the interests of the cities at court and the interests of the court in the cities, deriving benefits from their membership of both systems. Indirectly, *philoi* could act as intermediaries between the royal power and embassies seeking audience at court. For such arbitration cities could reward *philoi* with public honours, citizen rights and gifts. At court, they could obtain military commands, landed estates, privileges and

---

79. Strootman 2011:68.
80. This comes from Strootman 2011:69, citing Herman 1987 and Meissner 2000.
81. Strootman 2011:70 (emphasis added).
82. Herman 1987:200, cited by Strootman 2011:70.
83. See the major study by Savalli-Lestrade 1998, which contains a prosopography of the royal friends in the Seleucid and Attalid kingdoms of Asia Minor and a description of their recruitment, titles, origins and family ties and the way they were transformed from an informal group of companions into an ordered structure of courtiers.

favours for themselves, their families, their cities and their own clients, and status.[84]

This aspect of their system of government indicates how Hellenistic kings employed courtiers as important mediating figures and were, accordingly, not the absolute masters of their own courts, a point Elias made in relation to the *ancien régime*, as noted above. Another aspect of the limitations on the ruler can be seen in Polybius' descriptions of Hellenistic kings being subject to forces operating at court, a picture that Herman considers an accurate one.[85]

The Court as a Site of Royal Representation

The patterns of membership and interdependence of king and nobles that characterized the French court and the ancient Near Eastern courts were accompanied by a major emphasis on display and representation, on "image-management."[86] The phenomena involved included "the whole range of symbolic communication, such as art and architecture, ceremony and costume, which legitimate the ruler's authority."[87] Speaking of French nobles, although in a way that equally applied to the king, Elias stated, "The most real way of asserting one's rank is by documenting it through an appropriate social appearance."[88]

One way that French courtiers publicly manifested such social differentiation was through their ownership of large and luxurious houses, in which they lived when not at court. The higher one's noble rank, moreover, the larger and more luxurious one's house had to be.[89] Social pressure drove them to such display even if they bankrupted themselves in the process.[90] No matter how impressive a nobleman's house might be, however, it was never permissible to "exhibit the magnificence reserved for the palaces of kings."[91] This indicates the extent to which in this regard, the French king was socially superior to the courtiers and to all of his subjects.

---

84. Strootman 2011:71.
85. Herman 1997:212.
86. A phrase used by Spawforth 2007c:87.
87. Spawforth 2007b:8.
88. Elias 1983:63–64.
89. Ibid.:59.
90. Ibid.:53–54.
91. Ibid.:58.

The social superiority of Louis XIV was also reflected in the issue of controlled access to his person. In a similar way, Brosius has suggested that limited access to the Persian king "meant that the person of the king was exalted above other members of the court."[92] Elias explained this dimension of the position of the French kings as follows:

> Glory for the king was what honour was to the nobles. But the glorification of his own social existence, his claim to prestige, surpassed those of all others in his realm in magnitude and intensity in the same proportion as did his power.... This immense need for domination and for glorification of his own existence as king, distinguishing him conspicuously from all others, in its turn placed chains on him that drew him inexorably into the social mechanism ... He could not subject other people to ceremony and display as means of power without subjecting himself to them as well.[93]

One indicator of the extent to which the king was caught up in this need for display was that in 1744 (early in the reign of Louis XV) the palace of Versailles was reported to have accommodated 10,000 persons.[94] Not only in France but also in the courts of Egyptian, Persian and Hellenistic kings, the ruler's residence, the palace, was an indispensable locus of royal representation and display.

Having now set out the approach of Norbert Elias to courts and courtiers in absolutist monarchies, with frequent references to Persian and Hellenistic courts as reflecting the social dynamics he explored, I will now examine 1 Enoch in the light of this model, beginning with the broad nature of the heavenly court (Chapter 3).

---

92. Brosius 2007:22; also note her discussion of the various arenas in which the Persian kings controlled access at 39–40.

93. Elias 1983:136.

94. Ibid.:80.

3

THE NATURE OF
THE HEAVENLY COURT

THE RAISON D'ÊTRE OF THE COURT

The initial link between model and text lies in the absolutist nature of God's rule. The God of 1 Enoch is a monotheistic God who does not share power with any other gods, even though he exists in the presence of other heavenly beings. He is, moreover, a king like those of both the *ancien régime* and the ancient Near East, ruling without an assembly or assemblies of his human subjects. God is referred to as a king on six occasions in 1 Enoch 1–36. The first reference comes at 9:4 when he is called "king of kings."[1] This is a "royal title with a long history in the ancient Near East."[2] Thus, the title of "king of kings" was one that Darius the Great of Persia applied to himself in the first line of the famous Behistun Inscription that was mentioned in Chapter 2: "I am Darius, the great king, king of kings, the king of Persia, the king of countries, the son of Hytaspes, the grandson of Arsames, the Achaemenid."[3] God is also "king of eternity" (βασιλεὺς τοῦ αἰῶνος; 25:3, 5,

---

1. This is the reading in the Syncellus fragment of the Greek, "king of those who rule as kings" (ὁ βασιλεὺς τῶν βασιλευόντων), but not in the Akhmim manuscript (Codex Panopolitanus), which at this point reads βασιλεὺς τῶν αἰώνων; "king of the generations," see Black 1970:23. Nickelsburg notes that the former version of the Greek is generally superior to the latter (2001:13) and the reading is supported by the Ethiopic manuscripts, "their king of kings" (ንጉሦሙ፡ ለነገሥት; *negušomu la-nagašt*) and appears again in 1 Enoch 84:2.

2. Nickelsburg 2001:211.

3. Translation from King and Thompson 1907, line 1.

7; 27:3).[4] This latter expression conveys the fact of his sovereignty over and through time and eternity, something Darius could not and did not claim for himself, whatever the spatial extent of his rule.

God is addressed in many other ways in 1 Enoch, including "lord of lords" (κύριος τῶν κυρίων, 9:4), which was also used by other Near Eastern rulers, as in the stelae erected by the Egyptian king Sesoôsis that refer to him as "king of king and lord of lords" (βασιλεὺς βασιλέων καὶ δεσπότης δεσποτῶν).[5] These two features are also combined in 1 Enoch 9:4. God is also "the Holy One" (1:2), "the Great Holy One" (1:3; 14:1), "the Most High" (9:2; 10:1), "Lord of all Lords in Majesty" (9:2), "Lord of the Ages" (9:4), "God of gods" (9:4), "God of the ages" (9:4), "Great Holy One" (10:1; 12:3; 24:3), "the Lord of majesty" (12:3), "Lord of heaven" (13:4), "Great One"(14:2), "Great Glory" (14:20), "Lord" (14:24; 18:14; 21:6), "Lord of glory" (22:14; 24:3; 27:3; 27:5; 36:4), "Lord of majesty and righteousness" (22:14), and "Lord of eternity" (22:14). In this volume we are focusing primarily on God's kingship, even though other expressions, such as "lord," were often used by ancient Near Eastern and Hellenistic kings.

In spite of the kingship of God being an important theme in 1 Enoch 1–36, and in spite of the arena of God's activity having a spatial extent that covers both heaven and earth, the expression "the kingdom of God" does not appear in this text. Nevertheless, George Ladd rightly recognized that 1 Enoch 1–36 should be included in an attempt to trace the development of the notion of the kingdom of God.[6] For the notion of God's kingdom is implied in 1 Enoch 1–36, with a spatial extent embracing heaven (its capital) and earth that together constitute the arena of God's kingship.

We are so used to the designation of the Israelite God as a king that even mentioning his kingship may seem banal. Yet Bradley Parker has recently noted that discussions of kingship in the ancient Near East are surprisingly rare in the scholarly literature.[7] Moreover, this way of understanding God was not inevitable, but the product of the social context in which the idea developed. In the ancient Mediterranean world monarchy was one of three well recognized types of constitution, the other two being aristocracy and democracy, with all three types having, as the Greek historian Polybius mentions, a degenerate counterpart: respectively, tyranny, oligarchy, and ochlocracy or mob-rule.[8] Even though monarchy was far more common

---

4. The Ethiopic reads here "king of eternity" (ንጉሥ፡ ዓለም; neguš 'ālam).
5. Diodorus Siculus, *Bibliotheca* 1.55.7, cited by Nickelsburg 2001:211.
6. Ladd 1952a and b.
7. Parker 2011:357.
8. Polybius, *The Histories* 6.3–10.

than the other two, especially in the Near East, there were known to be other possible constitutions. At an early stage in their history, it is worthy of note, the Romans had, with the expulsion of their last king Lucius Tarquinius Superbus and his whole family in 510 BCE, decisively rejected the institution of kingship in favour of a democratic model. This circumstance usefully reminds us how heavily the Enochic (and wider Israelite) representation of God as king was context-dependent. This point will gain greater focus in the process of comparing the picture of God in 1 Enoch 1–36 with the courts of Near Eastern and Hellenistic kings.

As Elias noted, for absolutist kings the court functioned as the household for the royal family and as the center for the state administration, while Spawforth has highlighted the court as encompassing the ruler's dwelling and the people there. All of these elements feature in 1 Enoch. God is, admittedly, unlike Near Eastern kings who had wives and concubines and children, and unlike other gods who were represented in a similar way. So here we have a royal family consisting of one person. While that is probably without parallel in the ancient world, it is not in principle impossible. And although God lacks a family, he is understood as being like any other king in needing somewhere to live. As early as 1 Enoch 1:3 we learn that "the Great One will come forth from his dwelling."[9] The words "his dwelling" are not extant in the Aramaic text,[10] but the Greek has "from his dwelling" (ἐκ τῆς κατοικήσεως αὐτοῦ), and the Ethiopic has the same (እምንበሩ; 'em ḫedru). In the nine instances of κατοίκησις in the Septuagint,[11] it means "dwelling" in a general sense, not "house." It even has that meaning of God's abode. Thus at 1 Kgs 8:30 Solomon asks God to listen to his people from the place of his κατοίκησις which is in heaven. In 1 Enoch 14, however, with its detailed description of the heavenly precinct which I will consider in Chapter 4, although the Aramaic is not extant, the usual Greek word for "house," οἶκος, appears four times in connection with the building where God is located (14:10, 13, 15, 21), translated by ቤት (bēt) in the Ethiopic. Like other kings, therefore, God has a house, which forms part of a larger palace complex to be discussed later.

In 1 Enoch we see God in his abode taking actions "which shaped the destiny of the kingdom," to quote Gabriel Herman's observation about the critical role of Hellenistic courts. Yet, like the kings of those courts, God does so with the help of others and we must now consider their identity

---

9. Nickelsburg 2001:142.

10. See Milik 1976:142.

11. Gen 10:30, 27:39; Exod 12:40; Num 15:2; 2 Sam 9:12; 1 Kgs 8:30; 2 Kgs 2:19; 2 Chr 6:21; and 1 Esdras 1:21.

and functions and relate all this to the court model presented in Chapter 2. While God lacks a family, he is not alone in heaven. It turns out, indeed, that his abode is really rather crowded with other individuals, expressly mentioned or implied, who have various responsibilities. On inspection, we will see that they are virtually indistinguishable from the courtiers of ancient Near Eastern courts.

The Members of the Court

General Characteristics

The Behistun Inscription of Darius the Great is replete with accounts of military campaigns that he undertook to secure his kingdom, either under his direct command or through subordinates he appointed for the task. Here is one example:

> King Darius says: After that I marched against Babylon. But before I reached Babylon, that Nidintu-Bel, who called himself Nebuchadnezzar, came with a host and offered battle at a city called Zazana, on the Euphrates. Then we joined battle. Ahuramazda brought me help; by the grace of Ahuramazda did I utterly overthrow the host of Nidintu-Bel. The enemy fled into the water; the water carried them away.[12]

This is the sort of action that Persian and Hellenistic kings routinely took to secure the safety and well-being of their realm. The Enochic God is no different. Indeed, the character of those who share heaven with God is colored by a military dimension that appears very early in the text, in the details of God's descent to earth at the end-time (1 Enoch 1:4–9). For, like any king, God goes on campaign when necessary for his purposes:

> The Great Holy One will come forth from his dwelling (κατοίκησις),
>   and the eternal God will tread from thence upon Mount Sinai.
> He will appear with his army,
>   he will appear with his mighty host (ἐν τῇ δυνάμει τῆς ἰσχύος) from the heaven of heavens.
> All the Watchers will fear and <quake>. (1:3–4).[13]

---

12. Line 19; translation from King and Thompson 1907. Ahuramazda is Darius' god.

13. Nickelsburg 2001:142. There is a textual problem here, since the Greek reads not "with his army" (ἐν τῇ παρεμβολῇ αυτου) but "from his camp" (ἐκ τῇ παρεμβολῇ αυτου), the latter reading being favored by Black (1985:106). Yet, as Milik (1976:144–145) and

Not only will God descend from heaven with "his army" and "his mighty host" (v. 4), but he will also come "with his myriads and his holy ones" (σὺν ταῖς μυριάσιν αὐτοῦ καὶ τοῖς ἁγίοις αὐτοῦ) to execute judgment, to destroy all the wicked and to convict humanity of their evil deeds (v. 9). The number of the angels is directly linked to the overwhelming power that God will demonstrate during his end-time visitation. They represent the mighty warband of an invincible king.

Nickelsburg interprets 1 Enoch 1:3–4 as part of a "theophany" on the part of "the transcendent King who descends to earth to execute judgment, which is construed as a military campaign by the heavenly king and his army."[14] He is issuing forth from his "heavenly temple."[15] Yet a more realistic picture, and one that prioritises ethnic over religious identity, is gained by giving proper weight to the military nature of the passage. Rather, what we have here is a military campaign by God and his army, culminating in judgment, which Nickelsburg construes religiously and theologically with the word "theophany." But God was simply doing what other kings did.

The thirteenth century CE painting of Raphael with a raised sword on the cover of this volume from a monastery in Gorgora on Lake Tana and discussed in the Prologue indicates the extent to which the Enochic tradition in Ethiopia appreciated the military dimension of God's angels and archangels. The tradents of this tradition did not mistake Raphael for a priest in the temple.

We should not be so pre-occupied with theological and religious interpretations of the Enochic language that we overlook the sharp, indeed brutal, realities of a king's responsibilities as a military leader. First Enoch, after all, will later describe (see Chapter 4 of this volume) an actual campaign in which God orders Gabriel to destroy the gigantic children of the Watchers (10:1–11:2) that extends even to the Watchers' witnessing "the destruction of their beloved sons" (1 Enoch 10:12).

Nickelsburg (2001:142) have noted, the Ethiopic reading (በትዕይንቱ; ba-te'eyntu) presupposes the former Greek expression. Milik plausibly suggests that the Greek reading is a correction of the original ἐν τῇ παρεμβολῇ by someone who has not realized that παρεμβολή should be understood in terms of people ("the army"), for example, as in Testament of Levi 3:3; and not place. Another issue, however, is that "with his mighty host" (ἐν τῇ δυνάμει τῆς ἰσχύος αὐτοῦ) can be translated "in the power of his might" (Black 1985:25). Yet even Black notes that the language here is military (1985:106). Even if one were to read "from his camp" and "in the power of his might," the image would still be that of God with his army (especially given the forces that other parts of 1 Enoch 1–36 show he possessed in such numbers).

14. Nickelsburg 2001:145.

15. Ibid.:144.

Nor should we overlook the clarity and originality of the Enochic presentation of God as a warrior king in 1 Enoch 1:4–9, as a comparison with somewhat similar phenomena in the Psalter, which is the major source for such features in the Hebrew Bible, will serve to illustrate. As Martin Klingbeil has pointed out, a number of Psalms contain material depicting Yahweh either as a warrior God, or as a God who descends from heaven, or as both: Pss 18:7–15; 29:3–9; 46:6–11; 68:14–21; 83:13–17; and 144:4–7.[16] In Psalm 18 Yahweh "bowed the heavens, and he came down" (v. 9), "he rode on a cherub, and he flew" (v. 11), and "he sent out his arrows, and scattered them" (v. 14). In Psalm 46 we are told "The Lord of hosts is with us" (vv. 7 and 11), that he "makes wars to cease," and "he breaks the bow, and shatters the spear, he burns the chariots with fire" (v. 9). According to Psalm 68, "When the Almighty scattered kings there, snow fell on Zalmon" (v. 15), and other mountains envied the mountain of God (v. 16). Furthermore, "With mighty chariotry, twice ten thousand, thousands upon thousands, the Lord is among them in Sinai in the holy place" (v. 17).[17] In Ps 83:13–15 the Psalmist urges Yahweh to treat his enemies in the following manner:

> O my God, make them like whirling dust,
>   like chaff before the wind.
> As fire consumes the forest,
>   as the flame sets the mountains ablaze,
> so do thou pursue them with thy tempest
>   and terrify them with thy hurricane. (RSV)

Finally, in Ps 144:5–6 the Psalmist prays as follows:

> Bow thy heavens, O Lord, and come down!
>   Touch the mountains that they smoke!
> Flash forth the lightning and scatter them,
>   send out thy arrows and rout them! (RSV)

It is noteworthy that none of these passages matches the detailed and unambiguous picture of a warrior God descending with his army that we find in 1 Enoch 1:4–9. In none of them do we have Yahweh expressly leading

---

16. See Klingbeil 1999:55–157. He also includes Pss 21:8–12 and 65:10–14, but these features are not so obvious there. I have modified his lineation and translations in line with those of the RSV.

17. Note that here I have replaced the RSV's "the Lord came from Sinai into the holy place" with "the Lord is among them in Sinai in the holy place" which accords closely with the MT and the LXX.

his army into battle. This is a major innovation on the part of the Enochic author.

Let us now look more closely at the beings in heaven apart from God. The most significant are those described at various places in the text as "Watchers" (עִירִין, *'yryn*) "holy ones" and "angels." The notion of "Watchers" is significant, since it almost certainly has a functional meaning. At 1 Enoch 20:1 reference is made in the Ethiopic version (but not the Greek) to "the holy angels who watch" (ይተግሁ፡ ቅዱሳን፡ መላእክት፤ *yetaggehu qeddusān malā'ekt*) with the verbal form here indicating a specific function. The Ethiopic word *tagha* means "be vigilant, wakeful." The verbal adjective *teguh* (frequently used nominally) means someone who is watchful, wakeful, vigilant. The Aramaic עִיר (*'yr*), which (in a plural form) is translated by ἐγρήγοροι (at 10:9 for example) and *teguh*, means "wakeful."[18] Nickelsburg suggests a range of possible dimensions of their watching, that they are beings who are on twenty-four hour service attending God: (a) to praise him; (b) to function "as a kind of bodyguard in the throne room"; (c) to supervise the functions of creation (20:1); (d) based on 82:10, to keep watch over the celestial beings in charge of the seasons; and (e) to guard the righteous.[19] Some of these are problematic, however. As to (a), in this text the angels are not described as praising God (a point to which I will return below). Items [c] and [d] should probably be amalgamated. Finally, dimension (b) especially requires greater emphasis and elaboration.

At 1 Enoch 9:2 we have the first reference in the text to the "gates of heaven" and more detail is provided in 1 Enoch 34:1—36:2 where we learn that there are three gates on each of the four sides of heaven corresponding to compass points. Such mention of gates necessarily entails that heaven is a large walled precinct, since gates pre-suppose walls. As the Watchers who left heaven were able to see what was happening on earth (6:2) and since the named (good) angels (Michael, Sariel, Raphael, and Gabriel) who remained were able to see what they did when they descended there (9:1), readers of the text are probably meant to imagine the Watchers looking down from the walls of heaven. Strong confirmation for this view exists in the statement at the start of 9:2 that these named angels then "having gone in (εἰσελθόντες) spoke to one another,"[20] which indicates that they were *outside*, on the walls, but they then moved *inside*, to some room or other, to confer. This means that in so far as they are "Watchers," they have a vital guard duty. They are on guard not so much over the throne room, but rather, by looking out on

---

18. Sokoloff 1990:405.
19. Nickelsburg 2001:140–41.
20. This is from the Syncellus fragment of a Greek text.

the earth and also the sky, they are lookouts with heaven and earth below in their sights. They are doing this from the usual position, from the walls constituting heaven's outer periphery. Thus they are "Watchers" in a sense similar to that conveyed by the Latin *vigiles*. In this respect they were performing a similar task to the military personnel charged with ensuring the safety of the court of every Near Eastern king. They are courtiers with a military function.

In addition, however, just as the French courtiers of the *ancien régime* lived in the palace of Versailles for much of the year, heaven is where the angels live. When God is instructing Enoch on what he must tell the Watchers, he makes this point explicitly on two occasions saying, "The spirits (πνεύματα) of heaven, in heaven is their dwelling" (κατοίκησις; 1 Enoch 15:7 and 10), by way of criticism of the Watchers' descent to earth. As noted above, the word κατοίκησις is also used of God's dwelling in 1 Enoch 1:3. Although to modern ears it is a remarkable anthropomorphism, the Enochic author accepts that both God and the angels need somewhere to live and that place is heaven. Admittedly, unlike the courtiers of royal courts on earth, the angels have no other residences nor (for that matter) families to return to away from the court. Nevertheless, they do share with them the fundamental fact that heaven was their dwelling-place, just as it was for God himself. That the angels had a permanent residence in heaven differentiates them from Israelite priests. The priests were divided into twenty-four divisions (1 Chronicles 24) and came up to Jerusalem to serve for a week at a time (1 Chr 9:25) and, like all Israelite men, were required to go up to Jerusalem for the three major festivals. Whether the priests who came up to the temple to undertake their turn of service actually lived in its precincts rather than somewhere else in Jerusalem is doubtful; there is archaeological evidence that in the first century CE the high priests lived in (luxurious) houses outside the temple area.[21]

Differentiation among the Angels

As with the courts of the *ancien régime*, Persia and the Hellenistic kingdoms, these angelic courtiers were not an undifferentiated group. The primary distinction is between those of them who stayed in heaven and the two hundred from their number (6:5) who left to marry human women. Although the word "Watcher" is applied to both groups,[22] "holy ones" is restricted to the former.

21. Avigad 1983.
22. "Watchers" is applied mainly to the bad angels at: 1:5; 6:2; 10:7, 9, and 15; 12:4;

But there is also a division between angels who are named and those who are not. Named good angels exist at the top of a hierarchy as seen in their being given special tasks by God (such as Michael, Sariel,[23] Raphael and Gabriel in 1 Enoch 10) or in taking various initiatives. The role of courtiers, the Friends of the King, in the social and political realities of a Hellenistic court, discussed in Chapter 2, provides a plausible model for these named angels. Clearly those who are tasked with specific responsibilities such as these have access to God in a way that the others do not. We learn in 1 Enoch 14:22 that "ten thousand times ten thousand" angels stood before him and, while no angel could enter his house (14:21), some angels are described as approaching him and attending him by day and night (14:23). Presumably, these latter are the named leaders of the angels. They exist near to and even in the presence of God in a manner similar to the courtiers in Persian and Hellenistic courts. It thus makes good sense to speak of an inner and outer court in relation to the angels. More generally, the gap between heaven and earth and the inability of human beings (except only Enoch) to bridge that gap replicate the social distance between those who were permitted to reside in an ancient royal court and the rest of the population of the kingdom who were not, even if the polarity is more extreme in the former case.

The Watchers who leave heaven, in circumstances to be investigated in Chapter 4, are also hierarchically organised. Shemihazah is their overall "chief" (6:3, 7), but he is designated as the first of twenty "chiefs of tens" among the two hundred Watchers who descend to earth (6:7–8). The "tens" referred to really only make sense as an army unit and this is further evidence for the angels having a military organization. Probably we are meant to assume that these named angels would also have formed part of the inner court if they had not chosen to abandon heaven for earth. I will return to the question of individuation among the angels further below.

The allocation of duties to courtiers at the Persian court was mentioned in Chapter 2. First Enoch 20 contains a list of named angels and the responsibilities with which they were charged that is very similar. If one were looking for a more realistic parallel in a "religious realm," one could cite the fact that Mesopotamian peoples "associated specific deities with the areas of the cosmos they deemed important, from nature to culture to government."[24] Here, then, is the list of the names of "the holy angels who

---

13:10; 14:3; 15:2 and 9; and 16:2. But at 1 Enoch 15:9 the Watchers who left heaven are referred to as "holy," which is a recognition of their initial high status. Additionally, the good angels are occasionally called "Watchers" (see 1 Enoch 12:2 and 3).

23. Sariel is Nickelsburg's highly plausible emendation of Uriel.
24. Hundley 2013:212.

keep watch," together with their specific functions in the cosmos, from 1 Enoch 20:

(a) Uriel, who is in charge of the world and Tartarus;

(b) Raphael, who is in charge of the spirits of men;

(c) Reuel, with responsibility for taking vengeance on the world of the luminaries;

(d) Michael, who is in charge of the good ones among the people;

(e) Sariel, who is in charge of the spirits who sin against the spirit;

(f) Gabriel, with responsibility for Paradise, the serpents and the cherubim; and

(g) Remiel, whom God has put in charge of those who rise.[25]

Although there are many uncertainties in the versions of this list, the details are less important than the fact that its function is undoubtedly to describe the particular portfolio held by each of these important angels in a manner very similar to the allocation of significant military and administrative responsibilities to senior courtiers of earthly monarchies. We also learn at 9:7 that God had given Shemihazah authority over the Watchers "who were with him," but whether he received that authority before their secession from heaven or afterwards is unclear. While all this is readily explicable in terms of the court model being advanced here, with various senior figures charged with separate responsibilities, none of the functions described has anything to do with a cult or a temple. It must be emphasised, indeed, that if the angels were understood in 1 Enoch 1–36 as having priestly functions, this section of the text is precisely where we would expect them to be outlined.

It is instructive to note from Chapter 1 just how different is the position when ancient Israelite authors set out quite deliberately and unambiguously to portray heaven as a temple served by priests, as is the case with the *Songs of the Sabbath Sacrifice* and the *Testament of Levi*. In both texts there are angels in a heavenly temple engaged in the priestly task of making offerings to God that produce a pleasing odor. If the author of 1 Enoch 1–36 understood the angels to be priests, why is none of them not given responsibility for the heavenly cult in 1 Enoch 20?

In addition, according to Carol Newsom, in the *Songs of the Sabbath Sacrifice*, "The primary task of the angels is the praise of God, a motif ubiquitous in the Shirot and prominent in most Jewish and Christian

---

25. I am following the translation in Nickelsburg and VanderKam 2012:40–41.

descriptions of the angels."²⁶ She also maintains that the "close combination of liturgical song and cultic sacrifice appears to have been a feature of the Second Temple cult."²⁷ For this latter point she cites 2 Chr 29:27–28, which forms part of a longer passage describing how King Hezekiah arranged for Levites to sing and play musical instruments and priests to blow trumpets to accompany the sacrifice in the temple (2 Chr 29:25–30).

By way of stark contrast, there is not a single instance of the angels in 1 Enoch 1–36 praising God. This element, so prominent in the *Songs of the Sabbath Sacrifice*, is absent from the Book of the Watchers. This is the case even though there is one point in the text where such a feature could have been introduced into the text very easily. Toward the end of the description of God on his throne, in 1 Enoch 14:21–23, there is a description of the angels gathered in a circle before God, with the holy ones among their number approaching him. While I will defer consideration of this passage till later in this chapter, it is enough to say at this point that this would have been an ideal location for some description of angelic praise being offered to God. The fact that the angels are *not* said to praise God stands in stark contrast to their portrayal in the *Songs of the Sabbath Sacrifice*. If the Enochic author had in mind the idea of relating heaven to the Jerusalem temple, how easy it would have been for him to mention something analogous to the singing of the Levites at this point in the text. Yet he does not.

Enoch Becomes a Sage in the Heavenly Court

But mention of the angels in heaven does not exhaust the number of those present. Just as Near Eastern courts received visitors, so too did this heavenly court, in the form of Enoch. The ultimate source for Enoch's presence in heaven is the enigmatic statement in Gen 5:24 that "Enoch walked with God; and he was not, for God took him." Nevertheless, 1 Enoch represents a massive elaboration of God's taking Enoch in ways that the nature of the French and Near Eastern courts helps explain, which the currently favored model of the Jerusalem temple does not. A remarkable feature of 1 Enoch is that it explicitly presents Enoch as a member of court society. Consider how far the statement that "God took him" in Gen 5:24 is pushed in this text:

> Before these things, Enoch was taken; and none of the sons of men knew where he had been taken, or where he was, or what

---

26. Newsom 1985:30.
27. Ibid.:18.

had happened to him. And his works were with the Watchers, and with the holy ones were his days. (1 Enoch 12:1–2).[28]

There are a number of possible referents for "Before these things." Probably the most likely one is the whole course of events starting with the fall of Watchers,[29] which would have the effect that Enoch was witness to the entire catastrophe. Yet even if the reference is more limited, say to the commission to the angels in 1 Enoch 10 or its presupposed fulfilment in the Flood,[30] the fact remains that Enoch's works were with the angels and he spent his days with them; he was, in short, part of their society. We must imagine communication passed between them since in the very next verse the Watchers speak to him (1 Enoch 12:3).

The material presented in Chapter 2 on the presence of various wise and learned figures, including specialists in astronomy, geography, and mathematics, at ancient Near Eastern courts from the early Mesopotamian and Egyptian monarchies through to those of the Hellenistic period, provides a viable, indeed natural context for understanding the presence of Enoch in the heavenly court. When Enoch is first addressed in the text as a "righteous scribe" (12:4), we must understand both aspects, his righteousness and his status as a scribe, to have preceded his translation to heaven, for there is no suggestion he became righteous or obtained such knowledge there. Both dimensions are necessary pre-conditions for God's translation of him to heaven. Like the wise men who were welcomed to ancient Near Eastern courts as mentioned above, Enoch is literate and professionally qualified.

The text does, however, reflect a variation on this pattern. Unlike figures such as Aristarchos and Eratosthenes, who came to Hellenistic courts already possessed of expertise in astronomy and geography, Enoch arrives with the intellectual capacity to understand such areas but obtains the requisite knowledge through speaking with angels and from his own observations as he is guided through the cosmos. Enoch's combination of intellectual capacity and angel-imparted learning is emphasised at the very start of the work:

---

28. Nickelsburg 2001:233. So run the Greek and, by and large, the Ethiopic (although it does reverse the order of "Watchers" and "holy ones"), with the Aramaic text not extant for these verses.

29. So ibid.

30. Two other possibilities suggested by Black 1985:141.

From the words of the Watchers and holy ones I have heard everything; and as I heard everything from them, I also understood what I saw. (1:2)[31]

In the Book of the Watchers, the content of what is shown to Enoch on his journeys in Chapters 17–36 includes both geographic information, as he is taken to the four corners of the earth, and astronomical information, since he is also instructed in the nature of the heavenly phenomena. He sees, in fact, everything that exists (19:3). He is accompanied by a number of angels and archangels with whom he engages in discussion. The archangels (Uriel, Raphael, Reuel, Michael, Sariel,[32] and Gabriel) explain phenomena to Enoch that are relevant to the separate portfolios each of them possess as described in 1 Enoch 20. Enoch is full of curiosity ("Concerning all things I wish to know," 25:2) and he even takes notes of some of the phenomena (33:3). He may not be a sage when he arrives in heaven but he certainly becomes one through what he learns there. The picture that emerges—of a discussion between various members of God's heaven concerning the nature of the cosmos—is fully consonant with the discussion of astronomy, geography, mathematics, medicine and so on that occurred in Mesopotamian, Achaemenid and Hellenistic courts. Such material has no possible bearing on heaven understood as a temple (in Jerusalem or elsewhere) where the angels are priests. On the other hand, the fact that such knowledge was revealed to Enoch in this way has the function of legitimating the possession of the distinctive astronomical learning characteristic of the Enochic scribal group (discussed in Chapter 7).

IDENTITY AND PRESTIGE FROM COURT MEMBERSHIP

Although it may not be abundant, there are data in 1 Enoch 1–36 to the effect that, just as surely as the courtiers of Louis XIV needed to live in Versailles, the angels enjoyed a particular identity and prestige that could only be preserved by their membership of this particular court. The primary evidence is found in what God says to Enoch when he is commissioning him to go to the Watchers who left heaven with the message that they will not be forgiven, a subject that I will examine more closely in Chapter 4:

Enoch, scribe of righteousness, go and say to the Watchers of heaven who, having abandoned the high heaven, the holy place of the eternal station, defiled themselves with women. (12:4)

31. ET Nickelsburg 2001:137, here based on the Aramaic.
32. "Sariel" is a plausible emendation by Nickelsburg for "Uriel" (2001:319).

God says something very similar later when he sends Enoch back to tell the Watchers that their petition for forgiveness has been rejected and to ask:

> Why have you abandoned the high heaven,
> the holy place of eternity (τὸν ἅγιον τοῦ αἰῶνος),
> and lain with women and become defiled with the daughters of humans,
> and taken wives for yourselves. (15:3)

Here we see that God has two causes of complaint against the Watchers: leaving their post in heaven and defiling themselves with women. Although much of the focus in the text is upon their sinning with human women, the fact of their having deserted their very exalted responsibility in heaven also features in their wrongdoing. I will explore this issue further in Chapter 4.

Nickelsburg and VanderKam render the first clause of this second quotation as "Why have you forsaken the high heaven, the eternal sanctuary,"[33] but there is no "sanctuary" mentioned in the text, which simply speaks of "the high heaven, the holy place of eternity." Their mistranslation reflects the omnipresence of the idea that heaven is understood in this text as a temple. The preferable view is that the notion of heaven as "holy" functions to differentiate it from earth. It serves to convey a reality divided into two very different realms—of heaven and earth, and as we will soon see, of spirit on the one hand and flesh and blood on the other—and the Watchers have wrongly abandoned the former, exalted and holy realm for the latter. That this very clearly entails their loss of identity and high status appears in what God goes on to instruct Enoch to say to them:

> You were holy and spirits, living forever.
> You have become defiled with the blood of women
> and with the blood of flesh you have begotten,
> and with human blood you have lusted,
> and you have done as they do—
> flesh and blood, who die and perish. (15:4)

And a little later:

> But you used to exist as spirits, living forever,
> and not dying for all the generations of eternity;
> therefore I did not make women among you.'
> The spirits of heaven, in heaven is their dwelling. (15:6–7)

---

33. Nickelsburg and VanderKam 2012:36.

One could just as accurately say of the court of Louis XIV, "The courtiers of Versailles, in Versailles is their dwelling," especially in relation to any who had left Versailles to live, for example, in a farming village. We are dealing with beings who have forsaken the holy place and institution that were fully matched to their spiritual nature and afforded them a particular duty and station and where they enjoyed an illustrious identity and status. Accordingly, the court model allows us to appreciate their predicament in a convincing way.

COURT RELATIONSHIPS, FUNCTIONING, AND CONTINUANCE

As with the courts discussed in Chapter 2, the situation in heaven in 1 Enoch also proved not to be static. While one alteration had occurred with the arrival of Enoch, the major change in view was that of two hundred angels leaving heaven to marry human women. While these events will be examined more fully in Chapter 4, the dramatic turn of events concerning the Watchers who abandoned heaven, as related in 1 Enoch 6, indicates that this was a court subject to a similar type of convulsion and change in status as occurred among the courtiers in France and in the ancient kingdoms. This was not the end of the disturbance, however, because thereafter we have the account of complaints being made by earth to heaven about the behaviour of their progeny, the Giants (7:6; 8:4); the discussion this causes among the angels and their bringing the matter to God (Chapter 9); God's response (Chapters 10–11); and God's commissioning Enoch to tell the Watchers that they have forfeited mercy and peace and that he has rejected their petition (Chapters 12–16). The text also envisages further events in the period up to the End, when the spirits of the slaughtered Giants will cause havoc on the earth (15:8–12), climaxing on the Day of Judgment (16:1). Yet it should be noted that the loss of status of the Watchers was entirely self-inflicted, it was not an act of royal whim. For even in this respect they are like courtiers who themselves choose to abandon a king and his court (on which, more in Chapter 4).

As already noted, moreover, courts were not anonymous groups of people. Some were more prominent than others and a keen interest was taken in the various individuals making up the court and in their respective positions. Similarly, in 1 Enoch the angels are individualised not only by their names, leadership functions, and specific areas of responsibility. The Watchers are further individualised in having knowledge in particular areas. Thus 1 Enoch 8 describes nine named Watchers who taught human beings various forms of knowledge and skill. All nine, beginning with Asael, come from the list of the twenty leaders of the Watchers in 1 Enoch 6:7.

Elias' phrase a "social figuration" is appropriate to this group of angels since it has the capacity to encompass both friendly and also tense and difficult relationships, such as develop between God and one group of angels, on the one hand, and the Watchers who secede, on the other. Elias was interested in this notion as a way of accounting for the continuance of a court for generations: the figuration persisted even though the individuals making it up changed. His answer focused on the interdependence between king and courtiers, which meant seriously questioning the alleged absolute power of "absolutist" kings, especially in view of the fact that the king only knew what was happening in his kingdom and exercised power through the mediation of his courtiers. Even though God does appear to be omniscient and omnipotent in the Book of the Watchers, so that we might initially assume that Elias' views could have no application to him, examination of 1 Enoch in this light indicates their relevance.

The Seclusion of God

The God of 1 Enoch 1–36 is a monarch who, like Louis XIV and the Persian kings beginning with Deioces, has distanced himself from his subjects. God exists in seclusion, not only from human beings but also from the vast majority of the angels. Let us consider the following passage.

> No angel was able to enter into this house and to behold his face
> > on account of the honour and glory,
> and no human being was able to look at him.
> Fire was burning in a circle and a great fire stood near him.
> No one approached (ἐγγίζει) him.

Ten thousand times ten thousand (μυρίαι μυριάδες) stood in a circle before him,
> but he needed no counsellor; his every word was deed.
> And the holy ones of the angels who approached (οἱ ἐγγίζοντες)
> > him did not depart by night, nor did they leave him. (14:21–23)[34]

---

34. This translation closely follows the Greek, except for the addition of "He needed no counsellor." This expression is in the Ethiopic, but not the Greek, while "his every word was deed" is in the Greek but not the Ethiopic. Both most probably both belong to the original version, as suggested by their joint existence in 2 Enoch 33:4 (Nickelsburg 2001:258, following R. H. Charles). Nickelsburg (2001:259) emends by adding "by day" to the statement "nor did they leave him," but this is speculation with no textual

The statements that God "needed no counsellor" and that his "every word was deed" deserve noting at the outset. In the normal course—the text necessarily conveys—a monarch in his position has counsellors and needs people to carry out his commands. The force of the statement to the opposite effect in the text derives from the Enochic God's being distinctive in this respect. We have seen in Chapter 2 that among the courtiers in the French court were the ministers and secretaries of state and the *conseillers d'État*, while the Persian king had nobles serving as the King's Councillors, as Royal Judges and as the King's Eye. As also noted in Chapter 2, the propensity of Persian kings to seek advice is parodied in the Book of Esther. The revealing protestation in 1 Enoch 14:22 that such arrangements have no application to God cannot displace the fact that we are here immersed in precisely this world: of the king, the court and his courtiers. Kings who did seclude themselves from their subjects were totally reliant on members of the inner court to provide intelligence on what was happening in the kingdom and to advise him on such matters, and then to carry out the king's commands when he had made his decision. In 1 Enoch 9 four archangels impart precisely such intelligence to God (although assuring him that he knows everything himself). So God may not have needed counsellors, but he had some anyway! In 1 Enoch 10 God gives these archangels the necessary instructions; his every word may have been deed but this did not preclude him using agents to effect his will.

A further indication that God's seclusion is not absolute comes with the statement in 1 Enoch 14:23 concerning angels who "approached him" and "did not depart by night, nor did they leave him." This verse is subject to some textual uncertainty.[35] Nevertheless, on any reading, we still have reference to certain angels who "approach" God; they may not "enter" but they do "approach."

Some scholars interpret this "approaching" in relation to priests approaching God in the Jerusalem temple. They do this largely on the basis that the Greek word used here (ἐγγίζει) and similar Greek words represent the notion expressed in the Hebrew Bible with words like קרב (*qrb*), meaning "approach," where there are "specific cultic connotations."[36] Thus Nickelsburg points to Ezek 44:13; 44:15; and 45:4. Yet the word *qrb* appears hundreds of times in the Hebrew Bible in a very wide variety of contexts, the vast majority of them non-cultic. There are some 160 instances of ἐγγίζει in the various versions of the Septuagint, with about 70 of them translat-

---

support.

35. See Black 1985:151 and Nickelsburg 2001:258.
36. Nickelsburg 2001:265.

ing *qrb*, but again they cover a wide variety of contexts. Nickelsburg also points to the continuous attendance of the angels, with Josephus noting that attendance by night and day was enjoined of the Levites and the priests by Moses.[37] Rendering this factor unconvincing is the fact that (in spite of Josephus) the Law of Moses nowhere prescribes priestly service night and day, and that another purpose for the continuous service of the angels on God readily suggests itself: their protective duty.[38]

A more likely explanation presents itself if we imagine heaven as a royal court. The fact that a small number of angels do have access to God evokes the comparable material on inner and outer courts that we considered in Chapter 2. In other words, the angels with access rights are like the limited number of courtiers with direct access to the king in the French and Near Eastern courts. It is certain that some angels in heaven were permitted to speak directly to God, because this is what happens in 9:4–11 when Michael, Sariel, Raphael, and Gabriel address God to complain to him about what the Watchers have done on earth and ask what he wants them to do. Then God addresses these angels in 1 Enoch 10 and in so doing he is acting on what they tell him, just as a king does with his courtiers. This is very different from the case of the temple in Jerusalem, the inner sanctuary of which was only entered once a year, and then only by the High Priest on the Day of Atonement (Leviticus 16; Exod 30:9–10).

Moreover, the reference to the number of angels present, "Ten thousand times ten thousand (μυρίαι μυριάδες)," echoes the mention of the μυρίαι who will accompany God on his descent to earth for the final judgment in 1 Enoch 1:9 (see above). This is a way of underlining the military might that God has at his disposal. The Ethiopian painting of Raphael with a raised sword on the cover of this volume visually evokes the military power at God's disposal. God on his throne surrounded, at a distance, by angels is like a Near Eastern king surrounded by a huge army.

This discussion leaves two important issues remaining from the model of a royal court and courtiers set out in Chapter 2: the way in which God obtains information and the mediating role of the angels between God and human beings. I will address them in turn.

---

37. Ibid.:265–66 (citing Josephus, *JA* 7.14.7 §367).
38. Nickelsburg (2001:266) acknowledges the last two factors yet still persists with the temple interpretation.

God's Access to Information

At one point when the four angels are addressing God in 1 Enoch 9 they say:

> And all things are manifest and uncovered before you.
> And you see all things, and there is nothing that can be hidden from you. (9:5)[39]

They continue by explaining that God has seen what Asael and Shemihazah have done, while repeating in their conclusion:

> You know all things before they happen,
> and you see these things ... (9:11)[40]

At first sight, such material depicts a king unlike any other in that he has direct knowledge of everything that is occurring in his realm, whether in heaven or on earth. Here is a king, one might think, who has no need of information concerning his subjects to be mediated to him by his courtiers. Yet two features of the text stand curiously in tension with this. First, his angels are still manning the ramparts to see what is occurring on earth below (9:1). Secondly, the Enochic God behaves as if he does not have such direct knowledge. Only when the leading angels, having gathered evidence concerning events on earth by direct observation, report their intelligence to him, does he act. In spite of his omniscience, his behaviour is like that of any other king who has isolated himself from his subjects and who requires information to be provided by the senior courtiers around him. Remarkably, the text itself reveals awareness of this anomaly, since immediately after the passage from 9:11 just quoted it continues like this:

> ... and you permit them
> and you do not tell us what we ought to do to them with regard to these things.

This amounts to a gentle complaint from the angels along these lines: you know all about this unsatisfactory situation but you give us no instructions in relation to it. From this analysis we recognize that Elias' understanding of the reliance of a king on his courtiers for knowledge has a close analogy in God's relationship with his angels in 1 Enoch 1–36. Even where the king possesses divine omniscience, the usual patterns of gathering and communicating knowledge at court are still in operation. As we will now see, a similar pattern appears in relation to the wider mediating functions

---

39. ET Nickelsburg 2001:202.
40. ET ibid.

of the angels. This area, in particular, is only explicable on the basis of the court model and entirely excludes the notion that heaven and the angels are meant to represent a temple and its priests.

The Mediating Role of the Angels and Enoch

One of the notable features of 1 Enoch 1–36, especially in the section dealing with the descent of the Watchers to earth and its consequences (1 Enoch 6–16), is the phenomenon of appeals that are directed to heaven from earth and the extent to which these become a focus of the narrative. There are two types of such appeals. The first type consists of appeals made by the earth or by human beings in the direction of heaven. These are initially reported by the narrator in consequence of the actions of the Giants (7:6 and 8:4). Later the four archangels mention this appeal while talking among themselves (9:2) or when addressing God (9:10) as they seek his permission to take action against the Watchers and the Giants. Later in the text there is another appeal by a human being to heaven—in the plea by the soul of Abel against his brother Cain (22:5–7). The second type, for which there is a larger body of textual evidence, consists of the appeals that the Watchers make to God through Enoch for forgiveness, the data covering both the appeal and also its rejection by God (13:2, 4, 6 and 7; 14:4 [*bis*]; 14:7 [*bis*]; 15:2 [*bis*][41] and 16:2). The appeal of the Watchers is different in character from that made by the earth or people upon it because, at their request, Enoch puts it into written form and actually reads it out to God (13:4).

In the case of the earth and its inhabitants plundered by the Giants and the Watchers' hope for forgiveness, these appeals take the form of what I shall call "intercession." By this is meant that X asks Y to say something to Z in the interests of X or to secure some benefit for X from Z.

How is all this material to be explained? Existing explanations are tied to the interpretation of heaven as a temple and the angels as priests. Thus, according to David Suter, "In 1 En 9:1 we encounter heaven as a sanctuary, the location of an angelic priesthood—Michael, Sariel, Raphael, and Gabriel—whose function seems to be to hear the prayers of the victims of violence on earth and to intercede before God for them."[42] Shortly after this he adds, "Theoretically, given the omniscience of God, the angelic priesthood and intercessory cultus are pointless; pragmatically, they provide a vehicle for the outcry of the victims of violence and for the execution of God's

---

41. The Ethiopic version has two instances of appeal language in this line, while the Greek only has one; the former is to be preferred.

42. Suter 2007:199.

commands in response to the outcry."[43] Argall considers that in relation to writing out the appeal of the Watchers, which is a request for forgiveness (1 Enoch 13), "Enoch the scribe has a priestly role."[44] On the basis of arguments by Suter and Nickelsburg, and drawing attention to the close parallels between Enoch's actions (in 1 Enoch 12–16) and those of Ezra (in Ezra 9–10), Helge Kvanvig has concluded that Enoch is the archetypical scribe and priest.[45] To like effect Boccaccini speaks of the "attribution to Enoch of priestly characteristics as the intercessor in heaven between God and the fallen angels."[46] According to Martha Himmelfarb: "The priestly role of the angels is implicit in the language of God's response to the petition of the fallen Watchers: 'It is you who should be petitioning on behalf of men, and not men on your behalf' (15:2). Intercession is a task for priests."[47]

Yet, in spite of the confidence with which they are advanced, none of these views carries any probative weight. While the angels are actively interceding with God for those who have died as a result of the Giants' wickedness and violence and Enoch is willing to do the same for the Watchers, it is a big step to say that such intercessions are priestly or an aspect of the temple cult. The major problem with this approach is that it rests on the assumption that Israelites directed prayers to God through priests, rather then praying to God directly themselves. Consider the case of Hannah who, in the temple of Shiloh, prays to God for a child and meets the priest Eli (who thinks her soundless lip-movements are a sign of drunkenness). There is no suggestion that Hannah's prayer has not been efficacious because she uttered it directly to God, even if Eli does offer his support to it once it has been spoken (1 Sam 1:9–18). Many other Israelites are reported making prayers directly to God. Thus Abraham's argument with God in Gen 18:23–32 is a form of prayer. Moses and the Israelites sing a song of praise to God (Exod 15:1–2). Jephthah makes his ill-fated vow (Judg 11:30–31). Solomon prays to God at the altar without the aid of priests (1 Kgs 8:22–29). In short, in ancient Israel private prayer—without any involvement by priests—and the temple cult happily co-existed with one another.

Priests did engage in what we might call intercessory acts, but they mainly did so through offering sacrifice, something that is entirely absent in the various actual or potential intercessions in 1 Enoch 1–36 discussed above. Each day the priests offered sacrifice on behalf of Israel and any

43. Ibid.:200.
44. Argall 1995:28.
45. Kvanvig 1988:99–103.
46. Boccaccini 2002b:92.
47. Himmelfarb 1993:20.

prayers they uttered were meant to be representative of Israel. In addition, Israelites commissioned priests to offer sacrifice on their behalf. But that is very different from asking priests to convey their prayer to God in a non-sacrificial context. It is possible that a priestly blessing (such as at Num 6:24–26) might be regarded as being, broadly speaking, intercessory, but such a blessing was for generalised well-being; it was not a request to God to assist his adherents in relation to a particular matter at hand.

None of the commentators just mentioned, moreover, offers any evidence for priests preparing written memoranda of intercession, as Enoch did for the Watchers. Such an activity is so alien to what we know of the responsibilities of Israelite priests that it is difficult to see how the notion could ever have been entertained, or why its unreality did not prompt its proponents to seek a solution elsewhere. In short, while there is an intercessory dimension to priestly sacrifice and perhaps to priestly blessing, neither sacrifice nor blessing appears in these sections of 1 Enoch. That such eminent scholars could all be maintaining a case without any evidence in its support is perhaps testimony to the powerful influence exerted by the prevailing view that the chief identity in play in 1 Enoch 1–36 is religious in nature, that of Judaism.

A highly plausible explanation for these appeals, however, emerges when we expand our view to the bigger picture of the ancient monarchy and to the way that the king and his courtiers interacted in the court. Courtiers played an essential mediating role between the king and his subjects. When the latter wanted to reach the king, or when he wanted to reach them, members of the court had to be involved. Both aspects of this process are evident in 1 Enoch 1–36, although here we have two types of courtier, the angels and Enoch. There is abundant evidence from the ancient Mediterranean world, some of which we will consider below, for the prevalence of people making appeals, which are perhaps best referred to as "petitions," to officials, either in the royal court or in other administrative centers, for various types of assistance. The papyri extant from Egypt contain thousands of such documents. Let us now work through the text in the light of the data. The language used of petitions in 1 Enoch derives from precisely this kind of political and social pattern, as we will now see. This linguistic evidence simply leaves no room for the temple and angelic priest alternative.

Corresponding to the difference between the unwritten nature of the appeals by the earth and its inhabitants, on the one hand, and the written form of the Watchers' appeal, on the other, is a sharp differentiation of the language used of each. The most common word used of the appeals in the former category is ἐντυγχάνειν.⁴⁸ One of the meanings of this verb in late Greek is "to intercede with," "to entreat" (for example, at 3 Macc 6:37; Acts 25:24; and Polybius 4.76.9).⁴⁹ It is also found in the sense of "make a petition" in the papyri.⁵⁰ It has this meaning in 1 Enoch 1–36. Thus, in 1 Enoch 7:6 it was the earth that made a petition (ἐνέτυχεν), while in 1 Enoch 9:3 and 9:10 we have the following:

> The spirits and the souls of human beings groan, making petition (ἐντυγκάνοντα) and saying, "Bring in our judgment to the Most High." (9:3)

> Now, look, the spirits of the souls of human beings who have died make petition (ἐντυγκάνουσιν), and their groan has gone up right to the gates of heaven. (9:10)⁵¹

The word ἐντυγκάνειν also occurs five times in 1 Enoch 22:5–7 in relation to the petition that Abel makes to heaven against Cain. The nominal form of this word, ἔντευξις, although it does not appear in 1 Enoch 1–36, is extremely common in the papyri. Indeed, Bernhard Palme has observed that "The *enteuxis* is the classical Ptolemaic form of petition."⁵²

When we turn to the written petition of the Watchers, we once again come upon the standard language of the period for written requests to officials to assist with a complaint or problem. Some of these petitions were to local officials, but quite often the complaint went to the members of court itself. Yet ἐντυγκάνειν does not occur in relation to the written petition of the Watchers. Now the language shifts to the idea of a ὑπόμνημα ("memorandum") of ἐρώτησις ("request," "petition"). There are four examples of ὑπόμνημα and seven examples of ἐρώτησις (or its verbal form ἐρωτάω) employed in relation to the petition of the Watchers.⁵³ Liddell and Scott give several instances of the verb ἐρωτάω in late Greek with the meaning "to beg, entreat, solicit" (1 Sam 30:21 (LXX); Luke 7:36; 8:37; and John 16:26), and there are several more examples in BDAG.⁵⁴ The use of ἐρώτησις in the sense

---

48. In 1 Enoch 7:6; 9:3; 9:10, and 22:5 (*bis*), 6 (*bis*) and 7.

49. See BDAG 341 for other examples.

50. As one example, see P. Par 26 ("Petition from the Serapaeum Twins," of 163–162 BCE), line 5, where it is followed immediately after by ἔντευξις (Milligan 1927:13). The word also appears with the meaning of petition in P. Fouad 26, P. Coll. Youtie 12, and P. Oxf. 4.

51. In both cases I translate from the Syncellus fragment of the Greek text.

52. Palme 2009:376.

53. ὑπόμνημα: 1 Enoch 13:4 (*bis*), 6 and 7; ἐρώτησις: 1 Enoch 10:10; 12:4; 13:4 and 6; 14:4; ἐρωτάω: 1 Enoch 15:2; and 16:2.

54. See BDAG 395.

of "entreaty" or "petition" seems rather rare outside this text.[55] Nevertheless, that it has this meaning in the text is clear given its derivation from ἐρωτάω used in this sense in 1 Enoch 15:2 and 16:2. Instead of ἐρώτησις we also find δέησις (13:6, 7), "entreaty," "petition," "prayer," and its verbal form δέομαι (13:6; 14:7).[56]

We encounter abundant material on this subject in the text. In 1 Enoch 10:10 God informs Gabriel that if the Watchers make a petition (ἐρώτησις), by necessary implication, to him via Gabriel, in respect of their progeny, the Giants, it will be rejected. Later the good angels instruct Enoch to go to the Watchers who left heaven and tell them that they will see the slaughter of their sons yet they will have no forgiveness or peace even if they will make petition (δεηθήσονται) forever (1 Enoch 12:6). In 1 Enoch 13:1-2 these angels tell Enoch to go to Asael to say he will have no peace nor will he have (sc. granted) a petition (ἐρώτησις). In 1 Enoch 13:4-5 the Watchers do indeed ask Enoch to write a memorandum of petition (ὑπόμνημα ἐρωτήσεως) on their behalf to God and to recite it to him, seeking his forgiveness (ἄφεσις). Enoch writes out their ὑπόμνημα ἐρωτήσεως and their requests (δεήσεις) about which they made request (δέονται), so they might have forgiveness (ἄφεσις) and longevity (13:6). Later he recites their memorandum of requests (ὑπόμνημα τῶν δεήσεων) to God (13:7). In 1 Enoch 14:4 Enoch tells the Watchers that he wrote up their petition (ἐρώτησις) but that it will not be granted. Of particular interest is what God says to Enoch later (1 Enoch 15:2-4):

> Go and say to the Watchers of heaven, who sent you to petition
> on their behalf,[57]
> "You should petition (ἐρωτῆσαι) on behalf of human beings,
> and not human beings on behalf of you.
> Why have you abandoned the high heaven,
> the holy place of eternity (τὸν ἅγιον τοῦ αἰῶνος) . . .

God later tells Enoch to put a similar question to the Watchers (1 Enoch 16:2).

According to Nickelsburg, in commenting on the memorandum of petition in 1 Enoch 13:4, "In our (sc. biblical) literature a memorandum is a written or verbal communication, intended to call one's attention to certain

---

55. The word does not appear in Papyri.Info and Liddell and Scott do not cite an example. But BDAG (395) has one example of the word meaning "request" and three examples where it means "prayer."

56. For instances of δέησις, see BDAG 213 and of δέομαι, see BDAG 218.

57. This question survives in the Ethiopic but not in the Greek of the Akhmin manuscript, from which it appears to have been omitted by scribal error.

facts."[58] He then cites examples from Ezra 6:2 (a "chronicle"), Tob 12:12 (a "prayer") and Mal 3:16 (a "book"). Yet none of these parallels the meaning of ὑπόμνημα in 1 Enoch 13 or elsewhere in the text. In Ezra 6:2 ὑπόμνημα refers to a memorandum or report of events when Cyrus ordered the temple in Jerusalem rebuilt. In Tob 12:12 τὸ μνημόσυνον τῆς προσευχῆς, "the remembrance of your prayer," means that the angel Raphael reminded God of a particular prayer made to him. The expression βίβλιον μνημοσύνου, literally "book of memory," in Mal 3:16 denotes a book God writes to record the names of those who feared him.

The meaning of ὑπόμνημα in the Book of the Watchers lies elsewhere. As papyrologist Paul Schubert puts it, a ὑπόμνημα is "a memorandum, most often a request submitted to a person of higher standing by an individual in a subordinate position."[59] Many are petitions directed to senior administrative and political figures, often located in the king's court, and written by scribes on behalf of clients who are seeking favors or relief of various kinds. Petitions of this sort are well attested in the papyri, with Palme noting "that petitions to officials are the commonest type of record except tax receipts. More than a thousand survive from the entire "papyrological millennium."[60] The petitions sought redress for abuses or help against injustice. A search of the Papyri.Info search engine revealed 677 instances of ὑπόμνημα in the period 300 BCE to 200 CE.[61] This subject matter very closely matches that of the fallen Watchers asking Enoch, a scribe, to write to God on their behalf seeking a particular favor, in their case, forgiveness (ἄφεσις).

A collection of 33 such petitions was published in *Select Papyri*, Volume 2, translated by A. S. Hunt.[62] A petition of 132 BCE from certain priests of Socnopaeus (one of the crocodile gods of the Fayum) to the *Strategus*, complaining of actions by the High Priest of the god, is called a ὑπόμνημα in the document.[63] A common word of approach to the official is δέομαι ("I entreat"), together with the nominal form δέησις ("entreaty"). As already noted, both of these appear in 1 Enoch 13:6, while the former also features in 1 Enoch 14:7 and the latter in 1 Enoch 13:7. In wider Greek literature ἄφεσις was occasionally used of a release of a debt and exemption from service (as an example, see Plutarch, *Agesilaus* 24), which are quite close in

---

58. Nickelsburg 2001:237.
59. Schubert 2009:200; this is in an essay on editing a papyrus.
60. Palme 2009:377.
61. See http://papyri.info/.
62. See Hunt 1934:226–331.
63. Ibid.:248–51. Other expressions used of the petition are ἔντευξις (p. 228) and βιβλείδιον (pp. 276–81).

subject-matter to the Watchers' request for forgivenness (ἄφεσις). A similar usage from the thirty-three papyri petitions is one from two men to the senate of the citizens of Antinoe seeking acknowledgment that they have been exempted from having to provide a liturgy, the Greek word relating to the exemption being a cognate of ἄφεσις. In another petition a lentil-cook asks an official for extra time to pay a tax.[64] The broad range of these petitions and the humble nature of some of them indicate that any scribe would have been able to draft one for a client.

The action that the Watchers ask Enoch to undertake, therefore, is simply the standard way in which anyone would bring a complaint or problem to an official, with ὑπόμνημα being the very word used for such a document. That we are dealing with the everyday phenomena of courts and courtiers, and not with anything to do with a temple, could hardly be clearer. In their view, Enoch, a member of the heavenly court, is, like other courtiers in the Hellenistic world, regarded as a person with the ability to receive and convey a petition to the king, here God, on behalf of those living in the kingdom and away from the court. But God does not agree that even the righteous Enoch has attained angelic status. When God instructs Enoch to tell the Watchers that they should petition on behalf of human beings, and not human beings on behalf of them (1 Enoch 15:2), he is underlining the reversal of the proper order in heaven, as an instance of a royal court, caused by their having abandoned their appointed stations to descend to earth. As the heavenly equivalent of the "Friends of the King" who frequented Hellenistic royal courts and were meant to receive petitions from subjects of the king and convey them to him, it is a reversal of the proper order of things for the Watchers to be asking such a subject (Enoch) to intercede for them. What caused them to end up in such a position? To answer that we must understand the nature of and reason for their secession from heaven, and that is the subject of the next chapter.

---

64. Ibid.:228–29.

4

THE DESCENT OF THE WATCHERS
Rebellion in the Heavenly Court

THE WATCHERS' SECESSION FROM HEAVEN IN 1 ENOCH 36

The most dramatic event that shapes the narrative of 1 Enoch 1–36 is the secession from heaven of two hundred Watchers, members of God's angelic host, led by Shemihazah, to take human women as wives and to father children upon them, with terrible consequence for humanity and the earth (1 Enoch 6-8). The aim of this chapter is to offer an explanation for these events. This will entail interpreting the text on the basis that the source domain providing the foundation for so powerful a narrative consists of the ancient court and its courtiers.

It is inaccurate to speak of the Watchers' "fall" from heaven, because it could suggest some kind of accidental or unplanned action. This was not a fall, but a planned descent by the Watchers to earth to marry human women (with whom they "defiled" themselves), preceded by a joint oath sworn by the Watchers not to turn back from this course (1 Enoch 6:4-5). The text describes two sets of consequences of this act, which I will now briefly mention and return to in more detail below. Firstly, there was the havoc unleashed by the progeny of the Watchers' unions with women, the Giants—on human beings, on themselves and on other living things—that rocks the cosmos to its foundations (1 Enoch 7:2-5). Secondly, and compounding the depredations of the Giants, was the revelation by the Watchers of knowledge. They taught their wives "sorcery and charms" (1 Enoch

7:1), and Asael, Shemihazah, and other named Watchers revealed a wide range of knowledge and skills to human beings (1 Enoch 8:1–3), with terrible consequences.

The fact that we have distinct sets of consequences, with Asael named first as the revealer of secrets to human beings (1 Enoch 8:1–2), ahead of other Watchers, led by Shemihazah (1 Enoch 8:3–4), even though Shemihazah was the leader of the secession, has induced scholars interested in source criticism to propose that the author has here integrated a Shemihazah tradition and an Asael tradition.[1] While that is possible, my interest lies in the text in this form. A clear sign that the author himself wished to link the Shemihazah and Asael material is that he concludes both the section on the Giants and the section on the revelation of secrets in a similar way. The former ends with this statement: "Then the earth brought accusations against the lawless ones" (1 Enoch 7:6), accusations that could only be directed to heaven, while the latter ends with the human cry going up to heaven (8:4). As a result of the Watchers' secession from heaven, the author thus depicts two different types and sources of evil leading to the same result: a plea to heaven for relief.

EXISTING EXPLANATIONS FOR THE SECESSION OF THE WATCHERS FROM HEAVEN

The dominant existing explanations are tied to the temple and priests model for the Enochic heaven. A currently popular interpretation of what is here called the source domain (see Chapter 1 above) for the descent of the Watchers was provided in articles by David Suter in 1979 and George Nickelsburg in 1981. Crispin Fletcher-Louis rightly noted in 2002 that since the publication of these articles, "the *Fall of the Watchers* cycle has been widely interpreted as a typological reference to the exogamy of priests who, like Watchers in heaven, have left their domain of cultic and racial purity by marrying non-Israelite women of the land."[2] More recently, a similar position has been developed by Martha Himmelfarb.[3] I will now critically assess the arguments advanced for this view before proposing an alternative explanation.

---

1. See Nickelsburg 1977.

2. Fletcher-Louis 2002:22 (citing Suter 1979 and Nickelsburg 1981). I would favour the replacement of "Fall" with "Secession" (as already noted) and "racial" with "ethnic" in this statement.

3. Himmelfarb 2007.

David Suter's Proposal: Priests Marrying the Wrong Women

In 1979 David Suter argued that the marriages of the Watchers to human women in 1 Enoch "seem to reflect a concern with illegitimate marriages on the part of priests."[4] At this time there was a view among some priests at least that priests should only marry the virgin daughters of other priests, meaning that priestly marriages were to occur within a small and closed circle.[5] Suter proposed that the Enochic author supported this view and critiqued those who failed to adhere to it under the guise of a narrative attacking the Watchers for similar behavior. The data that Suter cited from 1 Enoch 1–36 for this view consisted primarily of the various statements that the Watchers had defiled themselves by taking human wives (for example, at 1 Enoch 7:1; 9:8; and 10:11; also cf. 15:3–4) and, from 1 Enoch 10:9, that their offspring were thought of as *mamzerim* (in the Greek, μαζήρεοι), "strange children," or "bastards." He suggested that it "would appear that a sociological (*sic*) code—the halakhic marriage rules—is being used to express the chaos that results when the cosmic order is violated by the marriages of angels with women."[6]

In addition, he drew in aid of his view 1 Enoch 15:2, which noted the irony that Enoch, a human being, was interceding for angels whereas angels should intercede for human beings. This meant that the "cosmic function of the angels as intercessors thus parallels the religious function of the priesthood."[7] He also cited other texts where angels and priests had similar functions, initially Jubilees 4:15, which reflected Mal 2:6–7 and 1QSb 4:24–27,[8] and then two other Israelite texts from the Second Temple period, the *Damascus Document* and the *Testament of Levi*, which contain extensive critiques of priestly misbehaviour.[9] To maintain his point that the angels were inspired by Jerusalem priests marrying the wrong women, Suter had to argue that: "The myth appears to be concerned with the purity of the angels themselves and with the pollution of their bodies that results from taking human wives. The effect of the angels' action on the human race is

---

4. Suter 1979:116. Suter's statement (116–17) that the myth of the Watchers is "a *paradigm* (rather than an etiology) of the origin of evil" (emphasis original) stands in refreshing contrast to the frequent and incorrect assertion by scholars to the contrary; in 1 Enoch 1–36 evil starts with Cain not with the Watchers—see Esler 2017b:171–75.

5. Suter 1979:119–22.

6. Ibid.:119. I would prefer "social" for "sociological."

7. Ibid.:123.

8. Ibid.

9. Ibid.:124–31.

secondary to their concern with purity."[10] Suter regarded his argument as fitting well into "the history of Judaism in the third century B.C.E."[11]

It is submitted that Suter has failed to prove his case. Merely stating that the angels had defiled themselves by marrying human women cannot itself raise a connection to priesthood, since defilement also necessarily ensued when beings who were "holy ones and spirits, living forever" had sexual intercourse with women, "with flesh and blood" (1 Enoch 15:4). Mary Douglas has shown that the core idea of impurity, including among Israelites, is that things are out of place, that boundaries have been transgressed, an issue to which I will return below.[12] Defilement or impurity is an inevitable way of describing the grievous boundary transgression involved in spirits having sex with flesh and blood. There is no need to import priestly holiness and no sign in the text that we should. It was equally likely that the notion of *mamzerim* ("bastards") would be attached to the products of such unions. In addition, Archie Wright has reasonably criticised Suter's view that the focal point of the narrative is the angels and the effects of their actions on themselves (not the consequences for the earth and its inhabitants) for the reason that it leaves too much of 1 Enoch 1–36 out of account.[13] In particular, how does Suter's explanation relate to the passages discussed above as to the revelations by Asael, Shemihazah, and the other angels to human beings that led to such devastation.

George Nickelsburg's Proposal: The Watchers as Priests Deserting the Sanctuary and Defiling Themselves

A somewhat similar argument was mounted by George Nickelsburg in an article published in 1981. He suggested that 1 Enoch 12–16 present God as living in a heavenly temple.[14] He likened 1 Enoch 14–16 to a "throne vision."[15] He regarded 1 Enoch 14 as similar to Ezekiel 40–48 and as describing Enoch's "ascent to the heavenly temple and his progress through its *temenos* to the door of the holy of holies, where the chariot throne of God is set."[16] Nickelsburg proposed that God is attended by angels "who

---

10. Ibid.:116.
11. Ibid.:134.
12. Douglas 1966.
13. Wright 2013:47.
14. Nickelsburg 1981:576–82.
15. Ibid.:576.
16. Ibid.:580, also at 582. We will later see (in Chapter 5) that Nickelsburg's notion of God's throne in 1 Enoch 14 being chariot in form, that is, that it had wheels,

are sometimes described as if they were priests," for which view he cited the word "approach" used of "the holy ones of the Watchers" coming near to God in 1 Enoch 14:23 on the basis that it had "technical cultic associations" and the fact of the angels being there night and day.[17] He did acknowledge, however, that in this section of 1 Enoch "we have no hymn of the angelic attendants."[18] He found further support for his theory in 1 Enoch 12:4 with its reference to the Watchers abandoning "the highest heaven, the sanctuary (ἁγίασμα) of their eternal station (στάσις)," with the latter word allegedly a reference to the priestly courses. More specifically, he discerned, in 1 Enoch 15:3–4 for example, a specific type of "cultic language" which "closely resembles explicit polemics against the priesthood."[19] He explained this on the basis that the Enochic author had "a grievance against the priesthood in his own time."[20] In summary, the text represents an attempt by the Enochic tradition, which associated itself with Mount Hermon in the north, to criticize the Jerusalem priesthood as impure and defiled, a view he noted that David Suter had recently reached independently.[21]

Nickelsburg did not specify the nature of or reason for the impurity and defilement of the Jerusalem priesthood. He came close to this, however, in discussing other Israelite literature that contains polemics against the priesthood. Here he mentioned Ezra's discovery on his arrival in Jerusalem that "many of the Israelites, but notably a significant number of priests and Levites, have married foreign women" and thereby polluted the holy people and the priesthood.[22] The people assemble, expressing remorse for marrying foreign women and agree to put away these wives and their children (Ezra 10). Nickelsburg regards this situation as similar to what the angels have done in marrying women forbidden to them and then asking Enoch to intercede for them.[23]

---

represents a mistranslation of both the Greek and Ethiopic texts.

17. Ibid.:585. First Enoch 14:23 speaks of the holy ones' presence by night and he has to emend the text to have them there by day as well (Nickelsburg 2001:259).

18. Nickelsburg 1981:582.

19. Ibid.:584.

20. Ibid.:586.

21. Ibid.:587; he was referring to Suter 1979.

22. Ibid.:585. It should be noted, however, that the numbers of priests and Levites involved were quite small. Among the priests who had married foreign women and put them aside were "Maaseiah, Eliezer, Jarib, and Gedaliah, of the sons of Jeshua the son of Jozadak and his brethren" (Ezra 10:18), while among the Levites "Jozabad, Shimei, Kelaiah (that is, Kelita), Pethahiah, Judah, and Eliezer" (Ezra 10:23) followed suit.

23. Ibid.

Yet this argument, like Suter's shortly before it, is unpersuasive for a number of reasons. Firstly, as we have seen in Chapter 3, the use of the word "approach" (ἐγγίζει) in 1 Enoch 14:23 is not probative of this position. The vocabulary of "approaching" is very common in the Hebrew Bible and cannot on its own support the notion of liturgical service; something in the context would need to suggest this meaning. But here the context does the opposite. It is not just any Watchers who approach God but the "holy ones" among them. These are probably the leaders of the angelic host—archangels like Michael, Raphael, and Gabriel and Sariel (1 Enoch 9:1)—and the statement (necessitating his emendation) that they were present day and night differentiates them from human beings (priests in particular) who must regularly break their attendance for one reason or another.

Equally problematic is Nickelsburg's reliance on 1 Enoch 12:4 with its statement that having abandoned τὸ ἁγίασμα τῆς στάσεως τοῦ αἰῶνος, literally "the *hagiasma* of the eternal *stasis*," the Watchers polluted themselves with women. It is true that on numerous occasions in the LXX the word *hagiasma*, when it means a place and not "holiness" or "something holy," does refer to the temple in Jerusalem. But this is not universally the case. On two occasions it relates to God's heavenly abode (Exod 15:17 [where it parallels κατοικητήριον] and Ps 77 [78]:54). This meaning is entirely appropriate for 1 Enoch 12:4. It could simply mean a holy place, since all of heaven must be holy, and need not carry a connotation of "sanctuary" or "temple."

There is no Aramaic fragment extant for this part of the text. Yet some support for Nickelsburg's position might appear to lie in Matthew Black's attempt to deduce the Hebrew or Aramaic expressions underlying the Greek. Black regarded the source of *hagiasma tēs staseōs* as the Hebrew word *maqom*, "place," especially the Place where God dwells. In particular, he pointed to מקום-הקדש (*maqom-haqodesh*), a biblical term for the Temple or Tabernacle (citing the LXX of Lev 10:17: τόπος ἅγιος).[24] In the LXX, however, *stasis*, which appears some twenty times, never translates *maqom*. The word has a range of meanings, including a place to put one's feet (Deut 28:65; 1 Macc 10:72), the place in the Temple where the Lord puts his feet (1 Chr 28:2), and the foundation of the house of the Lord (2 Chr 24:13), a condition of immobility (Josh 10:13), and even a sedition (Judg 9:6). It is also used, however, of the station of the Levites (2 Chr 30:16), the priests (2 Chr 35:10) and the psalm-singers (2 Chr 35:15) in the temple. It would be a mistake, moreover, to assume that *stasis* had any technical association with the station of priests or other functionaries in the Temple. Although it can have that meaning, it is really a word of general application that takes

---

24. Black 1985:143, although he cites the LXX here as τόπος τοῦ ἁγίου.

its specific meaning from its context. Thus it can also refer to a group of servants in Solomon's house standing in their place (III Kings 10:5; 2 Chr 9:4); the place where the king stood (2 Chr 23:13); the place where Daniel was standing when he received a vision (Dan 8:17); the place where the people prayed (3 Macc 1:23); and the place where the people heard the law read (Neh 8:7) and stood in their place (Neh 9:3). In short, a common meaning of *stasis* is a place where one stands for some particular purpose, with that purpose only being deducible from the context. What was the purpose of the station occupied by the Watchers in 1 Enoch 12:4? The fact that it is specified as "eternal" does not carry us much further forward since eternity was a state to be expected of such heavenly beings.

While the word *hagiasma* may seem to carry a cultic connotation if interpreted as "sanctuary," that seems a less probable interpretation than if it is read in a more neutral sense of "holy place." Although one may easily appreciate that the location where the Watchers stand eternally on duty in the heavenly realm is necessarily a holy place, the notion that this location is a "sanctuary," with its connotation of cultic practice, produces a rather ungainly picture.

Lastly, as we have already observed in Chapter 3, the idea that Enoch's interceding for the Watchers is a priestly function is unsustainable, given that he is described as performing this task as a scribe, whereas priests, while they offered sacrifices for Israelites and (to an extent) "interceded" for them in this way, did not write petitions for them.

Martha Himmelfarb's Proposal: Repristinating David Suter's Position

Martha Himmelfarb has been one of the leading advocates of the idea that the Jerusalem temple and its priests inspired the picture of heaven in the Book of the Watchers. I will critically appraise her proposal that the architecture of heaven is based upon that of the temple in Jerusalem, which she initially expressed in 1993, in Chapter 5 of this volume. In an essay published in 2007, however, Himmelfarb has returned to her advocacy of a temple and priests model for the Enochic heaven, although this time directly in relation to the precise phenomena in Israelite life and society that inspired and shaped the portrayal of the defection of the Watchers from heaven. Initially she discusses the ideas of David Suter (1979) and George Nickelsburg (1981).[25] She recapitulates Suter's proposal that the myth of the descent of the Watchers is an attack on priests for defiling the temple by tak-

25. Himmelfarb 2007:223.

ing wives forbidden to priests, by violating the laws of menstrual purity, and by misappropriating offerings brought to the temple (in reliance on 1 Enoch 6–11 and 12–16). She also notes what she claims is Nickelsburg's variation on the theme (focused on 1 Enoch 12–16) to the effect that the illicit wives are foreign women, rather than the wrong sort of "Jewish" women. While (as noted above) this view is an implication one must draw from Nickelsburg's argument rather than something he explicitly states, I will adopt Himmelfarb's interpretation for the purposes of the argument here. She finds this problem with the views of both Suter and Nickelsburg: "Before I attempt my own account of the criticism of priests implicit in the Watchers' marriage to women, it is important to note one difficulty with reading the story as critical of priests. In the context of the myth, the problem with the Watchers' marriages is not their choice of wives, but the very fact of marriage."[26]

This is a convincing submission that sounds heavily against the explanations of both Suter and Nickelsburg. So too is her observation that human beings need marriage for procreation but Watchers are spirits for whom marriage is inappropriate, for which she aptly cites 1 Enoch 15:4–7,[27] verses that quote what God said to Enoch to which I will return below. The problem was that the Watchers abandoned both their dwelling in heaven and the celibacy that were appropriate to their spiritual, holy and eternal natures in favor of defiling themselves with women on earth. We are dealing with the stark juxtaposition exposed by their fundamental choice, in that they have moved from the right to the wrong realm and identity. The problem had nothing to do with any particular characteristic of the women they chose.

Yet even though Himmelfarb then states that "(w)ith this problem in mind" she is turning back to Suter and Nickelsburg,[28] she hereafter largely forsakes the power of the objection and actually offers an explanation of her own that falls foul of it. For she continues by noting that, *contra* Nickelsburg, there is little evidence that intermarriage (between priests and foreigners) continued to be a problem in the Hellenistic period and this, she says, "lends support to Suter's view" that the issue is the wrong sort of "Jewish" women.[29] But how can Nickelsburg's "wrong" interpretation in any way help Suter's when she has just noted—quite rightly—that 1 Enoch 15:4–7 is convincing evidence against the explanations of both Nickelsburg and Suter, for the reason that they ignore the circumstance that the problem is the very fact of the Watchers' marriages, not the choice of their wives.

26. Ibid.
27. Ibid.
28. Ibid.:224.
29. Ibid.

Even less convincing is what follows, for she now proposes that from the criticism of priestly marriages in *Aramaic Levi* and 4QMMT, the Book of the Watchers takes the position that priests should marry only women from priestly families.[30] She must mean by this that the Watchers represent priests who have married women who were not from priestly families. Accordingly, having rightly just noted that the views of Suter and Nickelsburg are inconsistent with 1 Enoch 15:4–7, she now proffers a solution that is really just a particular version of Suter's approach and is subject to the same fundamental objection that it is. Moreover, the only positive evidence she proceeds to cite for her view comes not from 1 Enoch 1–36 but from two Qumran texts. For, having examined *Aramaic Levi* and 4QMMT and argued that this is their position, she states:

> Aramaic Levi and 4QMMT provide a plausible context for the Book of the Watchers' criticism of priests' marriages. Aramaic Levi is probably roughly contemporary with the Book of the Watchers, and it refers to Enoch (103), though not necessarily to the Book of the Watchers. 4QMMT dates from the middle of the second century, considerably later than the Book of the Watchers, but it comes from a group that valued the Book of the Watchers. It is clear from the polemical tone of Aramaic Levi and 4QMMT that their view that ordinary priests must marry priestly women was a minority view. The priests who were the objects of criticism probably chose wives from non-priestly families with a clear conscience and viewed those who criticized them as extremists. The Book of the Watchers, then, takes a restrictive view to priestly marriage that must have set it at odds with many priests of its day.[31]

It is axiomatic that one cannot simply impute to one text (here 1 Enoch 1–36) a view alleged to be found in others (*Aramaic Levi* and 4QMMT) simply because they have a high view of that text or its purported author or because they are roughly contemporaneous with it.[32] Of the last sentence in this quotation, one must respectfully reply: *non sequitur*.

The failure of Suter, Nickelsburg and Himmelfarb to offer a persuasive case for a connection between the imperfections of the Jerusalem priesthood and the secession of the Watchers prompts one to bring forward

30. Ibid.
31. Ibid.:226.
32. I argued in Chapter 1 that although the author of the *Testament of Levi* had a high regard for 1 Enoch 1–36, he knew that text did not contain references to the temple and its priests and he introduced those dimensions himself when describing Levi's visit to heaven.

another explanation. Taking our lead from Norbert Elias, that explanation will be found in the operation of royal courts.

CONFLICT AND REBELLION AT COURT IN THE ANCIENT MEDITERRANEAN WORLD

While a royal court, in both the early modern and ancient periods, could persist for generations, sometimes the whole system came under severe strain. At the French court, for example, there were strong pressures to behave correctly, to act in accordance with notions of court rationality, and to restrain one's emotions and affect in order to preserve one's vital interests.[33] Elias even suggests that "the privileged monopoly elites were frozen in the equilibrium consolidated by Louis XIV."[34] Nevertheless, in spite of this, the order of rank within court society was in constant flux. Sometimes large-scale convulsions changed the positions of people.[35] Eventually, indeed, the whole system collapsed in the French Revolution. Elias, arguing for the contribution of elites as well as non-elites to this transformation, links the success of the Revolution to the "stalemate of the competing monopoly elites" that "prevented them from taking account of developments in society as a whole that were increasing the social strength of hitherto underprivileged strata."[36]

An ancient king's control over his kingdom could be shaken by forces from without and from within his court. Typical threats arising external to the court came in the form of foreign aggressors, typically from a neighboring kingdom, or in a rebellion by a subject people led by one of its members. Threats from within took the form of rebellion by members of the court. In speaking of "rebellion," however, it is necessary to be alert to the two broad meanings encompassed by that word, as recognized by all major dictionaries. On the one hand, according to the OED ("the first meaning" hereafter), "rebellion" refers to "organised armed resistance to the ruler or government of one's country; insurrection, revolt." On the other hand ("the second meaning" hereafter), it refers to "Open or determined defiance of, or resistance to, any authority or controlling power;"[37] this latter formulation is well suited to defiance directed towards *the people in power*. The second meaning covers defiance to those in authority and also "against the rules,

33. Elias 1983:106–16.
34. Ibid.:273.
35. Ibid.:91.
36. Ibid.:271, 275.
37. OED Vol. 13, 1989:300.

or against normal and accepted ways of behaving."³⁸ This latter formulation reflects defiance or dissent towards *the system of rules and regulations established by those in power*.

In this section I will explore evidence from the ancient Mediterranean world relating to both types of phenomenon that threatened a monarchy (an attack by another kingdom and rebellion from within one's own) and will assess the likelihood of one or both providing a subject domain for the target domain from 1 Enoch 1–36 currently occupying our attention: the defection of the Watchers from heaven.

Conflict between Kingdoms

One of the curiosities of Enochic scholarship is that only four years before George Nickelsburg proposed the defiled priests of the Jerusalem temple as the source for the presentation of heaven in 1 Enoch 12–16, he had proposed a different source for the myth of Shemihazah in 1 Enoch 6–11. Shemihazah was the leader of the Watchers who descended to earth bringing evil and violence in their train, as their progeny the Giants battled against human beings and other living things and with one another (1 Enoch 6:1–7:5). In 1977 Nickelsburg, having recounted the broad features of the Shemihazah narrative, offered the following astute observation: "The author lives during a time of great violence and bloodshed. The terrible plight of his people has led to a crisis of faith, expressed in the angelic prayer (*sc.* 1 Enoch 9:1–11)."³⁹ To contextualize this situation he made the following proposal: "If we look for events that bear similarities to the battles of the Giants, two possibilities emerge: the wars of the Diadochi (323–302 B.C.E) and the Seleucid-Ptolemaic struggle for the control of Palestine (217–198 B.C.E)."⁴⁰

He opted for the former alternative: "The cast of warrior chieftains is large. These two decades are a period of continued war, bloodshed, and assassination. Palestine especially felt the brunt, and changed hands at least seven times in twenty-one years."⁴¹

The latter alternative only involved two persons or factions, who engaged in two sets of battles that were separated by more than a decade (218–217/201–198 BCE), and seemed too late to have allowed for the growth of the Enochic tradition.⁴² Nickelsburg has found some support for

38. CED: http://dictionary.cambridge.org/dictionary/english/rebellion.
39. Nickelsburg 1981:389.
40. Nickelsburg 1977:391.
41. Ibid.
42. Ibid.

this view, although often the wars of kings and generals after the Diadochoi are included. Thus Albertz considers that in the Giants "anyone could recognize the battles of the Diadochoi and the never-ending chain of Syrian wars."[43] Similarly, Portier-Young interprets Nickelsburg to be talking about "the Diadochoi and their successors" and essentially agrees with him.[44]

Nickelsburg's proposal has the great advantage of connecting a central feature of 1 Enoch 1–36 with the vigorous, real world politics of the Hellenistic period. This is a much larger social canvas than the purity rules for the priests in the temple in Jerusalem. Yet the major difficulty with it is that it does not proffer a particularly apt comparator for the notion of an exodus of angels from heaven, who thus abandoned God and the other angels. The wars of the Diadochoi, on the other hand, were rather between powerful rival forces. After the death of Alexander there were a number of generals with their own troops, and hence with solid claims to power and status, jockeying for position in relation to one another.[45] The source domain we need for the narrative of the Watchers is rather one in which members of a monarch's inner circle desert him and thereafter cause havoc in some part of his realm. In short, we are looking for examples of rebellion from within a royal court. This is the second type of disturbance that was mentioned above, where the kingdom could be shaken by forces from within the royal court. Yet, in addition, it relates far more closely to the second meaning of "rebellion" than to the first. I will now cite evidence for phenomena of rebellion from the Achaemenid and Hellenistic periods and then analyse the narrative of the Watchers in the light of the discussion.

Rebellion by Members of a Royal Court

Rebellion under the Achaemenids

In the record of his achievements carved in a cliff-face in Behistun, Darius the Great, the Persian (or "Achaemenid") king from 522 to 486 BCE, records how he suppressed numerous attempts to seize power after the death of Cyrus the Great and his son Cambyses II in the first years of his reign. Every instance involves the first sense of "rebellion" mentioned above—a group openly and with violence seeking to replace the existing government of a country. While most of the rebellions were by members of the diverse peoples under Persian rule, on two occasions Darius indicates that courtiers

---

43. Albertz 1994:579.
44. Portier-Young 2011:19 n62.
45. See Waterfield 2012.

took part in the rebellion. This occurred in the Persian heartland territories of Media and even Persia itself:

> Then did the Medes who were in the palace revolt from me and go over to Phraortes. He became the king in Media. (line 24)
>
> . . .
>
> Then the Persian people who were in the palace fell away from allegiance. They revolted from me and went over to that Vahyazdata. He became king in Persia. (line 40)[46]

On another occasion Darius states that "A man called Tritantaechmes, a Sagartian, revolted from me, saying to his people: 'I am king in Sagartia, of the family of Cyaxares'" (line 33).[47] Darius put down this revolt, but although he had Tritantaechmes punished in the usual way prior to his crucifixion, with the removal of his nose, ears and one eye, he did not have his tongue cut out. This suggests that he was not lying when he claimed to be the rightful king of Sagartia. It is likely that in this role he had previously acknowledged allegiance to Darius (or at least to this brother Cambyses II) and would have been an honored member of Darius's court had he chosen to visit it. But now he had abrogated that allegiance, a defection strongly implied in the statement, that Tritantaechmes "revolted from me" (line 33).

It is worth noting a sample of the actions that Darius took against the various people who revolted against him. One some occasions Darius himself led the forces against the rebels. He did this against Gaumata the Magus, who led the first rebellion and whom he captured and slew (line 13). He rebuilt temples and restored to the people the pasture lands, herds and dwellings which Gaumata had taken away (line 14). He also led his army against Nidintu-Bel, whom he likewise captured and slew (lines 16–20). But in relation to the revolt by Phraortes of Media, mentioned above, his approach was different. Here he initially sent a Persian army led by the general Hydarnes, who won a battle but in the absence of Phraortes (lines 21–25). Later he sent another army that captured Phraortes. Darius had his nose, ears and tongue cut off and one eye put out and kept him in fetters at his palace entrance where all the people beheld him. Then he had him crucified, flayed and his skin stuffed with straw hung out (lines 31–32). He also sent an army under the Armenian Dadarsi and another under the Persian Vaumisa to put down a revolt by the Armenians (lines 26–30). Against Tritantaechmes he sent out a Persian and a Median army under a Mede named Takhmaspada, his servant. They captured Tritantaechmes and subjected him to the punishment

---

46. Translations from King and Thompson 1907.
47. Translation from ibid.

mentioned above (lines 33–34). Similarly, he sent out the Persian Dadarsi, then satrap of Bactria, on a successful campaign against Frada the Margian (lines 38–39).

When describing the start of the rebellions, Darius sometimes used the expressed "X rebelled against me" (lines 24 [of the Medes in his palace], 33 [of Tritantaechmes]), or "revolted against/from me" (lines 35 [of the Parthians and Hyrcanians], 38 [of the province of Margiana] and 49 [of the Babylonians]). At times the bonds of loyalty that were being breached become explicit, as when he mentioned his father Hytaspes leading out "the troops which had remained faithful" (line 35), meaning faithful to him, or when the Persian people revolted from him and went over to one Vahyazdata, so that "the Persian people who were in the palace fell away from allegiance" (line 40). On other occasions, however, he used the expression "he rebelled" (line 11, 40) or "he revolted" (lines 22, 24), or "he raised a rebellion" (line 16; *bis*), as if the personal dimension, the breach of a relationship with him, although real, was not so prominent or needed highlighting.

While the importance of loyalty to the Persian king appears quite starkly in the case of the armed rebellion of Tritantaechmes, Maria Brosius has shown how loyalty to the monarch had a much wider ambit than dramatic events such as this. As already noted of courts in general from the argument of Norbert Elias, the system was in a state of flux, with some courtiers going up in royal estimation and some plummeting downwards. Within the Achaemenid court (like most others, we might reasonably surmise) were found both supporters and opponents of the king.[48] Such opposition could represent "rebellion" in the second sense—dissent from authority or the prescribed rules, which, we might add, the monarch was likely to interpret as disloyalty. As Brosius notes, whereas royal favour and gift-giving constituted spurs to individual ambition, such privileges could just as easily be revoked, so that "the nobles had to reaffirm their loyalty in order to confirm their worth and status. Failure to do so led to the withdrawal of royal favour." In addition, "No court official was exempt from punishments for disloyalty, running from loss of status and landed wealth to banishment from the court, and even death (potentially for all male members of the family too)."[49]

---

48. Brosius 2007:55.
49. Ibid.

Rebellions in Hellenistic Kingdoms

As already mentioned above, after Alexander's death in 323 BCE, the Hellenistic world was convulsed by wars among his generals (his "Diadochi," successors) for some twenty years. Over the next two centuries wars between the descendants of the Diadochi—the kings of the Seleucid, Ptolemaic, Attalid and Antigonid dynasties—continued. Yet we must not forget that some conflicts were endogenous, fomented by members of a king's own court. In the second century BCE, for example, the territorial contraction of Hellenistic kingdoms meant that loyalty could no longer be guaranteed.[50] No matter how well-informed a monarch might be of developments in his court and his kingdom, attempts by courtiers to advance their own position (an instance of "rebellion" in the second sense) or even to supplant the king or to carve off and take control of part of his possessions ("rebellion" in the first sense) were common.[51] Here are five examples recorded in Polybius' *Histories*; they indicate the rebellions from within Hellenistic courts began in the third century BCE. Polybius, it should be noted, was writing only several decades after these events had occurred.

(a) When Antiochus III succeeded to the throne in 222 BCE, he entrusted the governorship of Asia Minor to Achaeus, his cousin, and the inland provinces of the kingdom to Molon and his brother Alexander, with Molon as satrap of Media and Alexander satrap of Persis.[52] This decision confirmed the positions they had held under the previous king.[53] Molon and Alexander then rebelled against Antiochus.[54] Strootman observes that such conflicts were normal: "Virtually every new reign sooner or later saw attempts of the new king to replace the men who had risen to positions of power under his predecessor by his own *philoi*, and hence also attempts by the predecessor's *philoi* to retain their positions."[55] After several successes, Molon's army was defeated by an army led by Antiochus himself and Molon committed suicide.[56] This was an example of the first meaning of rebellion.

(b) Philip V of Macedon (reigned 221–179 BCE) inherited a certain Apelles from his father as one of his guardians.[57] Yet the relationship be-

---

50. Spawforth 2007b:16.

51. See the discussion in Herman 1997:215–24, with particular reference to the evidence in Polybius.

52. See Polybius, *The Histories* 5.39.

53. Strootman 2011:72.

54. Polybius, *The Histories* 5.40–41.

55. Strootman 2011:72.

56. Polybius, *The Histories* 5.54.

57. Polybius, *The Histories* 4.76

tween the two soon soured and Apelles worked hard to frustrate many of the king's plans. Apelles is an excellent example of a very senior courtier who was disloyal to his king but did not express this disloyalty through leading an actual rebellion. This was, accordingly, rebellion in the second sense. At one stage he went so far as to sabotage Philip's plans for conducting war against the Aetolians, the Lacedaemonians and the Eleans by cutting off Philip's supplies.[58] Eventually, in 220 BCE, Philip, neutralized Apelles by denying him access to his presence.[59] Shortly afterwards, Apelles took his own life.[60]

(c) Cleomenes of Sparta, who had been a close ally of Ptolemy III Euergetes, was treated badly by his successor, Ptolemy IV, especially by not being permitted to leave the court in Alexandria to return home to help his people in war. So, in 219 BCE he attempted a coup (= an instance of the first sense of rebellion); it failed and he and his companions killed themselves.[61]

(d) Not long after these events, the Ptolemaic governor of Coele Syria, one Theodotus from Aetolia, plotted with the Seleucid king Antiochus III to betray the cities of Coele Syria to him. Theodotus despised Ptolemy IV for his dissolute lifestyle and the king had recently come close to killing him, even though Theodotus had performed faithful service to him, by successfully defending Coele-Syria against the advance of Antiochus' army in 221–220 BCE.[62] In the war between Antiochus III and Ptolemy IV, Theodotus betrayed his king by handing over the important fortresses of Tyre and Ptolemais to Antiochus and then becoming a successful general in his army. This was closer to the second meaning of rebellion than the first, since Theodotus aimed to weaken the position of Ptolemy IV rather than to bring down his rule.

(e) Achaeus had rebelled against Antiochus III in 220 BCE.[63] He achieved major successes in a string of campaigns.[64] This was an instance of the first meaning of rebellion. Antiochus was initially too distracted by his war with Ptolemy IV over Coele Syria, which ended with his defeat at the Battle of Raphia in 217 BCE, to deal with Achaeus. Upon the cessation of hostilities with Ptolemy IV, however, he moved against Achaeus, whom he captured and had killed in 213 BCE.

58. Polybius, *The Histories* 5.2.
59. Polybius, *The Histories* 5.26.
60. Polybius, *The Histories* 5.28.
61. Polybius, *The Histories* 5.34–39.
62. Polybius, *The Histories* 5.40; see Strootman 2011:78.
63. Polybius, *The Histories* 5.57.
64. Polybius, *The Histories* 5.72–78.

In the late third century BCE, therefore, a possible date for 1 Enoch 1–36, there were several prominent instances of disloyalty by senior courtiers of Hellenistic kingdoms, two of them resulting in full-scale armed rebellions and protracted military campaigns across wide sweeps of the Seleucid kingdom. There were rebellions in both meanings of the term.

I will now proceed to analyse the departure of the Watchers from heaven in the light of this evidence for rebellion and disloyalty in the Achaemenid kingdom under Darius the Great and in the Hellenistic kingdoms in the late third century BCE. This analysis of rebellions from within or against a single court will provide a closer parallel to what we find in 1 Enoch 1–36 than the Wars of the Diadochi a century earlier (323–302 CE) that George Nickelsburg has proposed underlie the narrative of the Watchers.

REBELLION BY THE WATCHERS IN THE ENOCHIC HEAVEN

The Nature of the Watchers' Secession from Heaven

The idea that the model for the secession of the Watchers from heaven was the phenomenon of rebellion against Achaemenid and Hellenistic monarchs, which must have been familiar to whoever created 1 Enoch 1–36, has a strong *prima facie* appeal. This arises primarily from the close structural similarity of source and target domains. Unlike those who seek to appeal to the Jerusalem priesthood, for example, we do not need to mount strained arguments from individual words in the Book of the Watchers that are alleged to contain cultic associations. In 1 Enoch 1–36 we find a divine king in his palace, surrounded by angels some of them forming an inner group and the majority an outer group, two hundred of whom resolve to abandon heaven. As we have already, on other grounds, argued in Chapter 3 for the appropriateness of regarding the context as one of a king in his court with his angels being his courtiers, it is equally appropriate to interpret the deliberate departure of some of those angels from the court as a rebellion against the king and his rule.

The Two Dimensions of the Watchers' Secession from Heaven

The action of the Watchers is precipitated by their seeing and desiring the beautiful women who had been born (by implication, on earth below heaven) and their wish to beget children for themselves from them (6:1). Shemihazah realized that this would entail a great sin (ἁμαρτία μεγάλη; 6:3).

That was why he had the two hundred who joined him swear an oath that they would not turn back from the deed (6:4–5). In the background here we sense other conspiracies to take action (sometimes evil in nature), ancient and modern, where the conspirators swear an oath to one another to maintain unity of purpose and to discourage defections from their ranks.[65] More pertinently, this oath brings us directly into the larger world of ethnic groups, nations and politics—rather than the much narrower realm of the Jerusalem temple—in which the writing of 1 Enoch took place. For during the Hellenistic period kings often swore oaths to confirm peace treaties with one another and these were very potent instruments for maintaining agreements. John Grainger has noted that "no Seleukid or Ptolemaic king broke such an oath over the whole period of Hellenistic history."[66]

But what was the nature of the "great sin"? It must relate to the Watchers' initial action in leaving heaven to take human wives, not to the trouble that this subsequently caused on earth, since there is no sign that the Watchers anticipated such a result when they made their oath. First Enoch 1–36 quite carefully distinguishes these two areas of misbehavior by the Watchers. Thus in 1 Enoch 12:4 God refers to the Watchers who (a) "having abandoned (ἀπολιπόντες) the highest heaven, the holy place of their eternal station" (for this translation, see above) became defiled with women by taking wives for themselves and (b) wrought great destruction (ἀφανισμός) on the earth. That great destruction itself has two dimensions: first, the generation of Giants who ravage the earth, and, secondly, the revelation by the Watchers of secrets to human beings that causes further chaos and destruction (in the form of superior weaponry and magic, for example).

I will now deal in turn with these two areas (the Watchers' abandonment of heaven for earth and marrying women, on the one hand, and the destruction that results, on the other), by considering them in the light of the perspectives on rebellion set out above.

The Watchers' "Great Sin" as Rebellion

Let us now focus on the character of "the great sin." Nickelsburg, having cited biblical and post-biblical passages to the effect that it could refer to

---

65. See Sommerstein and Torrance (2014:203–4) for oaths between divinities for various common enterprises in Aeschylean tragedy. Equally revealing, since it is an exception that proves the rule, is the opposition that Brutus expresses to Cassius' proposal that the conspirators planning to assassinate Julius Caesar, in Shakespeare's play of that name, should swear an oath (Act II, scene i), for the reason that if they are doing the right thing for the right reason they have no need of an oath.

66. Grainger 2017:14.

adultery, incest, idolatry, and perhaps murder, then confidently states that in 1 Enoch 6:3 the great sin is "sexual relations between forbidden degrees, i.e. between species."⁶⁷ Yet this is an incomplete and inaccurate answer. The full details of that sin are elucidated by no less an authority than God himself in the highly significant passage mentioned above, 15:3–7:

> Why have you abandoned the high heaven,
> the holy place of eternity (τὸν ἅγιον τοῦ αἰῶνος),
> and lain with women and become defiled with the daughters of humans,
> and taken wives for yourselves.
> You have acted just like the sons of the earth
> And you have begotten children (τέκνα) for yourselves, sons (who are) Giants.
> You were holy and spirits, living forever.
> You have become defiled with the blood of women
> and with the blood of flesh you have begotten,
> and with human blood you have lusted,
> and you have done as they do—
> flesh and blood, who die and perish.
> Therefore I gave them women,
> that they might implant seed into them,
> and so beget children by them,
> so that nothing might fail them on the earth.
> But you used to exist as spirits, living forever,
> and not dying for all the generations of eternity;
> therefore I did not make women among you.
> The spirits of heaven, in heaven is their dwelling (κατοίκησις).

It is noteworthy how close is God's attitude to the manner in which Norbert Elias characterized the situation of the courtiers in the court of Louis XIV: "*[I]t was only by going to court and living within court society that they could preserve the distance from everything else on which their spiritual salvation, their prestige as court aristocrats, in short, their social existence and their personal identity depended.*"⁶⁸

Since the Watchers were not engaged in open and violent action aimed at bringing down God's rule and establishing a new one, we encounter here a form of the second sense of rebellion, which, it will be recalled, encompasses

---

67. Nickelsburg 2001:177.
68. Elias 1983:99 (italics original).

both defiance towards an authority or controlling power and resistance to the rules and normal and accepted ways of behaving.

Yet comparison with the evidence of the attitudes of Darius the Great to rebellion against his rule reveals one striking omission: there is no sign here of any personal investment by God in what the Watchers have done. He does not say that they had rebelled *against him*, or that they had *fallen away from allegiance or been disloyal*. There is no sign that the Enochic God takes the desertion of the Watchers personally! We noted above that Darius did not mention personal loyalty to him in relation to some of the rebels in the Behistun Inscription. Perhaps in 1 Enoch 1–36, however, this is to be understood on the basis that this God is too far above even his angelic creatures to regard himself as being in a relationship of loyalty with them. Rather, we have here an illustration of the second aspect of the second meaning of rebellion: resistance to, or rather abrogation of, the rules. This rebellion is the "great sin" of the Watchers to which Shemihazah admits in 1 Enoch 6:3. In particular, God's negative attitude towards the Watchers arises from the rebellion entailed in their having breached the established order—with God by necessary implication the being who has established that order—and breached it in two respects.

The first is simply that they had abandoned the place where they should be (1 Enoch 15:3). Although what they have left is here described as "the high heaven, the holy place of eternity," this is to be understood in relation to the more focused description at 12:4: "the highest heaven, the holy place of their eternal station." As we have noted in Chapter 3, we must take seriously the "watching" function of the Watchers: they are like the Latin *vigiles*. Moreover, as we will see in Chapter 5, heaven consists of an area of space within which is a walled and gated precinct. The Watchers become aware of what is happening on earth from their posts on those walls. The first aspect of their great sin, therefore, is in deserting their post. They have committed a fundamental dereliction of their duty. Nickelsburg overlooks this dimension in his characterisation of the great sin (noted above) as "sexual relations between forbidden degrees, i.e. between species" and to this extent his explanation is incomplete.

Yet there is a further aspect to God's displeasure in relation to the departure of the Watchers that reveals Nickelsburg's explanation, even in relation to this inter-marriage dimension of the problem, to be incomplete (as well as inaccurate). In the last line of the passage God states, "The spirits of heaven, in heaven is their dwelling (κατοίκησις)" (1 Enoch 15:7). Here God is focusing not on heaven as a site for the duties of the Watchers as guards but as the place where they live. The underlying sentiment reflects the court-and-courtiers source metaphor for the narrative. Norbert Elias has noted that at Versailles a section of the court society "had lodgings in the king's house permanently allocated to them. Louis XIV liked to see his nobles living in his house whenever he held court there."[69] The position of the Enochic God is essentially identical. It is not certain that any personal pique is being imputed to God in his response to the Watchers' departure from their home, that he wants them living in heaven *with him* and is offended that they are not. Nevertheless, it is the case that this is part of the order that he has created and which the Watchers have defied by descending to earth to live there with their women. This is a feature of the text well explained by the court and courtiers model.

But the Watchers have not merely abandoned heaven for earth. The second respect in which they have rebelled, and hence greatly sinned, is in their actions on earth—coupling with human women. This certainly involves their defiling themselves, but Nickelsburg's characterisation of the sin is, again, inaccurate as well as incomplete. It is inaccurate to describe the Watchers and the women as representing different "species" or "degrees" for the reason that this does not do justice to the magnitude of the difference between these two orders of being. Both the expressions "species" and "degrees" imply a context of biological organisms, the former of different organisms within one class and the second of different social categories within one species, in this case the species *homo sapiens*. All scholarly views that the Watchers somehow refer to the priests in the Jerusalem temple and their marriage practices need some version of Nickelsburg's explanation of the "great sin" to be correct. But the text points to a very different issue, for the Enochic God is concerned with the fact that *immortal spiritual beings not needing to engage in reproduction* have joined themselves with *mortal physical beings, beings of flesh and blood, who do need to reproduce*. No biological framework for including Watchers and women of the sort Nickelsburg proposes is possible here. The only thing these two types of being have in common is that they have both been created by God, and even that commonality must be implied from the text.

Nevertheless, the notion of defilement is prominent in 1 Enoch 15:3–7 and, as mentioned above in critically analysing David Suter's approach, Mary Douglas's ideas of purity help us to clarify what it means in this context. Douglas fruitfully explained pollution in terms of dirt, meaning matter that is out of place. Dirt, and pollution and defilement with it, is "the by-product of a systematic ordering and classification of matter."[70] She proposed that such classifications were ways of keeping phenomena in their proper place,

---

69. Elias 1983:80.
70. Douglas 1966:35.

meaning within their own boundaries, and thus of reducing or eliminating anomalies, meaning phenomena that did not fit, that fell between boundaries or represented a dangerous blurring of them. In short: "For the only way in which pollution ideas make sense is in reference to a total structure of thought whose key-stone, boundaries, margins and internal lines are held in relation by rituals of separation."[71] Breaching such boundaries entailed defilement and could aroused strong negative feelings in a particular context. The Enochic picture of the appropriate place for angels being heaven and for human beings earth represents a divine arrangement naturally construed as one of Douglas's "rituals of separation." God's displeasure in 1 Enoch 15:3–7 is primarily provoked by the Watchers' having grievously disregarded the fundamental boundary (by implication, created by him) separating them as immortal, spiritual and non-reproducing beings from mortal, physical and reproducing human women. Douglas's views on defilement are, accordingly, ample enough to illuminate a situation even where the difference between the two types of being is as stark as in 1 Enoch 15:3–7.

The Consequences of the Watchers' Rebellion

When the Watchers descended to human women, they did not merely defile themselves but, as noted earlier in this chapter, also fathered the Giants on the women (1 Enoch 7:2) and taught them sorcery, charms, knowledge and skills (1 Enoch 7:1 and 8:1–3). The text proffers graphic details of what the arrival of the Giants led to:

> They (*sc.* the Giants) devoured the labor of all the sons of human beings, so that the human beings were not able to supply them. And the Giants assailed the human beings and devoured them. And they began to sin against the birds and beasts and creeping things and the fish, and to devour one another's flesh. And they drank the blood. (1 Enoch 7:3–5)[72]

As a result, "the earth brought a petition (ἐνέτυχεν) against the lawless ones" (1 Enoch 7:6), meaning a petition to heaven.

---

71. Ibid.:41.

72. This is a translation of the Greek in the Akhmin manuscript, except that in the expression "all the sons of human beings" the words "sons of" are found in an Aramaic fragment (Milik 1976:150). The Greek for "human beings" in each instance in the quotation is ἄνθρωποι, which Nickelsburg and VanderKam (2012:25) at this point translate as "men." I prefer "human beings" to make it clear that the Greek translator includes women as also responsible for the labor that is being devoured, otherwise he would have used ἄνδρες.

Secondly, and compounding the depredations of the Giants, was the teaching of sorcery and charms to the women (1 Enoch 7:1) and the revelation by Asael and Shemihazah and other Watchers of various secrets and a wide range of knowledge to human beings (1 Enoch 8:1–3). Asael revealed secrets relating to swords of iron, weapons of war and body-armor, jewellery and cosmetics (8:1). As a result: "there was much godlessness, they committed fornication, they were led astray and they were obliterated in all their ways" (1 Enoch 8:2).[73] The other Watchers taught them spells and sorcery, and knowledge of the phenomena in the heavens and on earth and they revealed these secrets to their wives and children (8:3). The consequence of all this was dire: "Therefore the cry of the human beings who were perishing went up to heaven" (8:4).[74]

The first question thrown up by this material is whether it can be as easily interpreted to constitute rebellion as can the "great sin" of the Watchers. This question should probably be answered in the negative. As far as I am aware, the accounts of revolts in Persian and Hellenistic courts do not precisely recount issues relating to the rebels having children with the women of the people into whose midst they have removed themselves or revealing new skills and knowledge to them. Nevertheless, these phenomena do follow on from a rebellion against a king, even if they are very distinctive, if not unique in character. No such connection exists if we follow the currently popular view and seek to relate this aspect of the narrative to the Jerusalem priesthood.

On closer inspection, moreover, it is possible to find some features of ancient revolts that are, in fact, reasonably close to the Watchers' behavior with the women and its consequences. One area of comparison lies in the extent to which women inhabiting ancient towns and cities captured by a hostile army were likely to be raped as a matter of course.[75] If some of these women survived their ordeal, a proportion of them would have been left pregnant to the conquerors. The army led by a courtier rebelling against his king that captured a town or city still loyal to the monarch was very likely to have acted in this way. Furthermore, the description of the Giants devouring

---

73. This is based on the Greek of the Akhmin manuscript with which the Ethiopic version coheres. But immediately before this quotation in the Greek version of Syncellus there is another sentence: "And the sons of the human beings made them for themselves and for their daughters, and they transgressed and they led the holy ones astray."

74. This is a translation of the Greek of the Akhmin manuscript (which is similar to the Aramaic, which also has humans perishing and a cry going up [to heaven]: see Milik 1976:158); in addition Syncellus (and the Ethiopic) has the additional statement that human beings began to grow few upon the earth. For the complex textual issues regarding 1 Enoch 8:4, see Nickelsburg 2001:190.

75. See Vikman 2010.

"the labor of all the sons of human beings, so that the human beings were not able to supply them" (1 Enoch 7:3) lies close to the proclivity of an invading army (led by a courtier rebelling against his king, for example) to take over or consume the property and food supplies of the peoples whom it subjugated or even through whom it marched. As noted above, Darius claimed in the Behistun Inscription that he restored to the people "the pasture lands, herds and dwellings which Gaumata, a Magus, had taken away" (line 14). Just as the Giants "assailed the human beings and devoured them" (1 Enoch 7:4), it was not unknown for rebels to murder people in their arena of action. Thus, Darius the Great records in the Behistun Inscription in relation to Gaumâta—whose rebellion entailed falsely claiming to be Smerdis, the son of Cyrus and brother of Cambyses—that "the people feared him exceedingly, for he slew many who had known the real Smerdis. For this reason did he slay them, 'that they may not know that I am not Smerdis, the son of Cyrus'" (line 13).[76] At the same time, rebels could gravely oppress people in other ways, for example by exiling them from their own lands. Thus in the Cyrus Inscription in the British Museum, Cyrus complains of Nabonidus, the king of Babylon whom he removed and who is presented as an inappropriate, in the sense of weak or counterfeit, king although not actually a rebel from Cyrus, that he had transplanted peoples to Babylon and oppressed them. Very similar to 1 Enoch 7:6 ("the earth brought a petition against the lawless ones") is the way Cyrus describes the result of the actions of Nabonidus: "He did yet more evil to his city every day; . . . his [people . . .], he brought ruin on them all by a yoke without relief. Enlil-of-the-gods became extremely angry at their complaints, and [. . .] their territory."[77]

Even in relation to the revelation of skills and knowledge by the Watchers to human beings, there exists a close parallel from the ancient Mediterranean world in the story of Prometheus. While scholars have already drawn attention to Prometheus in this connection,[78] my interest here lies in the extent to which what Prometheus did was an act of rebellion against his king. In the fullest statement of this myth, Aeschylus' play *Prometheus Bound*, Zeus is presented both as the father of the gods (4, 969) and also as their sovereign/ruler/king in a variety of nominal and verbal forms (10, 96, 170, 202–203, 221, 305, 310, 756, 956, 996). A word frequently used of Zeus is τύραννος ("sovereign") with τυραννίς ("sovereignty"), deployed with

---

76. King and Thompson 1907.

77. See http://www.britishmuseum.org/research/collection_online/collection_object_details.aspx?objectId=327188&partId=1.

78. See Nickelsburg 1977:399–404 and Portier-Young 2014:41–43.

respect to his rule. He has a court (αὐλή, 122), frequented by all the gods (120–122), and a throne (ἕδρα, 389).

The rebellion of Prometheus did not involve an armed attempt to depose Zeus; indeed, he helped him achieve his pre-eminence among the gods (216–218). Rather, his was a rebellion in the second sense: he had defied the rule of Zeus by showing his love for human beings in secretly bringing them fire that would allow their civilization to advance. This act represented defiance of the sovereignty of Zeus (10–11), a failure to obey him (40). In giving privileges to human beings Prometheus was acting, according to other characters in the drama, "contrary to right" (πέρα δίκης, 30) and against the laws (νόμοι) of Zeus (149, 403). Prometheus did not fear Zeus but fulfilled his own purpose of helping human beings (542–544).

The behavior of the Watchers in revealing skills and knowledge to people on earth, an act very similar to that of Prometheus, was similarly an instance of rebellion in its second sense. Although it is not said to involve the breach of an explicit instruction of God against so acting, the text leaves us in no doubt that it was a contravention of the order he had established. Here is what Michael, Sariel, Raphael and Gabriel say to God on this matter, when they bring the petition of the earth to the attention of God:

> And you see everything that Asael has done,
> who has taught every type of injustice on the earth,
> and has revealed the eternal mysteries which are in heaven . . .
> (1 Enoch 9:6)[79]

The implication is clear: Asael has brought to earth knowledge that should have stayed in heaven. Just as the Watchers erred in blurring the divinely established boundary between heaven and earth by abandoning the former for the latter and taking human wives, so too did they breach that boundary by bringing to earth knowledge that properly belonged in heaven.

In sum, both aspects of the consequences of the Watchers' action in descending to earth—the production of the Giants and the revelation of knowledge, which together constitute the "great destruction" (ἀφανισμός) on the earth mentioned in 1 Enoch 12:4—also fall to be interpreted as rebellion (in its second sense) by courtiers against the king's rule. Now that we have determined that both the action of descent and the havoc it caused reflect rebellion against a king of the sort with which we familiar from Persian and Hellenistic monarchies, the final substantive task in this chapter is

---

79. This is a translation of the Greek of the Akhmin manuscript. The corresponding passage in Syncellus is somewhat longer but concurs on the critical feature, that Asael "taught the mysteries and revealed to the world that things that are in heaven."

to compare the typical responses by such sovereigns with the way that the Enochic God reacts to the defection of the Watchers.

God's Response to the Rebellion of the Watchers

In 1 Enoch 1–36 we encounter with respect to the rebellion by heavenly courtiers not only a carefully articulated explanation by the divine monarch of the nature of the disorder it represents (15:3–7) and consequences for humanity and the earth itself (1 Enoch 7:1—9:2, 9–10), but also firm action taken by that monarch to punish the rebels. At a general level, it is instructive to recall Elias' observation from Chapter 1 that "A courtier's position . . . depended on the favour he enjoyed with the king, his power and importance within the field of court tensions."[80] There is no doubt that the Watchers had fallen entirely out of God's favour; that is why God will later instruct Enoch to tell them that they will never be forgiven (1 Enoch 12:4–13:4 and 15:1–16:4). To contextualize the character of God's punishment more closely within the setting 1 Enoch 1–36, however, it will help to cite an example of how an ancient Near Eastern king confronted by such a situation might react. My point is not that the example I will cite ever came to the attention of the Enochic author. Rather, I am suggesting that in this world kings tended to act in certain ways when facing rebellion and that such actions formed a well-known cultural script with which the author was aware and to which he resorted in narrating how God dealt with the Watchers. Here, then, is another passage from the Behistun Inscription of Darius the Great from 522–521 BCE:

> King Darius says: A man named Tritantaechmes, a Sagartian, revolted from me, saying to his people: "I am king in Sagartia, of the family of Cyaxares." Then I sent forth a Persian and a Median army. A Mede named Takhmaspâda, my servant, I made their leader, and I said unto him: "Go, smite that host which is in revolt, and does not acknowledge me." Thereupon Takhmaspâda went forth with the army, and he fought a battle with Tritantaechmes. Ahuramazda brought me help; by the grace of Ahuramazda my army utterly defeated that rebel host, and they seized Tritantaechmes and brought him unto me. Afterwards I cut off both his nose and ears, and put out one eye. He was kept bound at my palace entrance; all the people saw him. Afterwards I crucified him in Arbela. (line 33)[81]

80. Elias 1983:90.
81. King and Thompson 1907 (slightly modified).

Now let us consider the orders that God gives to the archangels in relation to the two leaders of the Watchers who rebelled, first in relation to Asael:

> Then he said to Raphael, "Go, Raphael, and bind Asael;
> bind together his hands and feet, and cast him into the darkness.
> Open the desert that is in the desert of Dudael. Go and throw him there.
> Put sharp and jagged rocks under him and cover him with darkness.
> Let him live there for an aeon. Cover his face and do not let him see the light.
> On the day of judgment he will be led off to the fiery conflagration."
> (1 Enoch 10:4–6)[82]

Next is God's instruction regarding Shemihazah:

> And he said to Michael, "Go, Michael, bind Shemihazah and the others
> with him who mated with the daughters of human beings,
> so that they were defiled by them through their uncleanness.
> And when their sons are perishing,[83]
> and they see the destruction of those they love,
> bind them for seventy generations in the valleys of the earth,
> until the day of their judgment,
> until the day of the final consummation,
> until judgment will be completed for ever.
> And they will be borne away into the fiery chasm, and into the torture and into the prison until the conclusion of the aeon."
> (1 Enoch 10:11–13)

The similarities between the actions of Darius and of God are quite striking. In all cases:

1. Eminent, named individuals have revolted from their king;

2. Some or all of the rebellion has occurred in a part of the kingdom a distance from the capital.

3. The king issues an oral command to a senior courtier from his court, despatching him to deal with the leader of the revolt and, in relation to Tritantaechmes and Shemihazah, to deal with those with him as well;

---

82. This a translation of the Greek text of Syncellus.

83. Diverging here from the Greek text of Syncellus to follow the Aramaic (Milik 1976:175), since the Greek has the unlikely reading "when their sons are slaughtering."

4. It is implied that the courtier has or will have the necessary arms, either via his army or himself, to achieve the mission (recall the painting of Raphael with a raised sword on the cover of this volume and discussed in the Prologue);

5. The planned action is either successfully achieved (on behalf of Darius) or the reader is left in no doubt that it will be (on behalf of God);

6. Violent punishment has been or will be inflicted on the defeated rebels, even to the extent that they will see their children die before their eyes. To appreciate the extremity of this it is worth mentioning the opprobrium that Alexander Jannaeus attracted to himself when he crucified 800 Judeans on a road leading out of Jerusalem and had them watch from their crosses as he had their wives and children killed before their eyes (Josephus, *JA* 13.372–383). This was a punishment not that dissimilar to what God has in store for the Watchers.

7. The punishment was or will be meted out over a period of time, with initial seizure and binding, physical punishment and discomfort to be followed in due course by eventual death or consignment to everlasting, fiery torment.

There are, admittedly, some differences but they are readily explained on the basis that the Enochic king is God after all and they hardly detract from these similarities:

1. In the case of Darius, the rebellion falls within the first sense, where the rebel tries to take over control of some of the king's territory, but in the case of the Enochic God, the second sense, in that they are defying the established order of things, no doubt because the sovereignty of God over his kingdom or any part of it can never be in doubt.

2. Darius sends Takhmaspâda with an army, but God appears to send Raphael and Michael on their own, presumably because as archangels they do not need any further assistance;

3. Darius records that he has received assistance from his god, Ahuramazda, which is irrelevant to the Enochic text where the king is God.

4. God's agents are capable of inflicting a punishment on the rebels that, in its character (binding them under the earth or in its valleys) or length (an aeon or seventy generations), is far beyond the capacity of a mortal king. (Yet it is exactly what one would expect of a divine king: thus at one point in Aeschylus' *Prometheus Bound* (lines 153–159) Prometheus expresses the wish that Zeus had instead sunk him under

the earth, beneath Hades itself, so that no god or creature could see him and rejoice at this suffering.)

The comparison of this section of the Behistun Inscription with 1 Enoch 10:4–6 and 11–13 reveals two ancient Near Eastern monarchs reacting in very similar ways to instances of rebellion by their courtiers. The similarities are many and significant and the differences are trifling and easily explained. It goes without saying, on the other hand, that this material in 1 Enoch 1–36—which is central to the meaning of the work since it adds the crucial conclusion to the rebellion of the Watchers that God intervened to punish them for their "great sin"—cannot and does not depend upon any aspect of the behavior or fate of the priests in the temple in Jerusalem. The author's canvas is the wider political arena of ancient kingdoms and their courts and the violent pressures that sometimes split them apart. It is not the far narrower issue of the temple, its cult and its priesthood.

CONCLUSION

In Chapter 2 I cited the observation of Norbert Elias that in the court of Louis XIV, "large-scale convulsions incessantly changed the positions of people and the distance between them."[84] The secession of the Watchers from heaven, the consequences of their actions on the earth and its inhabitants and their eventual punishment that constitute one of the two primary narratives of 1 Enoch 1–36, represent just such a convulsion. The other such narrative, concerning the journeying of Enoch through the cosmos in Chapters 17–36, presupposes what we have already learned of this story in Chapters 1–16.[85] The currently dominant view that seeks to relate the story of the Watchers to the Jerusalem temple and its priesthood has been exposed as based on very little evidence in the text, mainly the strained and unconvincing attempt to build an edifice on a few words here and there alleged to have cultic associations. It is an explanation that also has no connection whatever with the structure and flow of the narrative concerning the Watchers.

The argument set out in this chapter, on the other hand, has shown that the source metaphor for this narrative was the common phenomenon of rebellion in the courts of Persian and Hellenistic kingdoms. On numerous points it has proven possible to show deep and abiding connections between source and target domains in relation both to the broad shape of

---

84. Elias 1983:91.

85. See references to the story and fate of the Watchers and the spatial organization of heaven in 1 Enoch 19:1–2; 21:10; 25:3–4; and 36:2–3.

the narrative and also to numerous individual details. In this aspect of the text, therefore, the picture of the king, his court and courtiers provides a persuasive framework for interpreting 1 Enoch 1–36.

This conclusion, finally, represents a stumbling-block to claims that apocalyptic texts like 1 Enoch 1–36 should be interpreted as opposing "empire." According to Anathea Portier-Young, to cite one example, for the writer and audience of the Book of the Watchers the revelation of forbidden knowledge and the violence that accompanied it "served as a type for their own situation, allowing them to critique the violence, power, and knowledge claims of the Hellenistic kings and generals who fought over Judea."[86] The investigation conducted above suggests that the text is best interpreted as advancing quite the opposite position. The Watchers were courtiers who rebelled against their divine king, wreaking havoc on the earth and its people in the process, and were punished by him with extreme violence as a result, a pattern virtually identical to the actions of Persian and Hellenistic kings in quelling rebellions in their own kingdoms. The text endorses without reservation the legitimacy of God in acting in this way. Far from the story of the Watchers representing an attempt by the author to oppose or subvert "empire," the text presupposes and even valorizes the existence of monarchies by finding in them an appropriate model upon which to base the representation of the divine king, with his court and courtiers, when faced with a grave challenge to his authority.

---

86. Portier-Young 2011:331.

5

THE SPATIAL AND ARCHITECTURAL DIMENSIONS OF THE ENOCHIC HEAVEN

DIVINE IMAGE-MANAGEMENT

In Chapter 2 I briefly described the "image-management" that was characteristic of kings in both the French and ancient Near Eastern and Hellenistic courts. The symbolic communication that this entailed included art, architecture, ceremony and costume that legitimated the authority of the sovereign. In this chapter I will consider data in the Book of the Watchers bearing on this subject. In so doing I will continue critically to interact with the view, currently dominant in scholarship, that heaven is portrayed in the text in terms of the Jerusalem temple and its priests. In Chapter 6 I will use these conclusions on the nature of the Enochic heaven to distinguish it from the Jerusalem temple, while showing its pronounced similarity to a Persian royal palace at Pasargadae.

Peter Schäfer has recently gone so far as to suggest that "it is very likely that the architectural structure in heaven is modeled after the First Temple on earth: God's heavenly residence is no mere palace but more concretely a temple, similar to the Temple in which he resides on earth."[1] Already in Chapter 3 we have seen that several aspects of this position, for example the notion that the mediating role of the angels in heaven was priestly, cannot be reconciled with the textual data, whereas interpreting them as courtiers in a royal court makes excellent sense of the evidence. Why Schäfer should

1. Schäfer 2009:59.

speak of a "mere palace" is particularly puzzling given the size of the central buildings, which were hypostyle halls, of the first two palaces (Palaces "S" and "P") constructed by Cyrus the Great at Pasargadae in the second half of the sixth century BCE (to name only one palace complex). The smaller of these (Palace S) was nearly three times as large (in terms of cubic volume) as Solomon's temple.

Accordingly, in this chapter our focus will be on the spatial and architectural dimensions of heaven and on the way God is presented, especially in relation to his enthronement and costume and the ceremonial practices that accompany his presence. The critical passage In this regard is 1 Enoch 14:8–23, although the investigation will at times entail consideration of other aspects of the text.

DIVINE ABODES AND PALACES IN THE ANCIENT NEAR EAST AND THE HELLENISTIC WORLD

Scholarly work on the heavenly abode in 1 Enoch regularly suffers from a failure to clarify the frameworks of investigation being applied. One major cause of confusion is the fact that in Israel and in other ancient Near Eastern states a temple was often called a house of the god. When reflecting on the heavenly abode of a god, the temptation, to which many critics commenting on 1 Enoch 1–36 text have succumbed, is to view it as a reflection of the terrestrial model. By so doing one can interpret angels in heaven as equivalent to priests in the earthly temple. But that is to invert the real position. For what seems a natural step actually conceals a major misapprehension of the true situation. On the reasonable assumption that the ancient people who produced our texts believed that God and his heavenly attendants actually lived in heaven, a supra-terrestrial zone, such an abode was real and the earthly temple was a substitute for, or a copy or metaphor of, that reality.

Instructive examples of this phenomenon come from Egypt and Mesopotamia. Michael Hundley has observed that in ancient Egypt "the gods' preferred abode was the sky or heaven," while the underworld was the abode of the deity's body to which his *ba* ("spirit") was united each night. Since the gods had little contact with the human sphere, the temple and, more precisely, the cult statue within it were hit upon as the solution to divine absence: by such a means the deity could be localized in the heart of the human community.[2] Similarly, in Mesopotamia human devotees realized the gods had temples on earth, but also abodes in heaven. Thus the sacred precinct of the god Enlil in Nippur was named "Duranki," meaning

---

2. Hundley 2013:41–42.

"the connection (between) heaven and earth."[3] For the most part humans had no access to heaven and the gods rarely appeared to human beings on earth. The temple, especially if constructed on a ziggurat, brought heaven as close to earth as possible.[4] Thus the deity "was sequestered in the deepest recesses of the temple to secure this unnatural incursion of heaven onto earth."[5] In other words, the natural home of the gods was in heaven and temples were a means to get round this troubling fact by creating a form of divine presence among the community on earth.

This distinction between the gods' heavenly abode and their "residence" (in a qualified sense) on earth provides justification for considering God's dwelling in heaven in 1 Enoch 1–36 on its own terms. Rather than interpreting this heavenly abode from the outset as a reflection of the earthly temple, we should rather first pay close attention to the heavenly dwelling itself. A later and different project might then be to investigate how it was shadowed in "temples" on earth. Accordingly, we will now return to the model of court and courtiers set out in Chapter 2 and consider the evidence in 1 Enoch 14 in relation to it.

Where does all this leave palaces? In speaking of the situation in Syro-Phoenicia, Michael Hundley notes as follows: "Although cities almost always had a temple, they did not always have a palace (e.g., LB I Megiddo). Thus, in such cases, city architecture suggested that the temple was the most powerful city institution. However, when both were present, they were commonly juxtaposed and the palace was often larger, thereby suggesting the relative power and interconnectedness of the two institutions."[6] In a footnote to this statement he adds: "Even the most pious kings constructed larger palaces than temples unless the temple institution was strong enough to prevent them. Since the palaces were built larger than temples, we may tentatively conclude that the monarchy was a more powerful institution."[7]

Although the French courtiers of the *ancien régime* maintained large, luxurious, and often ruinously expensive houses as a necessary incident of their high status and importance, none of them was permitted to maintain an establishment that rivaled in size or grandeur the palace or palaces of the king. Such a prohibition reflected the social and political superiority of the monarch.

3. Ibid.:77.
4. Ibid.:83.
5. Ibid.:84.
6. Ibid.:124.
7. Ibid.:124 n81.

THE PALACE PRECINCT IN THE BOOK OF THE WATCHERS: TEXTUAL ANALYSIS

The Sequential Logic of the Narrative

1 Enoch 14:8–24 relate how Enoch is translated to heaven in a vision and makes his way through various spatial and architectural features until he is brought near to the presence of God, who then, in 1 Enoch 15–16, gives him instructions on what he must say to the Watchers. The fact that all this happens in a vision requires a brief comment. Although Enoch describes various features that he sees, much of the depiction is rather schematic and many of the details that are provided, especially the paradoxical combination of fire and ice in the construction of the structures of heaven, do have an other-worldly quality. On the other hand, the basic features of the space and architecture of heaven are, as will be seen, quite clear and Enoch's movement across them exhibits a strong and realistic narrative logic tied to his encountering one feature after another in their expected spatial order. The latter point requires considerable emphasis given the number of scholars who appear not to appreciate this dimension of the text.

The significance of this feature of 1 Enoch 1–36 is also underlined by a comparison with the two texts (discussed in Chapter 1) where heaven is depicted in terms of a temple and priesthood, the *Songs of the Sabbath Sacrifice* and the *Testament of Levi*. In relation to the former Newsom notes that "The most striking aspect of the description of the heavenly temple in the Sabbath Shirot, however, is the reference to *seven* territories, sanctuaries or debirim . . ."[8] Curiously, however, there is a fluctuation between singular and plural in describing the heavenly sanctuaries. From this Newsom argues that while one of the seven sanctuaries is probably exalted over all the others, that alone seems an inadequate explanation for the fluctuation between singular and plural forms. It seems more likely that we have here plurals of majesty and even deliberate violations of ordinary syntax and meaning "in a text which is attempting to communicate something of the elusive transcendence of heavenly reality." Newsom next comments as follows, with her exemplary sensitivity to the text:

---

8. Newsom 1985:48 (emphasis original). She notes that "It is extremely difficult to supply parallels for the notion of seven heavenly sanctuaries. In most descriptions of multiple heavens, each heaven contains different inhabitants and/or distinct structures with the heavenly temple located in one of the heavens, not necessarily in the highest (cf. T. Levi, 3 Apoc. Baruch, 2 Enoch; b. Hag. 12b; Re'uyot Yeheziel; etc.). One can at least find references in two texts to seven heavens, each with its own throne, though in neither text are the heavens themselves described as sanctuaries" (1985:50).

> It is important to keep in mind that the Shabbath Shirot do not present their conceptions with the rationality of sober exposition or even with the sequential logic imposed by the narrative framework of a visionary's heavenly journey. Instead, allusions to heavenly realia are incidental to descriptions of angelic praise. The entire composition seems at times to be a rhapsody on the sacred number seven, so that one may simply have in the Shirot a fluctuation between a vision of heaven as one and as seven holy sanctuaries.[9]

In 1 Enoch 14, on the other hand, we do have "the sequential logic imposed by the narrative framework" of Enoch's journey through heaven and, in addition, we have a sober account of the architectural structures he encounters, even if particular details are paradoxical and extraordinary. The architectural realism of the narrative provides further confirmation for the source domain of the heaven in 1 Enoch 1–36 lying not in the temple in Jerusalem but in a royal court with its king and courtiers.

The Representation of Heaven in 1 Enoch 14

Arrival in Heaven (1 Enoch 14:8)

Our first task is closely to examine the textual evidence in 1 Enoch 14 concerning the spatial and architectural dimensions of heaven and the divine presence there and the way in which Enoch encounters them. Enoch's translation to heaven is hardly conventional. In his vision clouds summon him, mists cry out to him, shooting stars and lightning flashes hurry him along and winds make him fly and lift him upward and bring him into heaven (v. 8).

Enoch Encounters the Perimeter Wall of Heaven (1 Enoch 14:9)

Enoch then says, "And I went in until I drew near to a . . ." (v. 9). Although the Aramaic is not extant for this statement,[10] the Greek has καὶ εἰσῆλθον μέχρις ἤγγισα . . . and the Ethiopic ወቦኩ፡ እስከ፡ አቀርብ፡ . . . (wa-bo'ku 'eska 'eqarreb . . .), which are equivalent. This is a significant detail since it indicates that Enoch journeyed through heaven before he reached and passed through the structure I will now consider. Heaven thus consists of some space outside this structure and some space inside it.

9. Newsom 1985:49.
10. See Milik 1976:195.

What was this structure mentioned in v. 9? The Aramaic, once again, is not extant, while the Greek (of the Akhmim manuscript here) and the Ethiopic are somewhat different. The Greek then has Enoch say "(I approached) τείχους οἰκοδομῆς ἐν λίθοις χαλάζης, meaning roughly "of a wall of a building in stones of hail." I say "roughly" because there are difficulties with the Greek grammar and syntax in these and in the remaining nine words to which I will return below. The Ethiopic, on the other hand, is much smoother: (I approached) ጥቅም፡ ዘሕንጹት፡ በእብነ፡ በረድ፡ (ṭeqm za-ḥenset ba-'a'bāna barad),[11] meaning "a wall that (was) built of stones of hail." The Ethiopic here presupposes underlying Greek (different from that in the Ahkmim codex) of τεῖχος οἰκοδομημένον ἐν λίθοις χαλάζης. It is worth noting at this point that τεῖχος was the usual Greek word for a city-wall (cf. Acts 9:25 and 2 Cor 11:33), as opposed to τοῖχος or τειχίον, which were used of a house-wall, with τοῖχοι actually used later, of the walls of the "great house" in 1 Enoch 14:10.

The Greek then continues: καὶ γλώσσης πυρὸς κύκλῳ αὐτῶν καὶ ἤρχσαντο ἐκφοβεῖν με. Some Ethiopic manuscripts also have "tongue" in the singular: ወልሳነ፡ እሳት፡ የዐውዳ፡ ወወጠነ፡ ያፈርሃኒ፡ (wa-lesāna 'essāt ya'āwwedā wa-waṭana yāferrehāni), meaning "and a tongue of fire were surrounding it and they began to frighten me (lit: "It began they were frightening me"). Not only is singular "tongue of fire" grammatically problematic here, but the Aramaic has "tongues" in the plural: ולשנ]י נור סחרין סחור סח[ור להון (wlšn] y nwr sḥryn sḥwr sḥ[wr lhwn), "and tongues of fire were encircling them all around."[12] Further support for the plural subsists in the appearance of "tongues of fire" later in the passage, in 1 Enoch 14:15.

Has Enoch come to a wall or a building and, if a building, what sort of building is it? According to Martha Himmelfarb, writing in 1993, the answer is a building, and not just any building but a constituent part of a temple closely parallel to the one in Jerusalem. Having noted that some critics have treated the two "houses" that Enoch will next encounter "as the *hekhal*, or sanctuary ('nave' in RSV), and *devir*, or holy of holies ('inner sanctuary' in RSV), of a temple,"[13] she maintains that "the correspondence is more exact than that. Both the First and Second Temples contained a third, outer, chamber, the *'ûlām*, or vestibule." According to Himmelfarb, the "building" that Enoch comes to (according to the Greek text; she notes in the Ethiopic he comes to a "wall") is this vestibule: "The Greek text,

---

11. Some Ethiopic manuscripts read *ba-'ebna barad* ("of stone of hail").

12. See Milik 1976:195–96.

13. Himmelfarb 1993:14. The scholars she mentions (119 n27) are Johann Maier, Carol Newsom, and George Nickelsburg.

The Spatial and Architectural Dimensions of the Enochic Heaven 115

then, provides a heavenly structure that matches a three-chambered temple quite nicely."[14] Himmelfarb plainly conveys that this "vestibule" building is physically contiguous with the "nave" and "holy of holies," and this is the case with the sources she cites for the First Temple (1 Kgs 6:3) and the Second Temple (Josephus, *JW* 5.207–219; m. Middot 4:7).[15] First Kings 6:2–3 states:

> The house which King Solomon built for the Lord was sixty cubits long, twenty cubits wide, and thirty cubits high. The vestibule in front of the nave of the house was twenty cubits long, equal to the width of the house, and ten cubits deep in front of the house. (RSV)

Since the Second Temple described in Josephus' *Judean War* and in the Mishnah was the product of Herod's prodigious rebuilding of the temple that had been constructed by the Judeans who had returned from exile and with which the author and original audience of the Book of the Watchers would have been familiar, we cannot be entirely sure that it contained a vestibule. But that remains highly probable, given that it was a feature of Solomon's temple and it reappeared in Herod's reconstructed version. Indeed, Michael Hundley has recently pointed out that the tripartite structure of inner sanctuary, outer sanctuary, and vestibule seems to be the organizing principle for all Mesopotamian temples.[16]

Himmelfarb has won widespread support for her interpretation of the first structure that Enoch comes to in heaven as a "building" equivalent to the vestibule in the Jerusalem temple, with Fletcher-Louis, for example, accepting without question her view that "the tripartite heaven which Enoch enters is modeled on the tripartite division of the second Temple sanctuary."[17] There is some uncertainty as to whether Himmelfarb herself still fully adheres to the position on the matter she expressed in 1993, since she has recently referred to this structure as a "wall" and not a "building," even while insisting that the series of structures Enoch encounters in heav-

---

14. Ibid.

15. This is based on the reasonable assumption that the porch is the structure described as "shoulders extending twenty cubits on each side" of the main structure behind (Josephus, *JW* 5.207). Most plans of Herod's temple present this feature as the porch or vestibule.

16. Hundley 2013:51 (citing Jean-Claude Margueron).

17. Fletcher-Louis 2002:23; also see Orlov (2005:71) and Kvanvig (2007:182). Himmelfarb's Princeton colleague Peter Schäfer, while accepting that the Enochic heaven is modeled on the Jerusalem temple (as noted above), mentions but does not expressly agree with her view that the "building" Enoch first encounters is equivalent to the *'ûlām* (2009:59 n25).

en reflect the Jerusalem temple's "arrangement of three areas of increasing holiness."[18] How a "wall" can in any way constitute an "area" such as she requires for her "three areas" (and, *a fortiori*, her vestibule) is passed over in silence.

What are we to make of Himmelfarb's theory? It is, in fact, inconsistent with the text of 1 Enoch 14, in particular with details that emerge in vv. 10–13. The major problem is that the first structure Enoch encounters, and I will consider its nature below, is not physically contiguous with the two "houses" that Enoch comes to next. Such contiguity was a feature of the vestibule-nave-sanctuary arrangement of Solomon's temple and almost certainly of the temple erected after the exile. Yet in 1 Enoch 14:10 Enoch says "And I went into the tongues of fire, and I drew near to a great house built of hail stones."[19] That Enoch went into the tongues of fire and then drew near to a great house can only mean that he passed through this initial structure (whose character will be addressed below). In addition, the expression "I drew near to a great house" (which is extant in the Aramaic, Greek and Ethiopic versions and is discussed below) necessitates that Enoch, having passed through the first structure, then moved through a distance of space before he came to the first "house." He then describes details of this house, including its walls and roof (as discussed below), *from the outside* (vv. 10–12), since it is not until v. 13 that he says, "And I went into that house." For these reasons, the first structure is not a vestibule of a heavenly building modeled on the Jerusalem temple, since there is a space between it and the "great house" that Enoch enters. In addition, however, the fact that the building Enoch is described as entering has (as we will soon see) two and not three sections constitutes a strong argument against any intention by the author to convey that the divine house he was describing was like, let alone modeled on, the Jerusalem temple.

Now we must return to the precise nature of this first structure Enoch that encounters (1 Enoch 14:9). Considerable assistance on this comes from information elsewhere in 1 Enoch 1–36. As already noted in Chapter 3, both Enoch 9:2 and 9:10 mention human complaints from earth that reach "to the gates of heaven." At 1 Enoch 9:2 all three major witnesses are in accord: the Aramaic has עד תרע[י שמיא ('d tr'[y šmy'), the Greek μέχρι πυλῶν τοῦ οὐρανοῦ and the Ethiopic አስከ ፡ አንቀጸ ፡ ሰማይ ('eska 'enāqaṣa samāy). We learn more about the gates of heaven later in the text, in 1 Enoch 34:2—36:1, where it emerges that there are three gates on each of the four sides of heaven that correspond to the compass points: the north (34:2), the west

---

18. Himmelfarb 2006:20.
19. ET Nickelsburg 2001:257.

and the east (35:1), and the south (36:1). In each case the Ethiopic expression is ኅዋኅዉ፡ ሰማይ (ḫawāḫewa samāy, "gates of heaven"), with neither the Aramaic nor the Greek being extant for this part of the text. *Since gates presuppose walls through which they permit passage*, the text portrays heaven as a precinct surrounded by a walled and gated perimeter. Since gates, though necessary, were inevitably a point of weakness in any defensive wall, it was a common, if not universal practice in the ancient Mediterranean world to erect them as quite elaborate and heavily fortified structures with the gates set in towers from which defenders could hail down arrows and other projectiles on an attacking army.

This vital textual evidence for the existence of gates and therefore a wall around heaven is not mentioned by Himmelfarb in relation to her argument that the first structure Enoch comes to when he is translated upward to heaven is the vestibule of a heavenly temple, nor by those who follow her in this interpretation. This is surprising given the obvious relevance of this data to the nature of the structure. The information concerning gates and an implied wall provides the context within which one must determine what it is that Enoch encounters. It is highly unlikely that the author simply ignores the wall he carefully situates around heaven, which would mean that Enoch initially comes to some other structure after he reaches the space that the built structures of heaven occupy. The only plausible interpretation of the text is that it is this wall, or one of the gates that punctuate it, that Enoch first encounters when he is translated to heaven and, after travelling some distance (meaning through that part of heaven that lies outside the perimeter wall), draws near to it (14:9).

The core of the issue is whether the correct reading is τεῖχος οἰκοδομημένον ἐν λίθοις χαλάζης ("a wall built with stones of hail"), as implied by the Ethiopic ጥቅም፡ ዘሕንጻት፡ በአሕባነ፡ በረድ፡ (ṭeqm za-ḥenset ba-'a'bāna barad), or τείχους οἰκοδομῆς ἐν λίθοις χαλάζης ("of the wall of a building in stones of hail"), as in the Greek of the Akhmim manuscript. Were we to give usual precedence to the *lectio difficilior*, we would favor the latter, since it is probably easier to imagine a scribe emending οἰκοδομῆς to οἰκοδομημένον than οἰκοδομημένον to οἰκοδομῆς, especially when οἰκοδομημένον appears in the next verse (v. 10) and οἰκοδομημένος a little later in the passage (1 Enoch 14:15). But the *lectio difficilior* principle is a general guideline rather than an absolute rule and it may well give way before dubious grammar or syntax. In the present case, leaving aside οἰκοδομῆς for the moment, a number of oddities in the Greek of the section in which these five critical words appear (τείχους οἰκοδομῆς ἐν λίθοις χαλάζης καὶ γλώσσης πυρὸς κύκλῳ αὐτῶν καὶ ἤρχσαντο ἐκφοβεῖν με) provide just such a reason to prefer the version represented by the Ethiopic text. These are:

(a) τείχους is in the genitive and it should be in accusative or the dative after ἤγγισα (τεῖχος, as noted above, is the usual Greek word for a city-wall).

(b) As for ἐν λίθοις χαλάζης, David Suter observes that "the instrumental use of the preposition ἐν with a dative . . . seems to call for a passive participle."[20] This is exactly what we find very soon after in 14:10 (οἶκον μέγαν οἰκοδομημένον ἐν λίθοις χαλάζης) and in 14:15 (οἰκοδομημένος ἐν γλώσσαις πυρός).

(c) The word γλώσσης is anomalous as a genitive singular. Charles amends to γλώσσαις, which seems required as that which began to frighten Enoch, while Nickelsburg reads "tongues" with reference to the Aramaic.[21]

This accumulation of anomalies provides solid ground for displacing the *lectio difficilior* principle and preferring the reading τεῖχος οἰκοδομημένον over τείχους οἰκοδομῆς. That is to say, Enoch has arrived at the (perimeter) wall of heaven: "I went in until I approached a wall built of hail-stones" (1 Enoch 14:9). Matthew Black reached much the same conclusion: "The writer is thinking of the περίτειχος i.e., the protecting outer wall of heaven, like that of a city (cf. Isa 26:1; Eth. *ṭeqm*)."[22]

Yet even if the alternative reading were correct, to the effect that Enoch had reached the wall of some structure, it would be explicable on the basis that the building was a gate-house. As noted above, they were formidable structures to protect the perforations of the wall they represented and they often, if not always, had their own walls as part of the defensive structure. To come to this conclusion, however, it would be necessary to extend the meaning of τεῖχος as "city-wall" to cover the wall of a gate-house in such a wall. On either view there is no justification for interpreting the structure as the vestibule to a building allegedly modeled on that of the Jerusalem temple.

Enoch and the "Great House" (1 Enoch 14:10–12)

Enoch then draws near to a "great house." As noted above, this drawing near after passing through the wall entails that there was an area of space between the wall and the "house." Enoch describes the appearance of this house (vv. 10–12) before he enters it (v. 13). The fact that Enoch does not

---

20. Suter 2007:203.
21. Charles 1906:39; Black 1985:146; Nickelsburg 2001:258.
22. Black 1985:146.

enter the house until v. 13 is significant, since as a matter of narrative logic we would not expect him to mention architectural features, such as a floor or a ceiling, which would only be visible to someone who was inside the building (at least in the absence of windows, which are not mentioned here). Accordingly, the flow of the narrative suggests that vv. 10–12 relate to the external appearance of the house. Let us test this *prima facie* view against a fresh translation of the text, unit by unit, in italics, justifying this version in the process:

(a) "I entered into the tongues of fire"

The Aramaic is not extant and the Greek is translated closely in the Ethiopic.

(b) "and I approached a great house"

The Greek has ἤγγισα εἰς οἶκον μέγαν, which the Ethiopic translates literally ቀረብኩ፡ ኀበ፡ ቤት፡ ዐቢይ፡ (*qarabku ḫaba bēt 'abiy*). The Aramaic for this clause is extant but unusual, since we do not have קרבת (*qrbt*), "I approached," as one would expect from the Greek, but: אדבקת לביא ר]ב[(*'dbqt lby'r[b]*), with אדבקת deriving from דבק (*dbq*), meaning "adhere" or "attach." Neither Milik, nor Black, nor Nickelsburg comment on this verb.[23] No one seems to doubt it means "approached" in this context.[24] Certainly the Greek translator understood what was before him in this sense and offered ἤγγισα as the appropriate translation.

(c) "built with hailstones"

The Aramaic is not extant. The Greek is οἰκοδομημένον ἐν λίθοις χαλάζης, while the Ethiopic ዘሕኑፅ፡ በአእባን፡ በረድ፡ (*za-ḥenuḍ ba-'a'bāna barad*) translates closely: "which (was) built with stones of hail."

(d) "and the walls of the house"

The Aramaic is not extant. The Greek reads καὶ οἱ τοῖχοι τοῦ οἴκου, which the Ethiopic translates with a minor alteration as "and the walls of that (ውእቱ [*we'etu*]) house." At this point it is important to register the transition to a common Greek word for the wall of a house, as opposed to τεῖχος, which was used in 1 Enoch 14:9 of the city-wall around the central precinct of heaven.

(e) "were like slabs of stone"

The Aramaic is not extant. The Greek reads ὡς λιθόπλακες. Milik notes that λιθόπλακες is a *hapax legomenon*,[25] and it is not mentioned in Liddell

---

23. See Milik 1976:198, Black 1985:147, Nickelsburg 2001:258.

24. Milik (1976:194) also surmises it appeared at 1 Enoch 14:9 (where the Aramaic is not extant).

25. Ibid.:198.

and Scott. Nor, it should be noted, does any word with the letters λιθοπλα- appear in Papyri-Info.²⁶ Milik and Black both plausibly suggest that the underlying Aramaic was לוחת אבנין (*lwḥt 'bnyn*).²⁷ Black further suggests as a comparator, less plausibly given the very different referent, the use of πλάκες λίθιναι in the LXX (translating לחת אבן; *lḥt 'bn*) of the stone tablets of the law at Exod 31:18.²⁸ The Ethiopic has ከመ፡ ጸፍጸፈ፡ ሰሌዳት፡ በአባን (*kama ṣafṣafa salēdāt ba-ʾabān*), "like a layer of slab(s) of stones," which seeks to interpret the Greek and is very similar to the way Milik understands λιθόπλακες ("'slabs of stone' [more accurately, the 'facing' of the walls in marble flagstones]") although he makes no reference to the Ethiopic.²⁹

(f) "and they were all of snow"

The Aramaic is not extant. The Greek reads καὶ πᾶσαι ἦσαν ἐκ χιόνος, "and all were out of snow." The available plural antecedents of "all" are the walls or the stone tablets covering them, but the latter is more likely and the reference possibly being to their white color or to their actually being (a facing of) of snow slabs on a base of hailstones. Ethiopic has እምበረድ (*za-ʾem-barad*), "(in stones) which were from snow." In Ethiopic *barad* usually means "hail" but sometimes "snow."³⁰

(g) "and the groundworks were of snow"

The Greek here is καὶ ἐδάφη χιονικά, with ἐδάφη being a neuter plural. At this point we encounter the first problematic feature of many English translations, which read "floor,"³¹ where I have "groundworks." A century ago, however, R. H. Charles translated ἐδάφη as "groundwork."³² We are fortunate that some of the Aramaic has survived at this point:]תלג י[. Milik reconstructs the immediate context as: [ד]י תלג ש[ן] (*d]y tlg š[n*).³³ As Milik himself notes,³⁴ the word אשן (*'šn*) appears later in this work, at 1 Enoch 24:1. Here, after a lacuna in the text that must have read something like "And he showed me the mountains," we find: [ד]לק אשן בינת[הון] (*d]lq 'šn bynt[hwn]*), "the אשן ['šn] burned [singular] between them"). Whereas the Greek describes the mountains themselves burning, the Aramaic is

26. See http://www.papyri.info.
27. Milik 1976:198; and Black 1985:147.
28. Black 1985:147.
29. Milik 1976:198–99.
30. Nickelsburg 2001:258, citing Dillmann 1955:507–8.
31. So Isaac 1983:20; Black 1985:33; Nickelsburg and VanderKam 2012:34.
32. Charles 1913:197.
33. Milik 1976:194.
34. Ibid.:199, 218.

different, since it presents something (in the singular) "between them" being on fire, with "them" necessarily referring to the mountains. What does אשן mean, therefore, in 1 Enoch 24:1? It is a word not listed in Sokolofff, *A Dictionary of Jewish Palestinian Aramaic*, nor in his *Dictionary of Judean Aramaic*, nor in the on-line *Comprehensive Aramaic Lexicon Project*. But BDB proposes a Hebrew word אשן, meaning "be hard," in the light of the Aramaic words אשונא ('šwn') and אשינא ('šyn') meaning "something firm" to explain אשינה ('šynh), the name of two cities in Judah (Josh 15:33 and 15:43).[35] With this background and given that the word means something between the mountains, at 1 Enoch 24:1 Milik reasonably translates אשן as "ground."[36]

Yet at 1 Enoch 14:10 Milik reconstructs אש[ן as אשן, "floor," in the singular.[37] There are three problems with this interpretation. First, unless the Aramaic was radically different from the Greek at this point, which is unlikely, Enoch has still not entered the house and is not in a position to know what its floor is like. Secondly, Milik unjustifiably assumes that אש[ן at this point in the text was in the singular (אשן), as at 1 Enoch 24:1, even though the Greek translator in 1 Enoch 14:10 has rendered the Aramaic word before him at this point in the (neuter) plural as ἐδάφη. Reinforcing but distinct from this point is the consideration that later in the passage, at 1 Enoch 14:17, when Enoch has entered the building and is looking from it directly into a second "house" that abuts the first, he uses ἔδαφος, in the singular, to mean "floor" (see below).

Let us consider ἔδαφος/ἐδάφη a little more closely. In Liddell and Scott ἔδαφος is described as having the following meanings: (1) "bottom" (as of a boat, a river or the sea), "foundation, base of anything;" (2) "ground-floor or pavement" (as of a house [Herodotus 8.137]); (3) "ground, soil"; (4) "text" of a manuscript, as opposed to the margin; and (5) background of a puppet-theater.[38] Usually the word is in the singular but in relation to meaning (3) there are plural instances in the form of "lands and tenements" and "masses of earth." In Liddell and Scott the related verb ἐδαφίζειν means (1) "beat level and firm like a floor or pavement;" (2) "provide with a floor;" and (3) "dash to the ground" (this meaning being found at Luke 19:44). Of two adjectival forms, ἐδαφιαῖος means "belonging to a floor" and ἐδαφικός "pertaining to land."

---

35. BDB, 80.
36. Milik 1976:218.
37. Ibid.:196.
38. Liddell and Scott, 477.

In the Septuagint ἔδαφος appears twenty-four times, always in the singular. On eleven occasions it means "ground" and on one occasion "pavement."[39] There are eleven instances of it as referring to the "floor" of a structure devoted to God or a god: the "floor" of the Tent of Witness (Num 5:17), the "floor" of Solomon's Temple (1 Kings 6:15 [bis], 16, 30 and 7:7, on all five occasions translating קרקע [qrq']),[40] the floor of Ezekiel's imagined temple (Ezek 41:16 [bis] and 41:20, each instance translating ארץ ('rṣ), the "floor" of the Second Temple (3 Macc 1:29 and 2:22) and the floor of the temple of Bel (Bel 19). Lastly, at Dan 6:24 (Theodotion) it refers to the floor of the lions' den. The word ἔδαφος also appears 68 times in the papyri included in *Papyri.Info* (often meaning "ground" in an agricultural setting); it never appears there in a plural form.[41] In the New Testament ἔδαφος appears once, at Acts 22:7, meaning "ground."

Although I will return below to the function of ἔδαφος in designating the floor of a structure devoted to God or a god, the fact that it carries this meaning in the Septuagint—with some version of which we may be confident the Greek translator of 1 Enoch 1–36 was familiar—on eleven times, and is not used there in relation to the floor of any other building or structure (except a lions' den), makes the appearance of the plural form ἐδάφη in 1 Enoch 14:10 in relation to another structure devoted to God all the more noticeable. This consideration renders it highly likely that at this point the Aramaic source read אש[in a plural form.

Ethiopic tradition rendered ἐδάφη χιονικά as ምድሩ፡ በረድ (*medru barad*), "its (sc. the house's) ground (was) of snow."[42] The word *medr* (= nominative singular) covers the meanings "earth, ground, soil, field, country, land, territory, district, region, floor (of a house) and bottom (of a pit)."[43] The person responsible for this translation appears to have been unable to make sense of the plural form and to have interpreted ἐδάφη as a singular with the common meaning of "ground," but here presumably conveying something like "its ground-floor level."

What then does ἐδάφη mean? We need to do justice to the plural form, the semantic range of the word and the fact that it must refer to some aspect of the building visible to an observer from the outside. "Base" is one possibility, as is Charles's 1913 suggestion "groundwork," but rendered into

---

39. "Ground": Judg 5:18 and 16:5; Job 9:8; Ps 118(119):25; Sir 11:5 and 36(33):10; Isa 25:12; 26:5; and 29:4; Jer 38(31):37; and 4 Macc 6:7; "pavement": Sir 20:18.

40. Of the seven occurrences of this word in the Hebrew Bible, six relate to the floor of the Temple and one to the floor of the sea (Amos 9:3): Lisowsky 1993:1285.

41. Papyri.Info.

42. Some manuscripts read *medr* (see Charles 1906:38).

43. Leslau, p. 330.

the plural, as either "base-structures" or "groundworks" to reproduce the effect of the Greek (and probably Aramaic) plural. "Groundworks" is preferable, however, as a recognized architectural term. The word "foundations" is probably not suitable here since it normally refers to structures under the building that are not visible to an outside observer.[44] Looking at the "house" from outside, Enoch identifies its groundworks as made of snow.

(h) "And the upper storeys"

The Aramaic has not survived, but the Greek reads αἱ στέγαι, which is translated in the Ethiopic as ጠፈሩ (ṭafaru), "its ṭafar," a word embracing the meanings "vault, roof, ceiling, covering, wooden floor, firmament."[45] This is the second place, it is submitted, where some translations, in this case those rendering the word "ceiling," are misleading.[46] First, Enoch is still outside the building looking at it. Again, we must take into account the force of the plural here, especially since the word appears in its singular form at 1 Enoch 14:17 where it certainly does mean "ceiling" (see below). Both of these considerations give us cause to doubt the appropriateness of the translation "ceiling" frequently offered by translators.

Liddell and Scott offer the following meanings for στέγη, omitting some specialist meanings with no possible application here: (1) a "roof;" (2) a "ceiling;" (3) a "roofed place, chamber, room" and a "covered vestibule:" (4) the "storey" of a house; and (5) "house, dwelling," frequently in the plural; and (6) the "deck" of a ship. In relation to meaning 4 they note one instance of the plural form of the word to mean the "storeys" of a house—in Papyrus 2 of the Flinders Petrie collection, dated to the third century BCE.[47] There are five instances of στέγη in the Septuagint with the meanings "roof" (Gen 8:13 and 19:8 A; 1 Esdras 6:4); "screens" (Ezek 40:43) and "house" (4 Macc 17:3). The word appears three times in the New Testament meaning "roof" (Matt 8:8; Mark 2:4; and Luke 7:6).

In the papyri included in *Papyri.Info* there are sixty-five instances of the word in the singular but none in any of its plural forms. Yet the pattern of usage for στέγη among these papyri is very interesting. Nearly all instances mean "storey" (meaning [4] above) and are designated by their level in the building, either "first," "second," "third" or even "fourth," with "upper" appearing with some. Although these are legal papyri from Egypt

---

44. I am indebted to Scottish architect Jerry Eccles for advice on the appropriate architectural terminology for building structures at ground level.

45. Leslau, p. 588.

46. Charles (1913:197), Isaac (1983:20), Nickelsburg (2001:257) and Nickelsburg and VanderKam (2012:34) all mistranslate στέγαι as "ceiling."

47. Liddell and Scott, p. 1636.

usually referring to one storey among several for the purposes of identification, since so many houses had many storeys it must have been commonplace to refer to the upper storeys of a particular building having more than one even though we have only one surviving example, from the Flinders Petrie papyri just mentioned.

There is a further consideration for giving due weight to the plural form of στέγαι, the fact that the words "their walls" that appear a little later, in 1 Enoch 14:12, require a plural antecedent that can only be provided by στέγαι. Prior to concluding the discussion of στέγαι, however, the remainder of 1 Enoch 14:11 should be considered, where there is a close alignment of the Greek and Ethiopic versions:

(i) "(And the στέγαι) were like shooting stars and flashes of lightning"

(j) "and among them were fiery cherubim"

Black comments here, "The Cherubim are mentioned among these celestial phenomena as at Ps. 18.10 or under the influence of Ezek. 1.12,14 (Lods). Their role, in the upper parts of the house as in the fore-court . . . was no doubt a protective one."[48] It is likely that in 1 Enoch 14:11 actual cherubim are meant, since the central role of the Watchers comprised vigilance and protection (as discussed in Chapter 3). Nevertheless, the idea that the source for actual cherubim lies in Ezekiel 1 is implausible, since in that text their role is connected with the mobility of the *kābôd*-conveyance, which I will return to later, not with protection. Psalm 18:10, with its statement that God rode on a cherub and flew, also has little to do with 1 Enoch 14:11.

Yet it is not impossible that representations of cherubim are intended. If there is a biblical source for representations of the cherubim, it could be Ezek 41:18–20, with its reference to the cherubim (and palm-trees) carved on the walls of the Temple that the prophet describes in his visions (Ezekiel 40–48). On the other hand, 1 Kgs 6:28–35 and 2 Chr 3:7 also mention carved figures in the Solomonic temple.

Ezekiel may have been the source for representations of cherubim in the heavenly temple of the *Songs of the Sabbath Sacrifice*. Carol Newsom notes: "In several places the text of 4Q405 14–15 refers to 'images' or 'likenesses' . . . which are said to be engraved in the vestibules . . . and which praise God . . . This combination of motifs suggests that the author has in mind the description of Ezek 41:15–16, a passage which mentions the vestibule of the temple in connection with the wall decorations of palm trees and cherubim engraved throughout the temple building."[49]

48. Black 1985:147, citing Lods 1892.
49. Newsom 1985:53–54.

The Spatial and Architectural Dimensions of the Enochic Heaven 125

Yet there is another, and more likely, source for such representations (upon which Ezekiel himself may have been dependent). Although I will return to these in detail below, they could simply reflect the fact that in Assyrian and Persian temples winged genies for the purposes of protection (watchers if you like!) were frequently represented in stone reliefs. A particularly good example is the Assyrian four-winged genie carved in the palace of Sargon II of Assyria late in the eighth century BCE at Khorasabad (see Figure 5.1). Similar reliefs were also situated in Persian palaces, including the one at Pasagardae to which I will return in Chapter 6.

Figure 5.1
Four-winged Genie from the Palace of Sargon II at Khorasabad
(late eighth century BCE); the Louvre; Wikicommons.

(k) "and their heaven was water"

This is a very memorable statement but it is difficult to know what is meant by it. Nickelsburg interprets it to meant that their heaven was clear as water or constructed of water, paradoxically co-existing with fire.⁵⁰ According to John Strong, citing Keel and Clifford, water imagery "was a standard feature in ancient Near Eastern temple courts, including the Jerusalem temple as symbolized by the Bronze Sea (1 Kgs 7:23–36, 38–39)."⁵¹

This brings us to 1 Enoch 14:12:

(l) "and flaming fire encircled all their walls and (all) their doors burned with fire"

First Enoch 14:12 states in the Greek version: καὶ πῦρ φλεγόμενον κύκλῳ τῶν τειχῶν, καὶ θύραι πυρὶ καιόμεναι, meaning, "and flaming fire encircled the walls, and the doors burned with fire." Here we find in the Akhmin Greek that, unlike previously, τειχῶν is used for the walls of a building. But this is a scribal error for τοιχῶν, the singular form of which is presupposed by the Ethiopic reading here of አረፍት (*'araft*), "wall," the same Ethiopic word used of a building's walls in 1 Enoch 14:10, as opposed to ጥቅም (*ṭeqm*) for a town wall in 14:9. If one had only this evidence for the original text, the structure or structures with such walls and doors would be uncertain, either the "house" mentioned in v. 10 or the "upper storeys" in v. 11. Fortunately, help is at hand in answering this question. Two words of the Aramaic are extant: כול כתליהו[ן] (*kwl ktlyhw[n]*), "all their walls." The only possible plural antecedent for "their" is στέγαι. This requires the translation: "fire surrounded all the walls" (*sc.* of the upper storeys). While we do not know if "doors" appeared in the Aramaic source with a plural possessive pronominal suffix (perhaps with "all") as in: "(all) their doors (*sc.* of the upper storeys)," this seems highly likely. It would also produce a very strained picture if the description in v. 12 suddenly jumped from the walls of the upper storeys back to the house in the previous verse.

This analysis produces the following translation for 1 Enoch 14:10–12:

> 10. I entered into the tongues of fire,
> and I approached a great house built with hailstones;
> and the walls of the house were like slabs of stone,
> and they were all of snow, and the groundworks were of snow.
> 11. And the upper storeys
> were like shooting stars and flashes of lightning,
> and among them were fiery cherubim and their heaven was water;
> 12. and flaming fire encircled all their walls
> and (all) their doors burned with fire.

50. Nickelsburg 2001:263.
51. Strong (2015:48), citing Keel 1997:136–44 and Clifford 1972:49–51.

Enoch Enters the First House (1 Enoch 14:13–14)

In 1 Enoch 14:13 Enoch enters the house, the external features of which he has just been describing. It combines fire-like heat and ice-like cold, with no "delight of life" in it, and he experiences fear and trembling. The Greek here reads τροφὴ ζωῆς, "nourishment of life," which seems odd and has reasonably been emended to τρυφὴ ζωῆς, "delight in life," on the basis of an Ethiopic reading at this point.[52] How is this an appropriate preparation for a human being about to approach the presence of God? The otherness and awesomeness of God regularly induce fear in those who experience them, which is why on most occasions when an angel comes to someone on earth the first thing he says is "Do not fear." Black and Nickelsburg suggest that the reference is to a saying that there is no pleasure (τρυφή) in Sheol.[53] Yet it is not obvious that it is appropriate to compare heaven with Sheol. A more likely reason is the *mysterium tremendum* aspect of the experience of the holy as described by Rudolf Otto.[54] Melissa Raphael sums it up this way: "the *tremendum* is analogous to and expressive of the awesomely dreadful and of overwhelming power and force."[55] So Enoch was shaking and trembling, he fell (on his face: Ethiopic).

Enoch Sees the Second, Larger House (1 Enoch 14:14–15)

But then Enoch's vision continues (1 Enoch 14:14). This is what he saw:

> Behold, another door was open opposite me,
> and the house was larger than the former,
> and it was all built with tongues of fire. (1 Enoch 14:15)

This is the Greek version and the Aramaic is not extant. For the first part the Ethiopic reads: ወናሁ፡ ካልእ፡ ቤት፡ ዘየዐቢ፡ እምዝኩ፡ ወኵሉ፡ ኆኅት፡ ርኁት፡ በቅድሜየ፡ (wa-nāhu kāl'e bēt za-ya'abbi 'em-zeku wa-kwellu ḫoḫet reḫut ba-qedmēya), "And behold, another house that was larger than that one, and its entire door was open before me." Black, like Charles before him, prefers the Ethiopic version, which reverses the order of the mention of house and door, alleging that the Greek text here is "confused and corrupt" and that the phrase "another door" does not makes sense when no other door has

---

52. Nickelsburg 2001:258.
53. Black 1985:147 and Nickelsburg 2001:263.
54. Otto 1923:12–24.
55. Raphael 2003:7.

yet been mentioned.[56] Yet these objections are unpersuasive and the Greek version is to be preferred. Enoch's entry into the first house in v. 13 implies a door. Then he falls (v. 14) and observes opposite him another door, through which he sees a "house" larger than the one he is in. As we will soon discover, Enoch is actually able to see inside this second "house," observing details of its floor and ceiling and, above all, God on his throne. The door, obviously open, is mentioned first because this is the only means by which Enoch is able to see into the second "house." He is some distance from this door, since later an angel lifts him to his feet (from his prostrate position) and brings him to it, to a point where he can see God on his throne within and from where God can address him (v. 25).

These details of Enoch's experience in the first "house" and his observations of the second require emphasis. This is a text in which the narrative logic is sensitive to the spatial positioning of Enoch vis-à-vis the various architectural features he encounters and to his movement through heaven. Although the text does not say so explicitly, the details provided necessitate that the second, larger "house" physically abuts the first, smaller house, which serves as a kind of antechamber to it. If this was not the case, we would have to imagine:

(a) that Enoch looked out through some door in the first house and across a space to the second "house" and saw into its interior through a door or window in it which the text does not mention;

(b) that from his vantage point in the first building he looked across this distance and through such an aperture in its exterior was able to see both its floor, upper part and ceiling, which is physically impossible unless the aperture was an unparalleled opening from the roof to the foundations, and

(c) that when God comes to address Enoch (v. 24) he is speaking from within one building, through an unmentioned opening in it, across a space and thence through the door in the first "house" to where Enoch is standing just inside.

These consequences that would result if the second "house" did not abut the first indicate beyond any doubt that it did. Nor, given the second "house" is larger than the first, could the second building have been a house within a house.[57] Taking all this data into account, it is possible provide an illustration of the arrangement of architecture of heaven, which is Figure 5.2.

---

56. Black 1985:148, citing Charles 1913:197.

57. So also Nickelsburg 2001:264. Yet Nickelsburg fails to realize that the architecture of heaven is inconsistent with the heaven-as-temple notion that he supports.

The Spatial and Architectural Dimensions of the Enochic Heaven

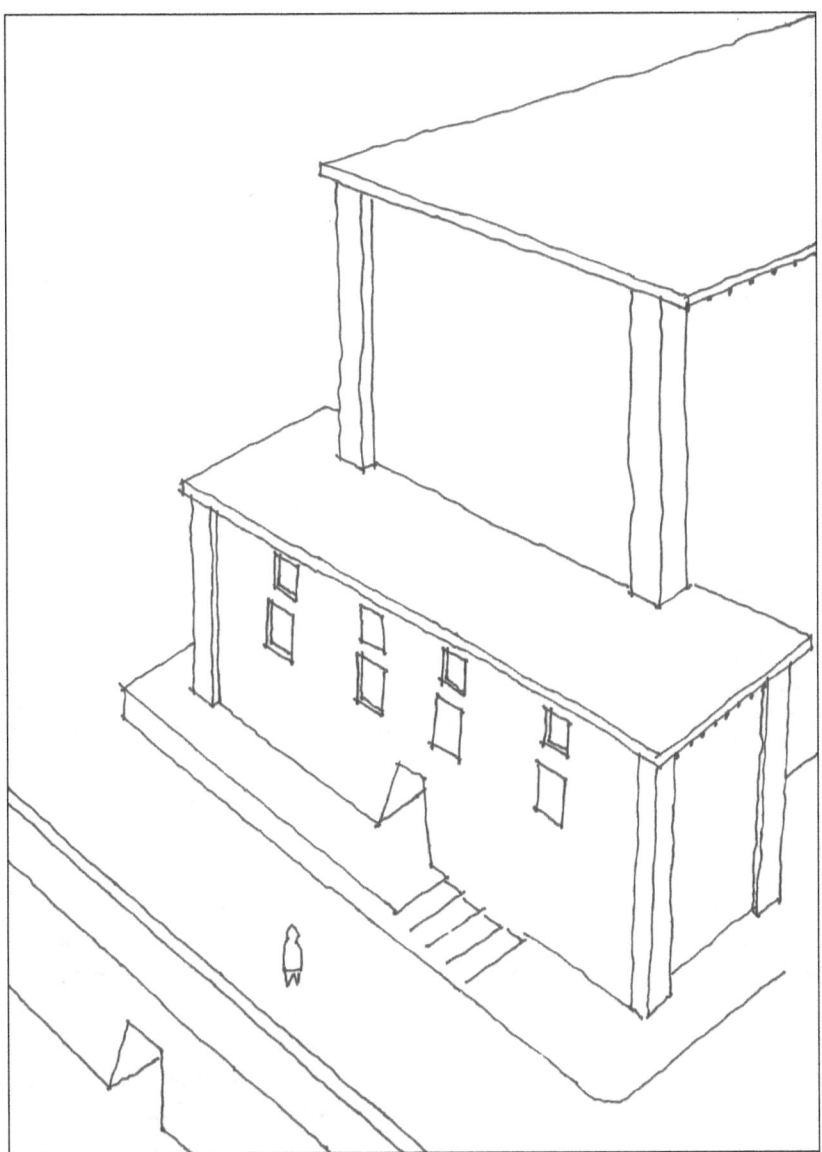

Figure 5.2
The wall of heaven and the building within in 1 Enoch 14.
Drawing by Jerry Eccles.

Description of the Second, Larger House (1 Enoch 14:16–23)

From his position on the floor of the first house and looking through the door to the second, Enoch begins by outlining the general impression it made on him:

> It completely excelled in glory and in honor and in greatness,
> so that I am unable to describe to you its glory and its greatness.
> (1 Enoch 14:16)

Then he describes some particular architectural features:

> Its floor (ἔδαφος) was of fire,
> and its upper part (ἀνώτερον) was flashes of lightning
> and shooting stars
> and its ceiling (στέγη) was a flaming fire. (1 Enoch 14:17)

Here we have ἔδαφος and στέγη in the singular, following their use in the plural, with a different meaning, in vv. 10–11 as already discussed. Black translates στέγη as "roof,"[58] but this translation is excluded by the fact that Enoch is looking into a larger structure that abuts the one he is located in and he therefore cannot see its roof, only its ceiling. By the same reasoning, the "upper part" that Enoch sees must refer to an inner wall, in particular the wall opposite the door he is looking through; it cannot, as Nickelsburg suggests, mean "the upper story" of this building.[59] This consideration also excludes Nickelsburg's comparison to the upper chamber that, according to Josephus (JW 5.5.5 §221) and m. Middoth 4:5, stood over the main room and the holy of holies of Herod's Temple.[60] There is, moreover, no veil between first and second houses. Newsom notes that Ezekiel contains no description of the veil, although it is described at length in the Priestly writer's account of the Mosaic tabernacle (Exod 26:31–35) and it is also mentioned in the Chronicler's description of the temple (2 Chr 3:14). But as far as the *Songs of the Sabbath Sacrifice* are concerned, like the walls and doors of the temple itself, the veil is also said to be worked with figures of the cherubim.[61] If the author had any intention of presenting the divine abode as similar to the Jerusalem temple, he would have mentioned a veil at the entrance to the second "house," perhaps drawn back to allow Enoch to see within. But, to reiterate a major argument of this volume, he had no such intention.

58. Black 1985:33.
59. Nickelsburg 2001:264.
60. Ibid.
61. Newsom 1985:54.

These features are a prelude to the primary aspect of this second edifice. In spite of its extraordinary details, Enoch is looking, not into the holy of holies of the temple, but into the throne-room of a royal palace where the king is seated on his throne:

> I was looking and I saw a high throne,
> and its appearance was like ice,
> and its roundness (τροχός) was like the shining sun,
> and the border[62] was cherubim.
> And from underneath the throne flowed forth rivers flaming with fire,
> And I was unable to see. (1 Enoch 14:18–19)

In vv. 20–23 we learn that the Great Glory sat on the throne, with his clothing like the appearance of the sun and brighter and whiter than any snow. Because of his splendor and glory no angel could enter into this house and look at his face, nor could any human being look at him. He was encircled by flaming fire and a great fire was next to him. None of those about him approached him and there were 100 million of them! Yet some of the Watchers, perhaps the most senior ones, did, somehow, approach him and did not leave him. Solar imagery is prominent in relation to God's throne and God himself, but not even Louis XIV, another Sun King it should be recalled, came anywhere near the awesome magnificence of the way God is presented in this passage.

One particular feature of the solar imagery deserves close attention. The major innovation in the translation of vv. 18–19 is the word "roundness" in relation to God's throne. In the first modern translation of 1 Enoch published by Richard Laurence in 1821 the clause I have translated as "and its roundness was like the shining sun" was rendered, in a rather similar manner, as "while its circumference resembled the orb of the brilliant sun."[63] "Disk" is another possible interpretation of τροχός, but there is reason to doubt its appropriateness here for reasons considered below. But in recent times many scholars have taken to offering "wheels" at this point.[64] It is dif-

---

62. The Greek reads ὄρος "mountain" which is unintelligible here; Milik reasonably suggested the modest alteration to ὅρος meaning "boundary," on the basis that the outer edges of the throne were cherubim carved as sphinxes (1976:200). The Ethiopic reads ቃል (qāla), "voice," for ὄρος, but we really need something that is visible, since this is one of the phenomena that Enoch saw.

63. Laurence 1883:19.

64. So Charles 1913:197; Milik 1976:199; Isaac 1983:21; Black 1985:18; Nickelsburg 2001:258 (who follows the use of wheels" in Dan 7:9 even though 1 Enoch 1–36 was written before Daniel) and Nickelsburg and VanderKam 2012:35. One scholar who translates τροχός correctly here as "roundness" is Stuckenbruck (2013a:32).

ficult to understand the confidence with which translators offer "wheels," even granted the existence of a four-wheeled arrangement in Ezekiel that is widely, if incorrectly, interpreted as a throne.[65] Although the Aramaic is not extant, the Greek word translated "wheels" *is in the singular*: τροχός. If Ezekiel was in the author's mind here, why does the Greek word (and, we must assume, the Aramaic behind it) not appear in the plural?

Liddell and Scott provide a range of meanings for τροχός: (1) a wheel; (2) a potter's wheel (although note that "disk" is a more appropriate designation for a potter's wheel); (3) a child's hoop; (4) a round cake, the sun's disk (as in Aristophanes, *Thesmophoriazusae* 17), although the word could also denote "roundness" there (since the sun is likened to the shape of the eye) and the coil of a serpent; (5) a large pill; (6) a circle or zone; (7) circuit of a wall or fortification; (8) a ring; (9) a whirlwind; and (10) a washpot. It is evident from this usage that τροχός frequently conveyed the meaning of "disk" (if the object was flat) or roundness (as in a round cake or washpot) rather than "wheel."

Yet we have more than the use of τροχός in the singular and the fact that it also conveys "disk" or "roundness" to assist us in determining its meaning in 1 Enoch 14:18. One of the principles of legal interpretation, based on common sense, is that the best dictionary for the meaning of a word in a document is the document itself. We can apply that principle to the present question since τροχός is used elsewhere in 1 Enoch 1–36, at 1 Enoch 18:4, while, as we will see below, the Ethiopic word that translates τροχός here appears instructively in the Astronomical book (although these other usages are rarely if ever mentioned by commentators):

> I saw the winds of heaven turning
> and bringing to their setting[66]
> the roundness of the sun (τὸν τροχὸν τοῦ ἡλίου)
> and all the stars. (1 Enoch 18:4)

This is extremely significant for interpreting τροχός in 1 Enoch 14:18. Not only is τροχός used here in the text in the singular with the meaning of "roundness" (or "disk"), but it is applied to the sun and solar imagery that are present in the description of God on his throne in 1 Enoch 14:18–22. It is not merely that the τροχός in v. 18 is said to be like the shining sun. In v. 20

---

65. So Black 1985:149.

66. This utilizes the emendation of the Greek διανεύοντας to δύνοντας with Charles (1913:200), but the correct reading here does not affect the point I am making about τροχός.

God's apparel is like the appearance of the sun, while at v. 22 "flaming fire" encircles him, thus continuing the imagery of disk or circle.

The reason for preferring "roundness" to "disk" comes from a consideration of the Ethiopic translation. First of all, it is worth noting that the Ethiopic translator did not understand τροχός to mean "wheels." At both 1 Enoch 14:18 and 18:4 he has translated the word, in the singular, as ከበብ (kebab). Leslau notes the derivation of this word from ከበበ (kababa), meaning "encircle, surround, go round in a circle, roll or wind into a ball." For kebab itself he offers the meanings "circuit, roundness, circumference, disk, ball, circlet, firmament, total,"[67] but not, one notes, "wheel." Moreover, the related word, makbab, means "circle, circumference, sphere," and also "community, congregation, assembly," but, again, not "wheel." Kebb means "round, circular" and kabib means "round." Leslau notes the related word in Arabic, kabbaba, meaning "to roll into a ball," while kubba means a "ball."[68] An Ethiopic word for "wheel," namely mankwarākwer (from 'ankwarkwara, "roll"), could have been chosen here but was not.

The decisive reason for preferring "roundness" to "disk" comes from the Astronomical Book. Here the word kebab is used both of the sun (e.g., at 1 Enoch 72:4) and the moon (e.g., at 1 Enoch 73:2). So we are talking about some aspect of their appearance common to each. While the sun is too bright too look at and therefore to determine if it is shaped like a disk or a ball, the moon is not. Observing the moon on a clear night reveals that it is three dimensional, like a semi-sphere, not like a disk. It is more likely than not that ancient observers would have regarded the sun as having a shape similar to the moon even though they could not observe it, than that they thought one was a disk and the other a ball; the very use of kebab for both militates against this latter view. It is interesting to note that Nickelsburg and VanderKam (inconsistently) translate kebab as "roundness" in relation to the sun and the moon.[69]

For these reasons, God's throne in 1 Enoch 14:18 had a roundness like the sun. Are there any parallels for such a representation? If the throne were being likened to a solar disk, there would be some similarities to the melammu of Akkadian art, a circular arrangement of elongated triangular rays around a divine figure.[70] This parallel would still be relevant if the Mesopotamian artists who depicted such a melammu actually intended a three-dimensional arrangement by their representation.

67. Leslau, p. 273.
68. Ibid.
69. Nickelsburg and VanderKam 2012:96 (1 Enoch 72:4) and 99 (1 Enoch 73:2).
70. See Aster 2006.

Is there a link to Ezekiel? Having referred to Dan 7:9 in connection with the Enochic throne, Black states "The imagery is drawn in both passages (whatever their relationship) from Ezekiel: the heavenly throne rests on wheels (Ezek 10:1, 2, 6, 9, 11) and is surrounded or accompanied by fire and flame (Ezek 1:27, 10:6)." There is no doubt that there is a wheeled throne of God (or a wheeled God!) in Dan 7:9: ὁ θρόνος αὐτοῦ φλὸξ πυρός, οἱ τροχοὶ αὐτοῦ πῦρ φλέγον, "His throne was a flame of fire, its (or "his") wheels were burning fire." The author of Daniel would have known Ezekiel. In addition, assuming a date for Daniel 7–12 in the mid second century BCE, it post-dates 1 Enoch 1–36 by as much as a century and its author may have been familiar with this text. But what would the author of 1 Enoch 1–36 and of Daniel 7 have found in Ezekiel relating to a throne with wheels? Scholars routinely misinterpret the winged *kābôd*-conveyance in Ezekiel. It is neither a "winged throne" nor, with its four wheels, a "winged chariot."[71] As John Strong has persuasively argued, the *kābôd*-conveyance is an hypostasis of Yahweh, not Yahweh on his throne.[72] The critical feature is that while Ezekiel does describe a wheeled conveyance for the *kābôd* of God beneath the firmament, as a way of emphasising its mobility, this is not God's throne. The divine throne is situated above the firmament and it is not said to have wheels. Note that in Ezek 1:5–23 there is a description of this conveyance, beneath the firmament, while only a few verses later we have the following:

> And above the firmament over their heads there was the likeness of a throne, in appearance like sapphire; and seated above the likeness of a throne was a likeness as it were of a human form. (Ezek 1:26; RSV)

This is a restrained (via the use of "likeness") description of God seated on his (unwheeled) throne, but separated from the wheeled structure by the intervening firmament. That the divine throne remains above the firmament is confirmed elsewhere in the text (Ezek 10:1).

A further argument against a wheeled throne for the God of the Enochic scribes in 1 Enoch 14 is that the notion is alien to how God is presented elsewhere in the text. God does not use a wheeled throne for transportation in 1 Enoch 1–36, nor will he avail himself of such a device when he does descend to earth. As to the first point, the evidence comes from 1 Enoch 1:3–4:

> The Holy and Great One will come forth from his dwelling,
> And the eternal God will tread upon the earth upon Mount Sinai.

---

71. Newsom talks about a "chariot throne" in Ezekiel 1 and 10 (1985:55). But it is rather the *kābôd*-conveyance that has wheels.

72. Strong 2015, and especially pp. 33–40.

That God will tread (πατήσει and ይከይድ [*yekayyed*]) from heaven to Sinai excludes his journey there by a wheeled throne. Probably the same event is in view in 1 Enoch 25:3:

> This high mountain that you saw, whose peak is like the throne of God, is the seat where the Great Holy One, the Lord of glory, the King of eternity, will sit, when he descends to visit the earth in goodness.[73]

On this occasion, God will use the mountain as his throne; he will not be reliant on a throne that has accompanied him from heaven.

While a text like Ezekiel cannot provide the source of the imagery applied to God's throne in 1 Enoch 14, the Enochic tradition itself can. The bearers of this tradition (see Chapter 7) cherished astronomical learning that derived from Babylon. The central interest of that learning was the sun, as reflected in the priority given to it at the start of the Astronomical Book (1 Enoch 72:2–37). The fact that Enoch had been taken to God when he was 365 years old (Gen 5:23), the number corresponding to the days of the solar year, rendered an interest in the sun entirely predictable. In understanding the character of God's presentation in 1 Enoch 14, therefore, we should not let distractions such as the erroneous idea that he sat on a wheeled throne prevent us from recognizing the true reason for the way God is depicted, namely, the deep and central astronomical instinct of the tradents of the Enochic tradition.

CONCLUSION

Based on the textual analysis conducted in this chapter, we have reached a number of views on the nature of the architecture of heaven, leading to a vision of God on his throne, that constitutes a form of divine image-management. Since the "house" in which God lives is an edifice composed of two contiguous rooms, the second (containing God on his throne) larger than the first (as in Figure 5.2), we can, at least in general terms and pending a closer look at the temple in Jerusalem in the next chapter, discard the idea of God's abode in heaven being based on that temple. We really need another model of or source for the "house" in 1 Enoch 14 and such is readily available—in the palaces of ancient Near Eastern monarchs, including Egyptian, Achaemenid, and Hellenistic kings. That proposal brings us to the next chapter.

---

73. ET by Nickelsburg (2001:312), based on a number of text-critical decisions.

6

THE ENOCHIC DIVINE DWELLING AS A ROYAL PALACE

In Chapter 1 numerous scholars were cited who have argued that the Enochic heaven is modeled on the Jerusalem temple and its priesthood. Part of their argument, especially under the influence of Martha Himmelfarb, is that the architecture of heaven reflects that of the Jerusalem temple. Aspects of that position were subject to critical scrutiny in Chapter 5 as we investigated the spatial and architectural dimensions of the Enochic heaven. The time has now come to summarize the nature of the Jerusalem temple in the third to second centuries BCE, and to see how sharply differentiated from that structure is the divine dwelling in 1 Enoch 1–36. That will occupy the first part of this chapter. In the second part I will propose that a better model for God's house in 1 Enoch 1–36 is the royal palaces of the Achaemenid and Hellenistic kings, especially a palace constructed by Darius I ("the Great") in Pasargadae in Persia.

DIFFERENTIATING THE JERUSALEM TEMPLE FROM THE DIVINE DWELLING IN 1 ENOCH 1–36

The Jerusalem Temple in the Third and Second Centuries BCE

The temple with which the author or authors responsible for 1 Enoch 1–36 were familiar was that constructed during the time that Zerubbabel, a Judean, was the Persian governor of Yehud, the province of Judea (Hag 1:1). The accession of Cyrus II ("the Great") as king of Persia in 559 BCE had made possible the return of Judean exiles to Jerusalem and the rebuilding of the temple that had been destroyed by the Babylonians in 587 BCE (Ezra 1:1-4; 2 Chr 36:22-34). The reconstruction of the temple was completed and its dedication occurred in 516 BCE (Ezra 6:15-18).

We have very little direct evidence for the dimensions of Zerubabbel's temple. The site of this temple and its complex of buildings were subject to massive enlargement by Herod the Great and there is little, if any, archaeological evidence for it. Even the literary sources are sparse. Nevertheless, we are able to make some reasonable surmises. We gain the impression that the Judeans returning from Israel aimed to do their best to rebuild Solomon's temple. Yet their rather difficult circumstances suggest that it is unlikely to have excelled the Solomonic temple in size or grandeur. This is confirmed by the prophet Haggai, when God tells him to say: "Who is left among you that saw this house in its former glory? How do you see it now? Is it not in your sight as nothing?" (2:3, RSV). Nevertheless, the best guide to what it may have been like is the picture of Solomon's temple found in 1 Kings and 2 Chronicles, and that structure must now be considered.

In the Solomonic temple (according to the account in 1 Kings, since there is little archaeological evidence for it) there was a core building subdivided into two parts, the outer part or nave, the *hêkāl* (forty cubits long, twenty wide and thirty high [1 Kgs 6:2]), and a smaller inner part, the holy of holies, the *dᵉbîr* (twenty cubits long, twenty wide and twenty high [1 Kgs 6:20]).[1] So the nave was twice the area of the holy of holies and 33% higher, which meant that going from nave to holy of holies was to pass from a longer and higher space to a shorter and lower one. On the widely accepted assumption that a cubit was equivalent to eighteen inches, the nave was sixty feet long, thirty feet wide and forty-five feet high, while the inner sanctum was thirty feet in length, breadth and height. This meant it was quite a small building, something I will return to later in this chapter. There was an altar of cedar plated in gold in front of the *dᵉbîr* (1 Kgs 6:21), and olive-wood doors with gold-covered carvings of cherubim and palm-trees (1 Kgs 6:31), separating the nave from the *dᵉbîr*.[2] The holy of holies contained the ark of the covenant and two cherubim: 1 Chr 28:18 speaks of "the golden chariot of the cherubim that spread their wings and covered the ark of the covenant of the Lord." The outstretched wings of the *cherubim* extended across the width of the room. It is possible that the ark of the covenant was a representation of the seat of God, "a sort of

---

1. Josephus provides an exaggerated account of the dimensions of Solomon's temple (*JA* 8.3 §§61-98).

2. 2 Chr 3:14, however, mentions a veil (worked with cherubim) but not carved doors.

empty throne."³ "Cherubim thrones," moreover, were well known in ancient Syria-Palestine.⁴ Nevertheless, there is no sign that the ark was regarded as a throne in a literal sense or that God was really enthroned there, for reasons advanced in Chapter 5. There was also a vestibule, the *'ûlām*, in front of this building that was twenty cubits wide and ten cubits deep [1 Kgs 6:3]). Although 1 Kings does not mention the height of the *'ûlām*, other texts (even if exaggerating its height) do give the impression that it was higher than the roof of the *hêkāl*.⁵ Surrounding this building was a large number of chambers, apparently arranged in three storeys (1 Kgs 6:5–6). All around the temple walls, inside and outside, were carved figures of cherubim, palm trees, and rosettes (1 Kgs 6:29). There was a bronze altar in the court in front of the temple (1 Kgs 8:64), which 2 Chr 4:1 suggests was of immense size (twenty cubits square and ten high). Also located in the court of the priests was a huge bronze "sea," or cauldron (1 Kgs 7:23–26; 2 Chr 4:10), which no doubt provided water for a variety of ablutions and purifications. There is no wall described as surrounding the temple area. Some parts of the Solomonic temple contained carved figures of cherubim (1 Kgs 6:28–35 and 2 Chr 3:4–7). The following plan (Figure 6.1) illustrates the architectural layout of Solomon's temple.

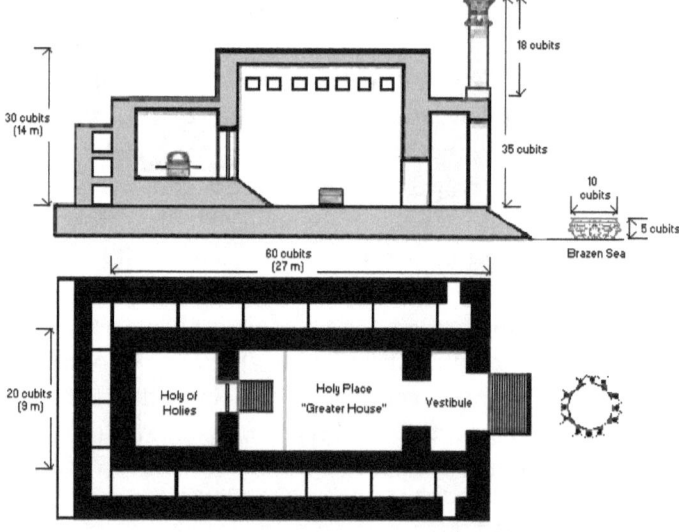

Figure 6.1
Plan of Solomon's Temple. Wikicommons.⁶

3. Haran 1978:246.
4. See *ABD* 1:389
5. See 2 Chr 3:4 that states it was 120 cubits high.
6. See https://commons.wikimedia.org/wiki/File:SolomonsTemple.png.

Moving now to Zerubbabel's temple, the first thing the returnees did was to erect the altar in the place where the Solomonic one had stood (Ezra 3:2–3). This suggests that in other respects also they followed the outline of the previous structure. When Nehemiah rebuilt the city wall, he followed the lines of the former wall, and it is likely that the old lines were followed when the temple was rebuilt. Redeploying the original foundations of the temple would have been a cost-efficient way to proceed with the rebuilding and those dimensions had been hallowed by nearly four centuries of cultic use. Although in Ezra 6:3 it is stated that the rebuilt temple was sixty cubits high and sixty cubits broad (with its length not being mentioned), these figures are likely to be exaggerated and the dimensions and shape of Solomon's temple are to be preferred. Zerubbabel's temple did not contain the ark of the covenant; the holy of holies was empty. The holy of holies seems to have been separated from the nave by a veil,[7] not by wooden doors.

God's Dwelling in 1 Enoch 1–36

A comparison of the temple erected by Zerubbabel in Jerusalem, probably following Solomon's design, with the arrangement in 1 Enoch 14 reveals two very different structures.

To recapitulate the views expressed in Chapter 5, the Enochic description of the architectural structures of heaven, although not their ornamentation, is stylized, even austere, yet makes good sense spatially. There is a perimeter wall, through which it is possible to pass, then an area of space, from which is visible a "house" of several storeys. This house is entered via an implied door and beyond, abutting it, is a second and larger house, into which there is access from the first house through a door. In the second house is a throne on which God is seated. The Enochic arrangement of heaven in 1 Enoch 14 can be expressed visually, as in Figure 5.2.

Here are the main differences between the Jerusalem temple of the third to second centuries BCE and God's house in 1 Enoch 14:

(a) Whereas the Jerusalem temple had three rooms, the Enochic structure had two.

(b) Whereas the third room one entered in the Jerusalem temple (the holy of holies) was smaller than the second (the nave), the second room in the Enochic structure was larger than the first.

(c) there is no veil mentioned between the two "houses."

---

7. See 1 Macc 4:51 and Josephus, *JW* 5.5.4—5.5.5 §§211–219.

(d) There was an actual throne in the Enochic structure, on which God sat. This was not the case with the Jerusalem temple.

(e) The Enochic structure lacked an altar.

Such examination reveals that the layout of the temple in Jerusalem, certainly in its Solomonic form and probably also as rebuilt by Zerubbabel, was unlike the structure that Enoch encountered in 1 Enoch 14.

There are two areas of similarity. The first is that there was likely to have been a wall around the temples of Solomon and Zerubbabel to create a court or courts within which the temple itself was situated. There was also a wall around God's house in 1 Enoch 14. But this really proves little, since the pattern of a central building with a wall around it was common in the ancient Near East for a wide range of purposes, including royal palace precincts within towns and cities, and was not restricted to temples. The second similarity is a feature of the ornamentation of the Solomonic structure that may have been replicated in Zerubbabel's temple, namely, the presence of representations of cherubim. Does the presence of cherubim on the first house in 1 Enoch 14, as mentioned in Chapter 4, indicate a dependence on the Jerusalem temple? This question must be answered in the negative. In 1 Enoch it is likely that real cherubim were intended, as guards for the structure. They appear on the outside of the building. In Solomon's (and perhaps Zerubbabel's) temple they featured as decorations on the inside of the nave. In addition, in the ancient Near East carvings of winged protective genies, presumably similar to those decorating Solomon's temple, were also a feature of Babylonian and Persian palaces, so there is another possible source for them apart from the temple in Jerusalem. I will return to these winged genies later in this chapter.

The importance of this conclusion for a major argument of this volume cannot be understated. If, in other respects, the author wished to present the Enochic heaven as like the temple in Jerusalem in relation to its personnel (which, I have argued, he did not), with the angels as priests for example, why not describe its architecture in terms of the three-room structure of the Jerusalem temple? This would not have been difficult. The fact that the author did not adopt this course is a strong argument that he had no intention whatsoever of evoking a connection with the temple in Jerusalem.

GOD'S DWELLING IN 1 ENOCH 1–36 AS A ROYAL PALACE

If the Jerusalem temple was not the inspiration for the architecture of God's house in 1 Enoch 14, is there another candidate? The argument being run in this book for Achaemenid and Hellenistic courts having provided the source domain for the Enochic heaven naturally prompts the thought that we should also look to palaces in the ancient eastern Mediterranean as providing the model for the divine house itself. Fortunately, the architecture of the palaces of ancient Near Eastern monarchies, Egyptian, Achaemenid and Hellenistic, has recently attracted increased attention from scholars.[8]

The Palaces of Near Eastern Kings

There were many palaces occupied by kings with which Judeans in the third and second centuries BCE would have been familiar—those of the Babylonian, Achaemenid, and Hellenistic kingdoms. Such familiarity could have arisen through collective memories of the past, some of it inscribed in historical and literary texts, only some of which have survived. Alternatively, Judeans, including the Enochic scribes to be discussed in Chapter 7, could have travelled to the capitals of the Seleucid and Ptolemaic kingdoms or could have heard word of those capitals from others who had visited them.

Maria Brosius has described how the palaces in the royal capitals of the Achaemenid kings—although her point is equally applicable to the Seleucid, Ptolelmaic, and Antigonid monarchs—were the physical manifestation of the court, so that the palace "was an expression of kingship, royal power and political control."[9] This statement applies with equal force to God's house in the Book of the Watchers.

In relation to Achaemenid and Hellenistic monarchies there were certain common elements that characterized the function of their royal palaces and their architectural form. As to function, they constituted the abode of the king and his family. They contained administrative and military staff who served and protected the king and his family. As to form, they tended to be in a walled precinct for security reasons and they also contained a throne-room. As far as the Achaemenid kings were concerned, these features were also present even though, due to both the geographical extent and the diversity of peoples encompassed in their rule, these kings had several residences in different regions and spent considerable time moving

---

8. See Nielsen 1998 (1st ed. 1994) and 2001; Kutbay 1998; and Brosius 2007.

9. Brosius 2007:46.

from one to the other.¹⁰ Prominent features of these palaces also appear in the architectural structure of the divine house in the Book of the Watchers.

The Achaemenid Capital at Pasargadae

It is not my aim to nominate any particular royal palace as *likely* to be the inspiration for God's house in 1 Enoch 14, but rather to suggest a *possible* source. In any event, by discussing one such example I will be able to show how a royal palace and its precinct can provide a match for what we find in 1 Enoch 14 in a way that the temple in Jerusalem cannot. The example taken up here is one of the two palaces from Pasargadae, the first royal capital which, according to Strabo (*Geography* 15.3.8), Cyrus II ("the Great"), the Persian king from 559–530 BCE, ordered to be constructed on the site where he had defeated the Median king Astyages in 550 BCE.¹¹ Building began around 546 BCE.¹² The site lay in a valley at an elevation of 6,000 feet, close to the center of his home territory. Although Darius I ("the Great"), who reigned from 522 to 486 BCE, built a new capital at Persepolis, 43 kilometers downstream along the Pulvar River, Pasargadae remained important, both because it contained the grave of Cyrus and also because it remained the place where Persian kings were consecrated to that role.¹³ In spite of other Persian capitals being erected later, it was still regarded as a significant place in Persian politics as late as the reign of Xerxes (486–465 BCE), since archaeological excavations uncovered a stone tablet containing a copy of Xerxes' attack on the cult of Daivas and praise of the cult of Ahuramazda that must have been sent there and displayed during his reign.¹⁴

It is worth briefly mentioning certain factors that help to establish the possibility of an influence from the royal architecture of Pasargadae before moving on to the architectural comparison that will form the core of the argument. The direct exposure of Judeans to the kingdoms of Babylon and then Persia began with the deportation of Judean exiles from Jerusalem in 587 BCE by the Babylonians. They were taken to various places and many no doubt settled down to a life of agricultural production, as has now been revealed in glorious detail from the cuneiform tablets in the David Sofer

---

10. See Boucharlat 2001:114 (and the references there cited).

11. See Stronach 1978 on the archaeological investigation of Pasargadae.

12. Stronach 1978:8.

13. On the grave of Cyrus at Pasargadae, see Stronach 1978:24–43 and 1985. Plutarch, *Life of Artaxerxes* 3.1, describes Artaxerxes going to Pasargadae for his consecration there as king conducted by Persian priests.

14. Stronach 1978:152.

collection.¹⁵ Yet the Babylonian monarchy did not last long. In 539 BCE the Persian king Cyrus II invaded and took control of Babylonia, turning it into a province of Achaemenid Persia. Cyrus' victory over Babylon is recounted in the Cyrus Cylinder in the British Museum, which also describes how he sent various peoples back home (although the Judeans are not specifically mentioned).¹⁶ As noted above, seven years earlier, around 546 BCE, Cyrus had begun the construction of his first capital, at Pasargadae. It is possible that children of the Judeans who had gone into exile in 587/586 worked on its construction or visited it. Even if they did not, word of the place must have permeated among the subject populations of Persia, in Persia itself and elsewhere.

There are signs of a strong interest in certain aspects of the ancient Near East in the earliest Enochic traditions, represented by the Book of the Watchers and the Astronomical Book. Prominent among them is the nature of the astronomy relied upon. As will be explained more fully in Chapter 7, this does not reflect Greek astronomical knowledge of the third or second BCE but older and more primitive learning from Babylon. Just as Judean leaders in Babylon borrowed from Babylonian astronomy in developing their own distinctive system (with the names of all the months in the traditional Jewish calendar derived from the Akkadian), so too are there signs that the Enochic tradents were also influenced by Babylonian astronomy in formulating their different approach, described by VanderKam as "somewhat schematic and inaccurate."¹⁷ If the Enochic authors could cherish a recollection of Babylonian astronomy, it is also possible that they retained memories of Persian architecture, especially that found in the first Persian capital of Pasargadae. This was the capital, after all, constructed by Cyrus, the Persian king who had made provision for some of them at least to return to Judea in 539 BCE (Ezra 1), and the many references to whom in Hebrew scriptures are very positive.¹⁸ Let us now proceed to Pasargadae.

The Central Area of Pasargadae

One part of the site at Pasargadae, a flat tract of ground, much of which was laid out as parkland, contains the ruins of three structures, namely, an

---

15. See Pearce and Wunsch 2014.

16. See http://www.britishmuseum.org/research/collection_online/collection_object_details.aspx?objectId=327188&partId=1.

17. VanderKam 1984:93.

18. See 2 Chr 36:22–33; Ezra 1:1–8; 3:7; 4:3, 5; 5:13–17; 6:3, 14; Isa 44:28; 45:1, 13; Dan 1:21; 6:28 and 10:1; and 1 Esdras 2.

impressive gate ("R") and two palaces ("P" and "S"). These buildings were set at some distance from one another, 200 meters or more. Figure 6.2 is a plan of this central area of the site and Figure 6.3 is a schematic reconstruction.

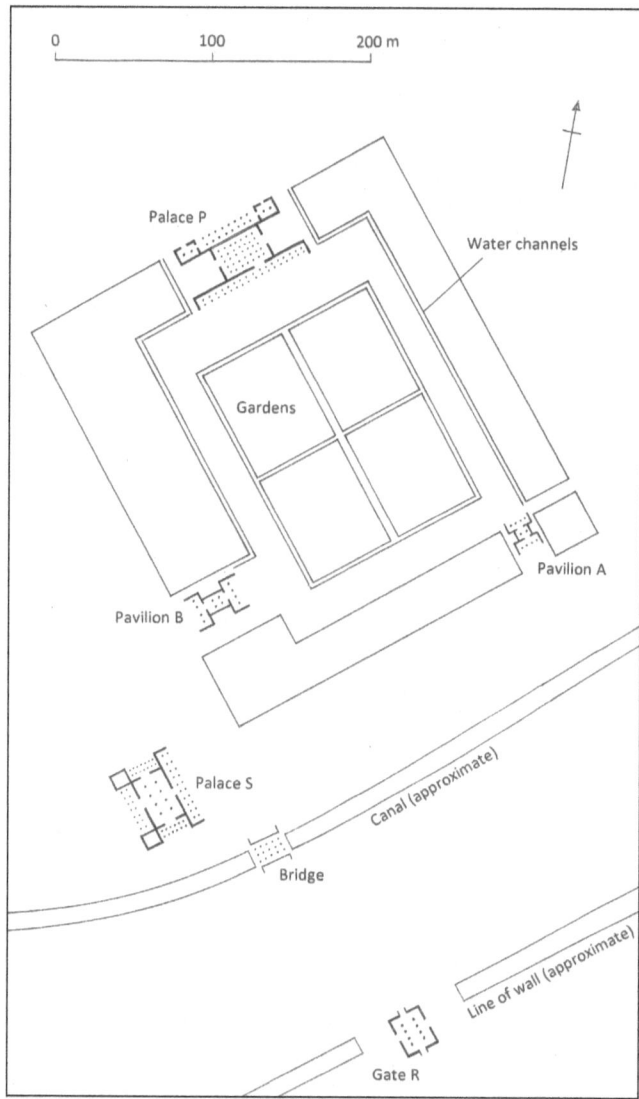

Figure 6.2 Plan of the central area of Pasargadae.
Drawing by Tessa Rickards after the plan by Marion Cox in Brosius 2007:48.

The Enochic Divine Dwelling as a Royal Palace 145

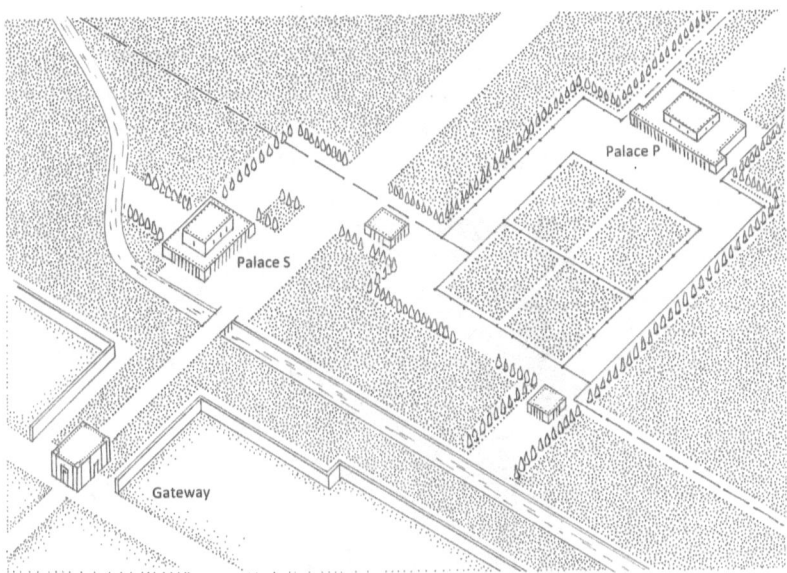

Figure 6.3 Schematic reconstruction of the central area of Pasagardae.
Drawing by Tessa Rickards after Stronach 1989, figure 3.

The lack of architectural remains on the surface has led many scholars to conclude that "the plan of the site conforms to the scattered organization of a tribal encampment."[19] While a geophysical survey of the site conducted in 1999 revealed the remains of more structures so far unexcavated,[20] it remains the case that a large area of Pasargadae was parkland. It is also likely that the Persians pitched tents here. Even Boucharlat, whose French-Iranian team found evidence of the structures just mentioned in 1999, agrees that "the use of tents for some royal activities, such as a banquet hall, and other more modest purposes remains probable."[21]

This was a palace complex surrounded by low stone and mud brick walls with entry through a monumental stone gateway.[22] Here guards controlled access and they would only permit admission to the royal compound for visitors approved by a courtier.[23] Brosius notes that "the construction of this walled palace complex with its entrance gate established an important feature of kingship: controlled access to the king. This vetting of access to

19. Stronach 1985:842.
20. Boucharlat 2001.
21. Ibid.:118.
22. Stronach 1978:10.
23. Brosius 2007:47. Also see Stronach 1978 and 1989.

the king turned him into a figure remote from his subjects."²⁴ This aspect of royal courts has already been noted in Chapter 2 and confirmed in relation to the Enochic God in Chapters 3 and 5. The two doorways of this gateway were probably close to 9 meters in height.²⁵ The door jambs contained reliefs of winged figures, one of which (in the north-eastern corner) survives. This is Figure 6.4.

Figure 6.4
A winged genie from Gate R at Pasargadae. Contemporary photo. Wikicommons.²⁶

It depicts a four-winged, bearded male figure facing left, inwards towards the center of the building, who is wearing an elaborate crown on his head attached to a close-fitting, ribbed cap.²⁷ The form of the crown is

24. Brosius 2007:49.
25. Stronach 1978:45.
26. https://upload.wikimedia.org/wikipedia/commons/b/b5/Pasargades_winged_man.jpg.
27. Stronach 1978:48–50.

Egyptian in origin.[28] Above the relief, as late as the middle of the nineteenth century and fortunately preserved in travelers' drawings, was carved a trilingual inscription in Old Persian, Elamite and Akkadian that read: "I, Cyrus, the King, an Achaemenian."[29] Figure 6.5 shows what the genie looked like in the nineteenth century before the inscription was removed.

Figure 6.5
Drawing of the winged genie at Pasargadae (Figure 6.4) before removal of the inscription. Drawing by Tessa Rickards after the nineteenth-century illustrations shown in Stronach 1978, Plate 43.

28. Brosius 2007:49.

29. For these details, see Stronach 1978:47–52.

148 God's Court and Courtiers in the Book of the Watchers

In spite of this inscription (which also occurs in Palaces S and P), the winged-figure does not represent a spiritual expression of the king, especially as it lacks all subsequent Achaemenian kingly attributes, such as a scepter or bow, a lotus that is held in one hand, a royal tiara, or a Persian robe.[30] The most probable interpretation of the figure is that it "was a genius: an apotropaic, protective spirit ultimately based on the magical guardians of Assyria."[31]

A good comparator to illustrate the Assyrian ancestry of the winged creatures on the doorway into the palace precinct of Pasargadae is the winged guardian from the palace of Sargon II (reigned 722–705 BCE) at Khorsabad (Dur Sharrukin), excavated by Paul-Émile Botta in 1843/1844 and now in the Louvre. This is Figure 5.1 in Chapter 5.

Palace S at Pasargadae

One of the two palaces erected in the walled area of gardens beyond the gate was a palace of Cyrus now called "Palace S," also known as the "the Audience Hall" or "Palace of Audience."[32] Figure 6.6 is the floor-plan of this palace.

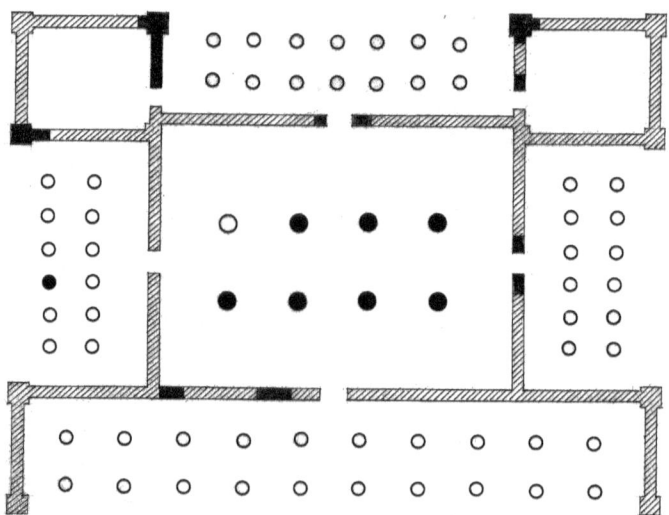

Figure 6.6
The floor-plan of Palace S in Pasargadae. Drawing by Tessa Rickards after Figure 26 in Stronach 1978:57 and plan by Marion Cox in Brosius 2007:48.

30. Ibid.:53.
31. Ibid.:54.
32. Stronach 1978:56.

Figure 6.7
Drawing of Palace S in Pasargadae.
Drawing by Tessa Rickards after the illustrations comprising Plate 53 in Stronach 1978.

Figure 6.7 is a drawing of Palace S. This palace consisted of a high, central hypostyle hall, 32 meters long and 22 wide and some 13 meters high, to judge from the one standing column of eight that once supported the roof of this hall.[33] A single doorway was situated at the mid-point of each of the four walls of the hall. The central building was surrounded by four porticoes and, on one side, two corner buildings of lower height that formed part of the total structure.[34] This means that, if the doors were left open, it would have been possible to see into the hall from the porticoes. Palace S is generally thought to have functioned as a royal audience hall.[35] As such, it must have contained a throne. Inge Nielsen has written that the "primary function of the royal palaces, namely the official and ceremonial function, was centred on the *chrematismos*, the audience, where business was concluded, embassies received, judgement pronounced, petitions considered, and council with the Friends held. Such audiences are well documented for the Achaemenid court..."[36]

She further describes the architectural context of the *chrematismos* in Hellenistic courts in a manner equally applicable to their Achaemenid precursors: "Official and ceremonial functions required reception and audience halls, was well as council halls and courtrooms; these all needed to contain a throne and had to be spacious, since the king's Friends, as well as his guard, were normally present on such occasions. All of these official activities probably often took place in the same hall, which at the same time served as a throne-room..."[37]

33. Stronach 1985:843.
34. Ibid.:843–44.
35. See Stronach 1978:56 and 1985:843; and Brosius 2007:49.
36. Nielsen 1994:18.
37. Ibid.:25–26.

If the throne in Palace S at Pasargadae was situated in a medial position in the hall and the door at the opposite end of the hall was open, the throne and Cyrus sitting on it would have been visible to someone standing in the portico at that opposite end. The central building alone was three times the size (in terms of cubic volume), of Solomon's temple.

A surviving corner pillar for the portico bears a cuneiform inscription the same as that noted above in connection with Gate R, containing the words in Old Persian, Elamite, and Akkadian, "I Cyrus, the King, an Achaemenian."[38]

There was also another palace at Pasargadae, Palace "P," known as the "Private Palace" or "Residential Palace,"[39] of somewhat similar shape, but larger and further from the entrance gate (see Figures 6.2 and 6.3). It was also a two-level structure, with porticoes. It contained a fixed throne seat (the only such installation found on the site) from which, David Stronach has surmised, Cyrus may have held private audiences but also contemplated the trees, grass and streams of the garden.[40] Brosius has differentiated Palace S from Palace P as follows: "The audience hall (*sc.* Palace S) was separate from the private palace of the king (*sc.* Palace P), itself set apart by a structured garden and accessible, we can assume, only to the king's attendants, his bodyguard and members of his family."[41] At Pasargadae, therefore, Cyrus chose to have a separate building for audiences, where he no doubt sat on a throne of some sort, but only for meeting those people who were permitted access by the courtiers stationed at Gate R. Palace P, where he lived, afforded him a greater measure of seclusion.

God's House in the Book of the Watchers and Palace S at Pasargadae

Comparing God's house in 1 Enoch 14, as represented in Figure 5.2, in the wider spatial context of heaven, with Palace S at Pasargadae, as represented in Figure 6.7 in the context of the whole precinct (Figures 6.2 and 6.3), reveals significant similarities between the two. In both cases, one must first pass through a wall to gain access to the building where the king is to be found, that king being God in the one case and Cyrus in the other. The edifice in question has two (not three) stages, with a lower and smaller outer structure: a room (or antechamber) in 1 Enoch 14 and porticoes and two

38. Stronach 1978:63.
39. Ibid.:78.
40. Stronach 1985:845.
41. Brosius 2007:49.

corner buildings in Palace S. Beyond this first structure, and contiguous with it, lies the larger house or hall wherein the king sits enthroned. Just as Enoch could see from the first room into the contiguous throne-room beyond, so too could someone in a portico of Palace S, depending on where the throne was set up, see the enthroned Cyrus. The lack of any other buildings mentioned in 1 Enoch 1–36 within heaven's perimeter wall, apart from God's house, nicely accords with the relative isolation of Palace S from other structures in the palace precinct of Pasargadae. Finally, the fact that there is nothing like Palace P in 1 Enoch 1–36 accords with God's nature as a monarch who lacks a family and does not have needs requiring attention.

There are some differences. We saw in Chapter 5 that there are angels mentioned in connection with the divine dwelling in 1 Enoch 14. No evidence of reliefs of winged figures turned up in the archaeological work on Palace S.[42] Rather than finding a source for these in memories of Solomon's temple or their actual presence in Zerubbabel's, they could simply reflect the fact that at Pasargadae it was thought enough to have such figures situated at Gate R, through which anyone going to Palace S needed to pass. Another difference is that the lower phase of Palace S consisted only of one storey, while in the Enochic divine house even the first building had more than one storey. This may, however, simply reflect the Enochic author's enhancing the magnitude of God's house.

CONCLUSION

From this I conclude that Palace S at Pasargadae represents a possible model for the divine dwelling in 1 Enoch 14. As set out in detail in Chapter 5, the building Enoch encountered makes good sense as a building of two rooms, the first being an ante-chamber and the second a throne-room of a royal palace. I have set out above reasons for suggesting that Judeans in the third century BCE may have been familiar with or aware of Palace S at Pasargadae. Yet even if we discount the possibility of such a link, the comparison with Palace S has the additional advantage of freeing us to imagine alternatives to the currently dominant notion of the Jerusalem temple constituting the source domain for God's house in 1 Enoch 14. As we will see in Chapter 7, authors who would turn to such a palace model were likely to have been scribes familiar with and perhaps actively engaged in the wider political world of their time beyond the boundaries of the temple. Finally, as an exercise in royal image-management, the extraordinary visual appearance

---

42. See Stronach's discussion of Palace S (1978:56–77). This does not, however, necessarily mean that they were never there.

of God's dwelling shown to the human observer Enoch takes features of ancient Near Eastern palace architecture, such as we see at Pasargadae, and elevates them to an entirely new level.

7

ENOCH THE SCRIBE AND THE NON-TEMPLE ENOCHIC SCRIBAL GROUP

In the previous chapters of this volume I have argued that the model (or "source domain") for the presentation of heaven in 1 Enoch 1–36 was not the temple in Jerusalem and its priests, but the royal court of Achaemenid and Hellenistic monarchies. In this chapter I move to consider the factor that may explain this circumstance—the portrayal of Enoch as a scribe in 1 Enoch 1–36 and in other parts of 1 Enoch and how this relates to the author or authors of these works. My aim will be to demonstrate that 1 Enoch 1–36 and the rest of the Enochic corpus were the product of a group of scribes who can be said, within a social identity perspective, to have regarded Enoch as an exemplar of their identity, but who were not connected to the temple in Jerusalem, nor had any priestly function.

THE CONSTITUENT PARTS OF 1 ENOCH

Since in this chapter we will be looking at other sections of 1 Enoch in addition to Chapters 1–36, it is necessary briefly to outline the various parts of the text and their probable dates of composition. The text, broadly speaking, comprises five major parts, a bridging exhortation and, finally, two short appendices:

1. 1 Enoch 1–36 (the Book of the Watchers), from the third century BCE or even earlier.[1]

---

1. VanderKam 1984:111–14.

2. 1 Enoch 37–71 (the Book of Parables), probably to be dated to the few decades either side of the turn of the first millennium CE.[2]

3. 1 Enoch 72–82 (the Book of the Luminaries), to be dated to the third century BCE or even earlier, and probably older than the Book of the Watchers.[3]

4. 1 Enoch 83–90 (Enoch's Dream Visions, comprising two apocalypses, the first concerning the flood [83–84]) and the second being the so-called "Animal Apocalypse" [85–90], and probably composed in the late 160s[4]).

Bridging Exhortation: Enoch 91:1–10, 18–19, perhaps written during the second half of the second century BCE.[5]

5. 1 Enoch 92–105 (Epistle of Enoch), probably from the end of the second or beginning of the first century BCE, although one part of it, the Apocalypse of Weeks (1 Enoch 93:1–10; 91:11–17), is likely to be an earlier and independent composition (from around 175–170 BCE) that has been incorporated into it.[6]

First Appendix: 1 Enoch 106–107 (the Birth of Noah), probably written sometime between the middle of the second century BCE and the last third of the first century BCE.[7]

Second Appendix: 1 Enoch 108 (The Eschatological Admonition),[8] which Stuckenbruck argues was composed "sometime during the late Second Temple period, perhaps around the latter part of the first century CE."[9]

Re-arranging these ten sections of 1 Enoch in chronological order produces the following sequence:

---

2. Nickelsburg and VanderKam 2012:62–63.

3. See VanderKam 1984:79–88. Also note Nickelsburg's view (2001:25–26, 64) that the Enochic tradition developed over three centuries from a core narrative concerning the Watchers.

4. VanderKam 1984:160–163.

5. Stuckenbruck 2007:156. Other scholars regard 1 Enoch 91:1–10, 18–19 as part of 1 Enoch 92; see the discussion in Stuckenbruck 2007:154–56. Whether this section is a bridge or a constituent part of 1 Enoch 92 does not affect my argument here.

6. See Stuckenbruck 2007:60–62.

7. Stuckenbruck 2007:616.

8. This is the designation given to this section by Stuckenbruck 2007:91–108.

9. Stuckenbruck 2007:694; Nickelsburg 2001:554 also suggests this date.

Enoch the Scribe and the Non-Temple Enochic Scribal Group

Third century BCE	Astronomical Book (72–82)[a]
Third century BCE	Book of the Watchers[b] (1–36)
175–170 BCE	Apocalypse of Weeks (93:1–10; 91:11–17)
Around or shortly after 160s CE	First Dream Vision (83–84)
Second half of second century BCE	Bridging Exhortation (91:1–10, 18–19)
Mid second century BCE—last third of first century BCE	Birth of Noah (106–107)
End of second or start of first century BCE	Epistle of Enoch (92–105)
Few decades either side of first millennium	Book of Parables (37–71)
Latter part of first century CE	Eschatological Exhortation (108)

[a] Stuckenbruck considers that the Astronomical Book "was written near to or slightly earlier than" the Book of the Watchers in its present form (2013b:323). In my view, in favor of this ordering of the two texts is that the various astronomical features to which Enoch is exposed during his journeying through the cosmos in 1 Enoch 17–36 appear to presuppose a pre-existing tradition of astronomical learning of the sort systematically set out in the Astronomical Book.

[b] Stuckenbruck refers to these two third-century BCE texts as comprising "the early Enoch tradition," with the Book of Giants, fragments of which were discovered at Qumran, arguably belonging to the same tradition (2007:1, 12–13).

Here we encounter a tradition that evolved over approximately 300 years. The dominant unifying feature is the connection with Enoch. Each of them is an Enochic pseudepigraphon. The Astronomical Book begins with a statement that it describes heavenly phenomena revealed by "the holy angel Uriel" to "me" (72:1), a "me" named as Enoch later in the text (beginning at 80:1). The Book of the Watchers and the Apocalypse of Weeks both begin with an express attribution to Enoch (1:1; 93:1). The Animal Apocalypse introduces itself as a dream that Enoch recounted to his son Methuselah (85:1–2). The First Dream Vision presents itself as recounted by an "I"-voice to his son, Methuselah (83:1), so Enoch by necessary implication, even though the name Enoch does not appear in the text. The bridging exhortation is delivered by Enoch to all his sons (91:3). The Birth of Noah is attributed to an "I" voice who is Methuselah's father and thus impliedly Enoch, as confirmed later in the text (106:13). The Epistle of Enoch describes itself as written by Enoch (92:1). The Book of Parables is "the vision of wisdom that Enoch saw" (37:1), while the Eschatological Admonition, finally, is "Another book that Enoch wrote for his son Methuselah" (108:1).

Yet a second feature that characterizes this succession of ten texts is that in them Enoch is presented as a scribe. Sometimes this is by his explicit designation as a scribe: the Book of the Watchers (12:3–4; 15:1) and the Epistle of Enoch (92:1). On other occasions, the fact that Enoch was a scribe emerges from his being a writer and/or the writer of or witness to books: the Astronomical Book (72:1; 74:2; 81:6 and 82:1); the Animal Apocalypse (89:76; 90:14, 17, 22); the First Dream Vision (83:2, 10) and the Eschatological Admonition (108:1). A third way of referring to Enoch's role as scribe is by mentioning his ability to read: the Birth of Noah (106:19; 107:1). The Book of Parables (37–71) is a little more complicated. Here Enoch is not described as a scribe and while he "sees," "hears" and "speaks,"[10] he does not write. Indeed, the text presents writing in a negative light, as a gift of the angel Penemue that led men astray (69:8–10). Nevertheless, Enoch is recorded as the recipient of written material that he can presumably read (39:2; 68:1).[11] The single exception to this pattern, a text in which Enoch is not presented as a scribe or as fulfilling the scribal functions or reading and/or writing, is the bridging exhortation (91:1–10, 18–19). But the brevity of this section this makes the omission less significant.

This picture of Enoch also appears in the *Book of Giants*, probably a third century BCE text like the Astronomical Book and the Book of the Watchers, in that it describes him as "a distinguished scribe" (4Q203.8). The same perspective is also found in the early reception history of the Enochic corpus. Thus, in Jubilees 4:17 (dated about the mid second century BCE) he is described as the person "who first learned writing and knowledge and wisdom from among the human beings born on earth." In the *Genesis Apocryphon*, moreover, Abraham reads from "the [book] of the words of Enoch" to the princes of Egypt who were visiting him in pursuit of wisdom, goodness and truth (1QapGen 19.24–25).

The notion of Enoch as scribe in the developing sequence of Enochic texts is a matter of the greatest moment in their interpretation. The source for this idea does not lie in the Hebrew Bible, where the sole portrayal of Enoch, in Gen 5:21–24, says nothing of his being a scribe. As far as we know, the depiction of Enoch as a scribe begins with the Astronomical Book where, as James VanderKam has pointed out, this entirely new role as a writer of heavenly discourses is attributed to him.[12] The likely explanation is that an author, or authors, who must himself, or themselves, have been a scribe or

---

10. See Stuckenbruck 2013b:325 for the textual data on these activities.

11. See ibid.:324–27 for a discussion of Enoch's scribal role in relation to the Book of Parables.

12. VanderKam 1984:104.

scribes, possessed a body of astronomical learning and wished to select a venerable figure from the past who might become its revered spokesperson. Enoch no doubt suggested himself because the number of the years during which he was on earth before God took him—365—was equal to the number of days in a solar year. The author of this part of Genesis may have been drawing upon a traditional Sumerian king list in describing the patriarchs and the seventh of these kings, Enmeduranki, was renowned as the inventor of divinatory techniques.[13] Enoch, the seventh patriarch, may be based on Enmeduranki (and their names have some similar features).

WAS A GROUP RESPONSIBLE FOR THE ENOCHIC WORKS?

Thus we have a tradition extending over three centuries in which texts containing angelic or visionary revelations concerning the heavens or past or future events were vouchsafed to Enoch who, being a scribe, wrote them down for future use. The earliest texts of this tradition thus inaugurate the attribution of a scribal role to Enoch. The first issue thrown up by such a phenomenon is how we are to understand the authorship of the texts in this tradition. Helge Kvanvig astutely poses this issue as follows: "There are two questions that need addressing. The first is whether it is possible or advisable to go behind the texts and try to reconstruct the collective bodies (groups, communities, milieus) responsible for the Enochic books. The second is what kind of criteria we should use when we talk about separate or rival collective bodies (and not simply about differing opinions between individual scribes, sages, or priests belonging to the same milieu)."[14] This will be my first focus of attention in this chapter. After dealing with it, I will proceed to the second issue, which is how the results so achieved bear on the subject of this volume, namely, the manner in which heaven is adumbrated in 1 Enoch 1–36.

Existing scholarship has not been slow to address the question of authorship. Michael Stone has noted that "The task we have undertaken, of trying to infer the existence of groups or trends in a society from opinions expressed in literary works is, of course, hazardous. We must try, however, for the issues are very central, but every caution must be employed."[15] Rising to this challenge is George Nickelsburg who, having noted that 1 Enoch provides little "explicit information about an Enochic community," has nev-

13. Ibid.:33–45.
14. Kvanvig 2005:81.
15. Stone 1988:167.

ertheless suggested that: "some textual evidence points in the direction of a community or group. Collective terms like "the righteous, the chosen, the holy" indicate a consciousness of community, though without any indication that the community had concrete manifestations in specific places."[16]

In addition, to account for the ongoing development of the corpus over three centuries "one must posit concrete channels of transmission."[17] Since the tradition depended upon composition in the name of Enoch, there seems to be some parallel in the Isaianic corpus, parts of the Qumran corpus and the developing Deutero-Pauline letters.[18]

On the other hand, some scholars have been sceptical of linking texts to communities or groups. Patrick Tiller opposes attributing 1 Enoch to a "sect" or "conventicle."[19] More than this he asserts that there was no group (of any kind) behind the Enochic texts and that, in any event, we cannot move from texts to groups responsible for them. He has argued that the existence of a succession of Enochic teachers: "does not imply the existence of a social group. When we speak of community or sociological group, we usually have in mind an organized social structure with defined boundaries and constraints. Having a common hero and a theology does not imply social structure."[20]

In an earlier formulation of this view Tiller said that nothing in 1 Enoch could be taken as evidence for a "community," unless "by community one means only an aggregate of individuals with similar interests."[21] John Collins, however, has criticized this view on the following basis: "But is this not at least part of what we mean by a group? We do not know whether the *maskilim* of Daniel were organized in any way, but they evidently shared some common understanding and purpose that was distinctive in their context."[22]

James VanderKam is also sceptical of the notion of a group or groups behind the Enochic texts: "There are references to groups in *later* Enochic booklets, but we do not know whether a social entity involving more than one person stands behind the Astronomical Book or whether the authors of the different units in the Book of the Watchers felt themselves to be part of

---

16. Nickelsburg 2001:64.

17. Ibid.

18. Ibid.

19. Tiller 2012:82. The idea of "conventicle" stems from Otto Plöger's *Theocracy and Eschatology* (1968).

20. Tiller 2012:98.

21. Tiller 2005:25–26.

22. Collins 2005:63.

a community with the astronomical writer. Perhaps they did, but it remains true that the sources say nothing about this."[23]

Yet this is not really accurate (except, perhaps, in some very narrow sense) for either the Astronomical Book or the Book of the Watchers. In the Astronomical Book Uriel informs Enoch that "the righteous will rejoice with the righteous" (1 Enoch 81:7) and Enoch tells Methuselah that he has given wisdom to him and his children (1 Enoch 82:2). In addition, the Book of the Watchers refers to the "righteous" and the "chosen" in 1 Enoch 1:8 and 2:6–8. The use of expressions such as "the righteous," "the chosen" and the children (of Enoch) are key concepts in later texts, and I will return to them below.

It will emerge in what follows that my support lies with the idea that one can plausibly discern in the Enochic works a group that is responsible for their production. Yet clearly there is debate about how to frame the discussion and Kvanvig's view (noted above) that it is necessary to clarify what kind of criteria we should use "when we talk about separate or rival collective bodies" is clearly correct. In what follows I will utilize social identity theory to that end. In addition, I will be relying on evidence relating to Enoch as a scribe and other descriptors attributed to him to make the case. This will allow me to bring into the discussion the circumstance that the application of terms like these to Enoch also spreads their relevance to those who saw in him the founder and exemplar of their group identity. For there is far more to having "a common hero" than Patrick Tiller seems to appreciate.

SOCIAL IDENTITY PERSPECTIVES FOR INVESTIGATING AN ENOCHIC GROUP

The diverse attempts to reach some view on those responsible for the Enochic corpus have, as already noted, generated terms such as "sect," "conventicle," "community" and "group." Yet these suggestions are really expressions of folk psychology, that is, efforts to postulate the relevant human collectivity without recourse to the abundant social-scientific literature that might be helpful here. It is at moments like this that recourse to the social sciences can introduce a measure of clarity and social realism, both in posing questions to be put to the ancient data and in making sense of the answers that result. For many years now I have found in social psychology, especially the

---

23. VanderKam 2007:19 (italics original).

social identity theory developed by Henri Tajfel and John Turner, valuable resources for such an enterprise.[24]

Social identity theory finds the word "group" the most useful way to refer to human collectivities and explores the identities that individuals derive from belonging to groups in the context of diverse inter-group and intra-group phenomena. But how should we characterize a group? Social-psychologist Rupert Brown, while noting the diversity of meanings associated with the word "group" in works on group dynamics, has isolated four dominant approaches.

First, for some theorists it is the experience of sharing a *common fate* that is decisive. On this view the Jews of Nazi Europe constituted a group. For other theorists, secondly, a group requires the existence of a formal or implicit *social structure*, with some form of status and roles, a family being a good example. A third view highlights face-to-face interaction among the members as the critical factor. While the second and third approaches, however, favor quite small groups and tend to exclude large-scale social categories like ethnicity, social class or nationality, this latter type of social category can impact on people's lives just as powerfully as small, cohesive, face-to-face groups. A fourth approach, which seeks to avoid the problem just mentioned, is that represented by social identity research, which proposes that *a group should be defined in terms of people's self-categorizations.*[25] "It is difficult to imagine a group," notes Brown, "in which its members did not at some stage mentally classify themselves as actually belonging to it."[26] According to this view, initially proposed by Henri Tajfel and John Turner, "a group exists when 'two or more individuals . . . perceive themselves to be members of the same social category.'"[27] On this approach, the Jews of Nazi Europe would constitute a group, as would the other two approaches mentioned.

For Brown, however, this definition is somewhat too broad, since it fails to capture an important feature of groups, namely, that their existence is usually known to others. He considers (and this is indeed a foundational theme of social identity theory) that a group does not usually exist as an independent social system but in relation to other groups. Accordingly, he adopts and develops the definition just cited and offers the following definition: "*a group exists when two or more people define themselves as members of it and when its existence is recognized by at least one other*," that "other" being

---

24. For a recent over-view of social identity theory, see Esler 2014b.
25. For these four approaches, see Brown 2000:2–3.
26. Ibid.:3.
27. Ibid., quoting Turner 1982:15. Also see Tajfel 1978b, 1981, and 1982.

either a person or a group.[28] While in the vast majority of cases Turner is right in his view that a group will be known by someone else outside it, there may be some exceptions to this, for example in the case of secret societies, where the fact that no one else does know about them is part of their reason for existing in the first place. That type of exception will not, however, be relevant to what follows.

The original research by Henri Tajfel was to the effect that the mere fact of inclusion in a group led to its members discriminating against outgroups. This result, demonstrated in his renowned "minimal group" experiments, has been conclusively shown to have application across cultures.[29] Tajfel developed the idea of "social identity," which is the identity that an individual gains from belonging to a group, not a reference to the identity of the group as a whole. It has three dimensions. The first, the "cognitive" dimension, refers to a person's awareness of his or her belonging to the group, plus (as Daniel Bar-Tal later argued)[30] the group beliefs to which one subscribed through membership. The second dimension, "evaluative," referred to how one valued one's membership compared with potential membership in outgroups. Thirdly, the "emotional" dimension concerned how one felt about belonging to such a group.

Tajfel had been interested in ethnic groups—as one type of group to which his theory applied—from the outset.[31] In speaking of ethnic groups, but capable of much wider application, Fredrik Barth (see Chapter 1) noted that such a group could persist for a very long time. Since the group's sense of itself as a group came first, a group could select various cultural features to express its identity and define its boundaries with outgroups and those features might change over time.

One of the group phenomena studied in social identity theory is how a group influences the thoughts, feelings and behavior of its members. A distinctive feature of this process is the role of norms.[32] Within a social identity framework, norms are those "regularities in attitudes and behavior that characterize a social group and differentiate it from other social groups."[33] Norms in this sense bring order and predictability to the environment and

28. Brown 2000:3 (emphasis original).

29. See Fischer and Derham 2016. This article represents a solid rejoinder to John Barclay's disparagement of social identity theory as a form of social analysis "based on necessarily artificial experiments on modern subjects" so that "its applicability across time and culture is extremely uncertain" (2011:7).

30. Bar-Tal 1990 and 1998.

31. Tajfel 1978b:2.

32. Hogg and Abrams 1988:157–58.

33. Hogg and Reid 2006:7.

thus help members to construe the world. They also encapsulate behavior appropriate to the group in new and ambiguous situations. Norms enhance and maintain group identity.[34] Various expressions, such as "the righteous" or "the chosen," that appear in parts of 1 Enoch from the Astronomical Book and the Book of the Watchers onwards would repay analysis as norms so understood. For present purposes, a related aspect of social identity theory holds great promise in understanding the Book of the Watchers: the notions of prototypes and exemplars.

A prototype is an abstract concept that is formed from multiple experiences with members of a group. It is a summary representation that encapsulates the central tendency of the social category. An exemplar, on the other hand, is a single example of the group in question, that is, an actual person, living or dead, thought to embody the identity of the group.[35] From a social identity perspective group prototypes and exemplars "describe individual cognitive representations of group norms."[36] To appreciate how prototypes and exemplars may assist with 1 Enoch 1–36 it is necessary briefly to consider John Turner's development of Henri Tajfel's social identity. Whereas Tajfel had mainly been concerned with intergroup phenomena, Turner explored the intragroup dimension. More specifically, he focused not on "a specific kind of group behaviour but on *how individuals are able to act as a group at all.*"[37] He formulated that interest in terms of these questions: "How does a collection of individuals become a social and psychological group? How do they come to perceive and define themselves and act as a single unit, feeling, thinking and self-aware as a collective entity? What effects does shared group membership have on their social relations and behaviour."[38]

Turner and his colleagues answered fundamental questions by appealing to phenomena they called self-categorization and depersonalization. The antecedent condition for individuals to act as a group was *the formation of in-group categories.*[39] For a group to form, two or more people in a particular context must begin to view themselves in terms of similarities and differences that they share as opposed to other people. That is, they must reach the view that they belong to one group ("social category") as opposed to other groups ("social categories") to which they do not belong.

---

34. Brown 2000:60.
35. Smith and Zarate 1990:244–46.
36. Hogg and Reid 2006:11.
37. Turner et al. 1987:42 (emphasis added).
38. Ibid.:1.
39. Ibid.:51–54.

When they do this, they are likely to internalize existing, culturally available information relating to that group. Inextricably bound to this process of "self-categorization" is that of "depersonalization." Turner and his colleagues defined this as "the process of 'self-stereotyping' whereby people come to perceive themselves more as the interchangeable exemplars of a social category than as individual personalities defined by their individual differences from others."[40] Via the process of depersonalization individuals self-stereotype themselves to become "the interchangeable exemplars of a social category."[41] This helps them to conform to shared in-group prototypes and this in turn leads to them manifesting in-group normative attitudes and behavior.[42] Yet depersonalization is not "a loss of individual identity, nor a loss or submergence of the self in the group." Rather, "it is the *change* from the personal to the social level of identity, a change in the nature and content of the self-concept corresponding to the functioning of self-perception at a more inclusive level of abstraction." Depersonalization actually enables individuals to *gain* identity, since it allows them to act in terms of social similarities and differences built up in human cultures over time.[43]

Prototypes and exemplars provide members with the models they must emulate in order to manifest in-group normative behavior and beliefs. The more they succeed in this, the more they will be positively viewed and treated as loyal group members. The existence of the group depends on such positive regard existing among the membership. As Turner and his colleagues explained, group cohesion (mutual attraction) requires the members of a group mutually to perceive that there exists a similarity (or identity) between themselves in terms of the defining or prototypical characteristics of that group (or social category).[44] Closely aligning themselves in beliefs, norms and behavior with the prototypes or exemplars of the group is an effective way to achieve this.

One final aspect of social identity needs mentioning. Most human beings belong to a number of different groups and acquire a social identity from each of them. The context in which a person finds him- or herself will determine which social identity is salient. As Stephen Reicher and Nick Hopkins have said in commenting on this aspect of the theory, "We all have

40. Ibid.:50.
41. Ibid.
42. Hogg and Reid 2006:11.
43. Turner et al. 1987:51 (emphases original).
44. Ibid.:60–61.

a number of self-categories, but in different situations different categories will be more or less important to us."[45]

To bring this discussion back to 1 Enoch 1–36, the question arises as to whether Enoch the scribe vested with angelically revealed knowledge of the heavens and human history functioned as an exemplar for a group of scribes who distinguished themselves from other scribes, indeed, other Israelites by possession of the same knowledge provided to them as the heirs of Enoch himself. Social identity theory prods us to consider whether the stress on so illustrious a figure from the past served as an exemplar for a group whereby the members derived a social identity they construed to be based on that of Enoch himself. In other words, social identity theory challenges Patrick Tiller's view that having "a common hero and a theology does not imply social structure" and suggests that it may very well imply precisely that. We should be open, moreover, to the possibility that the group existed over a long period, even if its members selected or developed some dimensions of its beliefs at different times (for example by moving into *ex post facto* surveys of Israelite experience in the Apocalypse of Weeks and the Animal Apocalypse). We must now assess the evidence in the light of this proposal.

A SCRIBAL GROUP BEHIND 1 ENOCH?

Some scholars have already suggested that the presentation of Enoch as a scribe matches the nature of those responsible for the texts written in his name. As David Orton notes, following F. Dexinger, it is likely that the emphasis on the scribal role of Enoch reflects the self-understanding of the apocalyptic author.[46] According to Randal Argall, "it is safe to assume that the Enochic authors were themselves scribes who patterned their roles on the biography of Enoch."[47] While these are highly plausible views, with Argall coming very close to the social identity perspective on Enoch as an exemplar, we need to examine more closely writing and scribal practices and attitudes to see how it impacts upon the interpretation of 1 Enoch 1–36.

---

45. Reicher and Hopkins 2001:38.
46. Orton 1989:82, citing Dexinger 1977:149.
47. Argall 1995:30.

Enoch the Scribe and the Non-Temple Enochic Scribal Group 165

The Group Dimension of Textual Composition in the Ancient World

As noted above, James VanderKam expresses doubt as to "whether a social entity involving more than one person stands behind the Astronomical Book or whether the authors of the different units in the Book of the Watchers felt themselves to be part of a community with the astronomical writer." It seems clear from this that he is seriously entertaining the rival possibility, of single authors (or, in some cases perhaps, editors), for the various parts of the Enochic corpus. No doubt many other critics would share this assumption. But is it correct? Or does it rather embody anachronistic notions of the "author" current in our post-Gutenberg and post-Enlightenment world, notions that also draw on nineteenth century understandings of the "genius."[48] These ideas have flowed into the modern view of the author as a highly creative individual who produces a written expression of his or her unique consciousness and who then receives protection in the form of copyright law.[49] That the VanderKam's single author approach is indeed anachronistic is suggested by the recent argument of Pieter Botha that the composition of texts in the ancient Mediterranean world was a collaborative exercise.[50]

Reading and writing was a thoroughly social process in antiquity. In the case of Rome, as Botha has shown, but clearly with much wider application, scrolls were usually read aloud and wealthy people often had lectors to read to them. If someone was writing a composition, this might entail listening to source texts, taking notes, planning the work and then possibly dictating it to a secretary to write down. It is likely that the person responsible for this draft would then circulate it to friends for their comments prior to the promulgation of the work.[51] When it came to this stage, what we call "publication," we must try to shed our preconceptions based on an author as working on the basis of "individual, introspective identity" where his or her output was represented as an instance of intellectual property protected by law. Instead, we must remember that works "were collective, traditional, cultural enterprises."[52] Their "publication" primarily took the form of having someone, who had carefully prepared the text in advance, read the work aloud to its intended addressees. Getting a work known thus

---

48. See Theissen and Winter 2002:46–48.
49. Botha 2012:115–16.
50. Botha 2012.
51. Ibid.:118–22.
52. Ibid.:123.

involved performance.⁵³ In short, we must acknowledge "the 'communal,' interactive authorship of ancient documents."⁵⁴ We are speaking here of works with something at least of a literary dimension, since commercial and legal documents were often produced by individual scribes without going through this process.

Although I will come to scribes in more detail further below, it is useful to note here that this process, in part or in whole, would also have obtained in relation to scribes when they were composing a work. Speaking of ancient Israelite scribal authors Karel van der Toorn has observed: "The author is a craftsman. Individual talent, which would be as real a gift in antiquity as it is today, was not an instrument to express the private and the personal but was a way to attain the pinnacle of a collective art."⁵⁵

It is also worth noting that the collective dimension prevailed no matter which of the six ways they prepared written texts that van der Toorn has identified:

1. Transcription of an oral lore;
2. Invention of a new text;
3. Compilation of existing lore, oral or written;
4. Expansion of an inherited text;
5. Adaptation of an existing text for a new audience; and
6. Integration of individual documents into a more comprehensive composition.⁵⁶

The first category needs to be understood as broad enough, however, to encompass all the many examples of scribes who wrote down a document, such as a letter, from material provided to them orally by those using their services.

The cooperative nature of the composition of texts in the ancient Mediterranean world predisposes us to think in terms of a plurality of people being involved at any given time in the production of each section of 1 Enoch. In addition, the fact that the various parts appeared over some three centuries or more and were redacted into a whole supports the existence of people taking responsibility for the Enochic tradition across a considerable period of time. This conclusion represents the first step in an argument for

---

53. Botha 2012:123–25.
54. Ibid.:129.
55. Van der Toorn 2007:47.
56. Ibid.:110.

a scribal group behind the Enochic corpus. The next step involves a closer look at how scribes operated in Israel and the ancient Near East generally.

An Ancient Comparator: The Scribes of Emar

The last two decades have witnessed growing interest in ancient Judean scribes.[57] This research extends to the importance of Judean scribes in the genesis of apocalyptic literature and in the formulation of the Jesus tradition.[58] Yet the evidence for the practices, social roles and status, and training of scribes in Palestine is rather limited. Given the relative paucity of direct evidence for ancient Judean scribes, and how they were trained and organized themselves, recourse must be had to what is known about scribes in other Near Eastern cultures, especially Syria, Mesopotamia and Egypt.[59] Justification for using such comparative information lies in the extent to which similar scribal practices, even in such areas as their training (including the curricula used in it) and the genres in which they composed documents, were common across the region and only changed slowly over time.

Yoram Cohen, speaking of the scribes of Emar in northern Syria during the fourteenth to twelfth centuries BCE but in a way that has far wider application, has noted that in the ancient Near East "the scribes viewed themselves as an established community of users of a shared writing system learned by means of a common curriculum." They could converse with one another in different countries using their linguistic skills. Many of them shared a religious milieu in honoring the local gods Nisaba, Nabu and Ea as their patrons. They recognized their power to control information in courts and other establishments and this assisted their integration into political institutions.[60] Let us now look more closely Emar, which has proved to be a particularly rich source of information on scribes and is the subject of a hugely revealing monograph by Cohen.[61]

Emar, modern Balis-Meskene, was a late Bronze Age town near the Euphrates in northeastern Syria that was destroyed in 1187 BCE. Emar was

---

57. See Schams 1998 (although she was writing before the publication of the documents in Aramaic and Nabatean-Aramaic from the Babatha archive, for which now see Yadin et al. 2002), Van der Toorn 2007, Tov 2009, and Czajkowski 2017:60–87. Also see my detailed analysis of the work of two Nabatean scribes and their highly skilled draftsmanship of the earliest four papyri from the Babatha archive (94–99 CE) in Esler 2017c.

58. See, respectively, Arnal 2001 and Horsley 2010 (although Horsley is unwilling to see scribal *groups* being involved).

59. Cohen 2009. Also see Cohen 2005 and 2012.

60. Cohen 2009:27.

61. Cohen 2009.

under Hittite control from about 1340 BCE to shortly before its destruction. It was a relatively minor city, compared with the much bigger sites of the period like cosmopolitan Ugarit and imperial Hattuša.[62] During excavations by a French team between 1972 and 1976 hundreds of cuneiform clay tablets in Akkadian were discovered and then published between 1985 and 1987.[63] Almost ninety per cent of these tablets came from an archive in a building closely connected with the Zu-Ba'la family of diviners and scribes. Many more tablets, looted from the site after the French left, later appeared on the antiquities market. The textual remains from Emar fall into three main types: "ephemeral" (meaning commercial and legal) documents (such as contracts of sale, wills, sales into slavery, debt notes, letters and dockets listing temple objects etc), cultic texts, and, thirdly, scholarly materials (including literary texts and school texts for training scribes).[64] In Emar, during a period of about 140 years, "there were around forty scribes drafting ephemeral documents, along with more than a dozen scholarly scribes and their students."[65]

Although the excavators named the building associated with the Zu-Ba'la family "Temple M1," Cohen has argued persuasively that it was a private dwelling, not a temple.[66] What makes this house such a uniquely instructive archaeological setting is that it included both schooling materials (including texts and student exercises) and an archive of ephemeral documents relating to a major family in the city.[67] The Zu-Ba'la family were, accordingly, conducting a scribal school in their own house. This conclusion has considerable bearing on the debate concerning the social context of scribal training during the Old Babylonian period (roughly 2,000 to 1,600 BCE). The scribal schooling at Emar was based on the blueprint of the Old Babylonian scribal schooling that had been disseminated throughout the region.[68]

Whereas the older view was that scribes were trained in a palace or some other administrative power center, like a temple, more recently the consensus has shifted towards the idea that the schools were family-run affairs, although the people running them might have held official positions. "The final end would be to provide an education that would ensure

62. Ibid.:243.
63. Arnaud 1985–1987.
64. For the details in this paragraph, see Cohen 2009:7–17.
65. Ibid.:21 (for the 140 years) and 27 (for the quotation).
66. Ibid.:54–56.
67. Ibid.:54.
68. Ibid.:240.

the younger members of the family means to continue in the professional footsteps of their elders."[69] Such was the case with the Zu-Baʻla family in Emar, in the thirteenth and twelfth centuries BCE.

Since Emarite scribes rarely used patronyms to identity themselves, we do not have direct evidence if their children followed as scribes in the footsteps of their fathers. Nevertheless, this may have been the position generally in Emar. There is evidence that one of the members of the later generations of the Zu-Baʻla family was educated by his father.[70] At Ugarit, to cite another city in northern Syria from much the same period, the scribes inherited their position from their fathers, "so perhaps schooling was conducted in the family domain."[71]

While it was in their house that their offspring and other members of the Zu-Baʻla family, were educated, at least one foreign teacher, Kidin-Gula, was employed in the school of the family.[72] He also took part in merchant activities in the town.[73] This means he must have been employed by the Zu-Baʻla family on a part-time basis, perhaps to provide areas of expertise not otherwise available in Emar.[74] We do not, however, know how much scribes at Emar earned or in what way they were remunerated.[75]

There were two broad types of scribal tradition in Emar, an older Syrian tradition and a newer Syrian-Hittite one, with the latter probably originating with scribes who had moved to the city from the Hittite provincial capital of Carchemish. In the textual remains from Emar different scribes are associated with each tradition.[76] Cohen observes that it would be wrong to understand the Syrian scribes at Emar (twenty-nine of whom are known by name) "as working exclusively for the palace or temple institutions. All the scribes to whom more than two or three documents were attributed wrote a mixture of documents, which leads to the conclusion that their clients were not necessarily associated with either the palace or the temple."[77] Some Syrian scribes only appear as the writers of private documents, although it is possible that they worked as scribes on a part-time basis.[78] The Syro-Hittite

69. Ibid.:49.
70. Ibid.:180.
71. Ibid.:51.
72. Ibid.:148.
73. Ibid.:116.
74. Ibid.:183–89.
75. Ibid.:28.
76. Ibid.:28–29.
77. Ibid.:89.
78. Ibid.:90.

scribes (thirteen of whom are known by name) were in a different position, as they were in a more important position and associated with the Hittite administration of the city.[79]

Scribes in Israel and Its Context

Scribes were needed in Israel just as they were in Mesopotamia, Syria, and Egypt. In addition, they had to be trained somewhere and evidence for their training also attests to their presence in that context. A handful of the tablets used for training scribes has been discovered at Ashkelon, Aphek, Hazor and Megiddo from the Middle to the Late Bronze Age (1650–1050 BC). Although this material does not allow the curriculum to be reconstructed, it is likely that it was based on the same principles as those in the cities of northern Syria and the Euphrates valley.[80] There is no reason to believe that scribes or the need for them to be trained disappeared in Israel at the start of the Iron Age.

In relation to the Second Temple period, prior to Schams' 1998 examination of the surviving evidence there was a tendency to make large generalizations concerning scribes without sufficient attention to the complexities and tendencies in the data.[81] The evidence for the Second Temple period covers *bullae* from the Persian province of Yehud from the seal of a scribe that contains (in Hebrew) the words "Belonging to Jeremai the scribe," references to scribes in biblical texts, such as Ezra-Nehemiah (for example, Ezra 4; 7:6, 11 and 12; Neh 8:1, 13; 13:13), 1 and 2 Chronicles; Septuagint translations of the biblical books; extra-biblical Judean literature; the Qumran documents; Philo and Josephus; the New Testament; the Targums; papyri; rabbinic literature; and Judean inscriptions.[82]

Finally, Yoram Cohen has identified an aspect of scribal attitudes that was a feature of Israel's Near Eastern context and bears directly on 1 Enoch 1–36. He has noted that the "scribal profession in Mesopotamia attached to itself great prestige based on a long historical tradition." This prestige

---

79. Ibid.:90.

80. Ibid.:53.

81. For example, Schams (1998:15–16) criticizes Emil Schürer's creation of the artificial category of *Schriftgelehrte* by assuming that the Greek term γραμματεύς and the Hebrew term *sofer* were equivalents and by collating evidence from the New Testament, Josephus, and rabbinic sources. She also offers critiques of the views on scribes propounded by Joachim Jeremias, Adolf von Schlatter, Martin Hengel, Jacob Neusner, and David Orton (1998:18–24), citing similar weaknesses.

82. See Schams (1998:36–273) for a detailed discussion of this evidence for Judean scribes in the Second Temple period.

meant that some Mesopotamian kings "boasted of their scholarly pursuits, taking pride in their control of the scribal skills." Some scribes connected themselves with great figures from the past: "Scribes active at the end of the practice of writing cuneiform during the Achaemenid and even later Seleucid periods traced their lineage to famous authors now long dead but still alive within scribal memory, a trend which started around the Kassite period. They viewed themselves as direct descendents of famous long-dead authors, such as Sin-leqe-unninni, the alleged author of the Epic of Gilgamesh, or claimed that their "father" or ancestor was Sumerian, surely for the sake of prestige."[83] The results of this discussion must now be brought to bear upon our understanding of 1 Enoch 1–36.

Implications of Scribal Authorship for 1 Enoch

It makes good sense to regard the scribes in an ancient Near Eastern city (like Jerusalem), or even in a kingdom or temple-state generally, as a group in the social identity sense previously outlined. The scribes in an urban context had a similar training and engaged in work that was distinctive and was characterized by a high level of literacy. They regularly defined themselves as scribes, and other groups and individuals also identified them as such. In writing of the scribes of Emar, Yoram Cohen has suggested that although their sense of being an elite group was more modest than those of the Mesopotamian scribes with their much older traditions, "it is evident that the scribes of Emar formed a distinct group in the city." Evidence for this comes from their insistence on using titles identifying themselves as scribes in everyday commercial and legal documents and "as diviners or experts in magic and medicine in the colophons of the scholarly works they copied."[84] Similarly, Karel van der Toorn has argued that in Mesopotamia and Israel, because the work of scribes expressed common ideological and artistic values, they belonged to and identified with a scribal social group.[85] While both these views are steps in the right direction, on the approach I am taking here it is the fact that scribes regarded themselves as belonging to a group and others in the local context would have recognized such a group that clinches the point.

The evidence from Emar points to the likelihood that in Judea, during the period that the texts comprising 1 Enoch were composed, there were scribal families, with the required skills of reading and writing passed down

83. Cohen 2009:26.
84. Ibid.:27.
85. Van der Toorn 2007:46.

from father to son in the family home. These skills would have covered both the needs of private individuals (for "ephemeral documents") and also of the state. Perhaps some of the scribes took part in wider commercial activities. There is no necessity to imagine that scribes were trained only in, or were restricted to, palace or temple contexts. From this we may suggest that the Enochic authors were scribes embedded in the broad social and commercial life of Judea. Nor should we be surprised to find that some of the Judean scribes of this period associated themselves with great figures from the past.

As noted above, it is possible to possess multiple identities with the context determining which one is salient at any given time. There is no contradiction in someone being a scribe and composing documents for any purpose, private or public, which might arise, while also belonging to a specific Enochic group that constituted a subgroup of the scribal group as a whole. The time has now come to adduce specific evidence for such an Enochic scribal group.

Specific Evidence for an Enochic Scribal Group

When discussing the meaning of a group above, I noted Rupert Brown's view that in addition to the members perceiving that they belonged to a group, it was also necessary that the existence of the group be recognized by at least one other group. Two areas of evidence exist for just such a recognition, the first being external to 1 Enoch and the second internal to it.

External Evidence

The external evidence is to be found in Sirach, for the reasons explained by Randal Argall.[86] Sirach is to be dated to the period 200 to 175 BCE, and was thus written at a time when the only Enochic texts in existence were the Astronomical Book and the Book of the Watchers (see above). Although the work proclaims its authorship by Ben Sira (translating the work of his grandfather), for the reasons already set out above, we should be wary of understanding this in terms of a solitary author but instead view him as existing within a circle of people who worked with him as he composed or translated the work. Sirach expresses Ben Sira's outspoken support of the Jerusalem priests and their cultic activity in Jerusalem, in 7:29-31 and

---

86. Argall 1995; also see Argall 2002.

35:1–11 and in the references to Aaron (45:6–22), Phineas (45:23–25) and the High Priest Simon II (50:1–21) in the Praise of the Ancestors.[87]

The relevance of Sirach is that it contains evidence for a clash between Enochic traditions and Sirach. For example, both 1 Enoch 32 and Sirach 24 talk about the Tree of Wisdom and both descriptions include material on four elements: height, foliage, fruit and fragrance.[88] Yet there are two differences: "First, Enoch saw the Tree while on a journey to the outer Eastern reaches of the cosmos. It was not present on earth. In Sirach, Personified Wisdom envisioned itself as this tree, a tree plotted at the temple in Jerusalem. Second, Enoch saw holy ones eating the fruit of the Tree of Wisdom. In contrast, Personified Wisdom invites all who desire her to eat her fruits."[89] In other words, in "1 Enoch, the great wisdom represented by the Tree is inaccessible to ordinary mortals. It is made known to angels and they, in turn, communicate it to Enoch through interpretations of his visions. Enoch then brings this wisdom from heaven to the chosen and righteous, who "eat" it (82:3b). In Sirach, the wisdom represented by the Tree is present in Israel and is accessible to all who desire it. Wisdom emanates from Jerusalem to all mankind though the activity of sages like ben Sira."[90]

There are other differences. First Enoch uses a solar calendar of 364 days (1 Enoch 72–82), whereas Sirach favours a lunisolar calendar of 354 days (Sir. 43:6–8) that requires periodic intercalations.[91] At Sir 24:4–5 it is stated:

> I dwelt in high places, and my throne was in a pillar of cloud. Alone I have made the circuit of the vault of heaven and have walked in the depths of the abyss. In the waves of the sea, in the whole earth, and in every people and nation, I have gotten a possession. (RSV)

This sounds like a direct riposte to Enoch's journeys. In addition, Ben Sira employs specific vocabulary that suggests his rivals teach esoteric wisdom. His vocabulary brings Enochic tradition to mind. Ben Sira warns his students not to study "things too marvelous," "secret things," "what is beyond you" and "what is too great for you" (Sir 3:21–23). He criticizes the parabolic interpretations of "dream visions" (Sir 34[31]:1–8). This is the language by which the authors of 1 Enoch characterize their wisdom ("beyond

---

87. Wright 2002:179.
88. Argall 1995:93.
89. Ibid.:94.
90. Ibid.
91. Ibid.:164.

their thought," 1 Enoch 82:2; "great wisdom," 32:3; "dreams ... and visions," 13:8, "mystery," 103:2a; 104:10a, 12a).[92]

Argall reasonably concludes that such "differences are the stuff of conflict."[93] Benjamin Wright is favorably disposed to Argall's position and follows Patrick Tiller and Richard Horsley in the view: "that Ben Sira was a member of a retainer class of scribe-sages that was in the employ of the aristocratic class in Jerusalem, a class made up primarily of the priests, who were in charge not only of the cult in Jerusalem, but who also administered government affairs."[94]

For each instance of "class" in this quotation we might reasonably substitute "group." It is likely that Ben Sira, a member of one group, was not just antipathetic to Enochic ideas but also to the authors of the works in which they were to be found, presumably a group of scribes differentiated from his group by such beliefs. We will return to possible conflict between scribes associated with the temple and Enochic scribes below.

Internal Evidence

1 Enoch 104:9–13 is dated to the period probably from the end of the second or beginning of the first century BCE (see above). It is thus at least one century later than the Book of the Watchers. It is also to be dated about seventy years after the composition of Sirach and seems to reflect continuing inter-group tension. Accordingly, I will assume that it still sheds light on the earlier period.

Enoch first issues a direction to certain people not to go astray (πλανᾶσθε) in their hearts and not lie (ψεύδεσθε), "nor change the words of truth (μηδὲ ἐξαλλοιώσητε τοὺς λόγους τῆς ἀληθείας), nor falsify the words of the Holy One," nor praise their errors, for their lies and errors lead not to righteousness but to great sin (104:9). The "words" used twice in 104:9 appear to be a reference to words in written form, a view confirmed by what is stated in the next two verses:

> And now I know this mystery (ምሥጢር; *meṣṭir*),
> that sinners will alter and refute (ἀντιγράφουσιν)
> the words of truth,[95]
> and pervert many and lie and invent great fabrications,

92. Ibid.:250.
93. Ibid.
94. Wright 2002:179–80.
95. For this interpretation of the text, see Nickelsburg 2001:531–34.

and write books in their own names (104:10).
Would that they would write all my words in truth {in their names,}
and neither remove nor alter these words,
but write in truth all that I testify to them (104:11).[96]

It is noteworthy that in v. 10 a precise reality emerges underlying the direction in v. 109 not to change the words of truth, namely, that the author, speaking in the guise of "Enoch," accepts the possibility that such lying and misguided people may come into possession of Enochic texts such as this and alter them. While castigating what is plainly a negatively viewed outgroup, he acknowledges that they do have access to Enochic texts. Although he is writing mainly for his own group, this recognition that his text might pass into outside hands means that the second person plural pronouns in v. 109 are not directed to purely imaginary parties.

He accuses them of altering texts, omitting aspects of them and adding to them. The texts in question are Enochic in the sense that "Enoch" is their author and claims to be such on their face (notwithstanding that for us, and possibly ancient readers, this is a pseudepigraphic maneuver). That the social setting is one of competition between rival groups is made manifest in the way that they mistreat the Enochic writings, especially to the extent that they refute, literally "write against" (ἀντιγράφουσιν) them, a dimension lost in Nickelsburg's mistranslation of this word as "copy."[97] Of critical significance for understanding the group dynamics in play here is the statement that they "write books in their own names" in v. 10. This carries two consequences: first, they are not presented as writing in the name of any great figure in the past (or, as we would say, they are not creating pseudepigraphic texts) and thus, secondly, they cannot be understood as writing in the name and under the guise of Enoch. Although we do not know what texts the author has in mind that they are producing, we can illustrate the reality of the phenomenon by pointing to a text from the early second century BCE by a Judean author in his own name, namely, Siracides, by Jesus, the son of Sirach, son of Eleazar, of Jerusalem (Sir 50:27), which was discussed above.

Enoch continues by saying that he knows "a second mystery," namely, "that my books (βίβλοι) will be given to the righteous (δίκαιοι), the holy (ὅσιοι) and the wise (φρόνιμοι) for the joy of truth (104:12), and all the righteous will believe them and rejoice in them and be glad to learn from them all the ways of truth" (104:13).[98] We see here an author seeking to legiti-

96. ET Nickelsburg 2001:531, but with changes in the first two lines. He favors "copy" for ἀντιγράφουσιν.

97. Nickelsburg 2001:531.

98. I have followed the Greek manuscript for vv. 12–13. The Ethiopic tradition is

mate a plurality of books from his tradition, since they come from "Enoch" himself, that are central to the identity of an ingroup described as righteous, holy and wise, as opposed to outgroups characterized by lies and errors and immersed in sin. These epithets are the norms (or "identity descriptors") pertaining to a particular group and its identity. As well as having some substantive meaning, they also serve to valorize the worth of their group and of belonging to it and to diminish the members of outgroups not characterized by such values.

1 Enoch 104:9–13 thus exists in a context where there are outgroups existing in tension with the Enochic ingroup. This second aspect situates the matter firmly within the realm of (often fraught) intergroup relationships upon which social identity theory focuses.

As mentioned above, the text envisages a battle between groups of scribes, with the one to which we have access upholding its understanding of the traditions handed down by Enoch in the face of attempts to remove, alter or add to those traditions. It is important to note that we are not dealing here with groups that have formed from the fragmentation of a larger Enochic group, in other words, almost intra-group differentiation and conflict. The reason for this is that representatives of the outgroup or groups write in their own names. They do not write in the name of Enoch and thus have no connection with him such as they would have if they were members of a group looking back to Enoch as prototypical of their group identity.

Enoch in the Book of the Watchers and an Enochic Scribal Group

The time has now come to apply the argument that I have developed so far by considering the way in which Enoch is presented in the Book of the Watchers (1 Enoch 1–36). This will require paying close attention to the theme of books and writing and the explicitly scribal role of Enoch.

Such phenomena are not explicit in 1 Enoch 1–5, which initially recount that Enoch had a vision (ὅρασις; 1 Enoch 1:2) and heard things from the angels and then proceeds to an oracle of judgment.[99] The theme does, however, surface in the next section, the rebellion of the Watchers in 1 Enoch 6–11, when God tells Raphael to write all Asael's sin "on (or over) him" in 10:8, which Nickelsburg interprets as a command to Raphael to write an epitaph over Asael's tomb or an indictment for use at the final judgment.[100] This is the beginning of a number of occasions in 1 Enoch when

---

somewhat different.
99. Nickelsburg 2001:129–34.
100. Ibid.:222.

angels engage in writing, mainly, however, on heavenly tablets recording human good and evil (which will later become a prominent feature of the Animal Apocalypse).

In 1 Enoch 12, however, the scribal theme becomes quite explicit in relation to a human being, Enoch. Enoch is first introduced as a scribe in 1 Enoch 12:3-4. In 1 Enoch 12:3 (in some Ethiopic manuscripts, but not in the Greek) Enoch says that the Watchers "called me, Enoch the scribe . . . (ሄኖክ፡ ጸሐፊ; *Henok ṣaḥāfi*) and said to me." This may have appeared in an earlier Greek version than we have but later dropped out through homoioteleuton.[101] Without these words, especially "and said to me" the transition to the 12:4 is rather compressed. Thus we have a self-designation by "Enoch" that indicates he regards being a scribe as a fundamental aspect of his identity; it is how he categorizes himself.

1 Enoch 12:4 contains the next reference to Enoch as a scribe. Here "the Watchers of the Holy One" (12:3) formally address Enoch as "the scribe of righteousness" (ὁ γραμματεὺς τῆς δικαιοσύνης; ጸሐፌ፡ ጽድቅ፡ [*ṣaḥafē ṣedq*]; 12:4).[102] Their mission for Enoch, however, does not entail his use of scribal skills. Rather they give him a message of condemnation that they want him to relay orally to the Watchers who have abandoned heaven for earth and who have defiled themselves with women (12:4—13:2). This Enoch does (13:3). No doubt it is his status as righteous that qualifies him to deliver such a message to those who demonstrably are not. It is actually the Watchers so condemned who request he activate his scribal skills by writing a memorandum of petition (τὸ ὑπόμνημα τῆς ἐρωτήσεως) for them that they might have forgiveness (*aphesis*) and then reciting this petition in God's presence (13:4). So Enoch writes out the memorandum (ὑπόμνημα) and the "entreaties" (δεήσεις) concerning themselves and their sons for whom they "were making entreaty" (περὶ ὧν δέονται; 13:6).[103]

This process represents an example of the first way in which scribes prepared written texts identified by Karel van Toorn (as mentioned above), the transcription of an oral message. Then Enoch goes and sits by the waters of Dan in the land of Dan, south of Mount Hermon, and recites "(to God) the memorandum of their petitions" (τὸ ὑπόμνημα τῶν δεήσεων αὐτῶν)

---

101. As Nickelsburg seems to suggest (ibid.:234). Isaac omits this instance of "scribe" (1983:19).

102. Stuckenburg notes that the underlying Aramaic was likely to have been ספר קושטא (2013b:322).

103. Nickelsburg (2001:238) reasonably emends 13:6 to include τῶν υἱῶν αὐτῶν ("their sons") after περὶ ὧν δέονται, partly because these sons (the Giants) are mentioned as part of their petition in 14:7.

until he falls asleep (13:7).¹⁰⁴ But Enoch learns in a vision that the Watchers' petition has been rejected and that he must reprimand them, which he does in their presence (1 Enoch 13:8–10). Enoch summarizes contents of the message from heaven in 1 Enoch 14:1–7. He reiterates (14:4) that he wrote their petition (ἐρώτησις) but that it will not be accepted (14:7).

In 1 Enoch 15:1 God himself calls him and then says, "Fear not, Enoch, righteous man and scribe of truth." This is Nickelsburg's translation on the basis of the Aramaic probably underlying the Greek, which actually has Ὁ ἄνθρωπος ὁ ἀληθινός, ἄνθρωπος τῆς ἀληθείας, ὁ γραμματεύς, "The truthful man, man of truth, the scribe."¹⁰⁵ It is noteworthy that truthfulness is now being attributed to Enoch (although the Ethiopic version persists with his righteousness at this point).¹⁰⁶ God tells him that he must go and say to the Watchers who sent him on their behalf that they should petition (ἐρωτῆσαι) on behalf of human beings, not human beings on behalf of them (1 Enoch 15:2). Later these Watchers are described as "those who sent you to petition (ἐρωτῆσαι) on their behalf" (16:2). Each such reference reinforces the image of Enoch as a scribe.

There is no further mention of Enoch's scribal activity until 1 Enoch 33, when Enoch sees the ends of the earth and the gates of heaven from which the stars come forth (vv. 2–3), clearly alluding to the opening verses of the Astronomical Book (1 Enoch 72:1). Enoch writes down what Uriel shows him, but Uriel writes down the various features as well (33:4). As Nickelsburg notes, the author is suggesting that Enoch was instructed in the matters described in the Astronomical Book at this point in his journey, but also (differently from 1 Enoch 72–82) that Uriel as well as Enoch was the author of the Astronomical Book.¹⁰⁷

It is now possible to bring all of the above discussion together. To avoid anachronistic construals of the composition of texts in the ancient Mediterranean, it is reasonable to propose at the outset that a text like 1 Enoch 1–36 should not be regarded as the creation of a single author writing in splendid isolation but rather as written by someone who was in regular contact with other (like-minded) people and with whom he discussed the text as it was being composed (even if that meant something like an editorial process of bringing together previous traditions or sources). As conceptualized within social identity theory, the sense that a collectivity of people has of themselves

---

104. ET Nickelsburg 237, but changing his "petition" to "petitions."

105. Nickelsburg 2001:267.

106. The Ethiopic is ብእሲ፡ ጻድቅ፡ ወጸሐፌ፡ ጽድቅ፡ (be'si ṣādeq wa-ṣaḥāfē ṣedq), "a righteous man and a scribe of righteousness."

107. Nickelsburg 2001:330.

Enoch the Scribe and the Non-Temple Enochic Scribal Group 179

as belonging to a group is the foundation for the view that they are indeed a group. I will now rehearse the solid evidence for the conclusion that those people with whom the author of 1 Enoch 1–36 was associated in writing were a group, with membership therein being characterized by distinctive cognitive, evaluative and emotional dimensions and were, to pick up Rupert Brown's point, regarded as such a group by outgroups.

There can be little doubt that the author of the Book of the Watchers was a scribe. Only a scribe would have had the education necessary for the task. Yet the fact that Enoch is portrayed, quite remarkably, as a scribe in this text and in the other constituent parts of 1 Enoch, when there is no indication of a scribal role for him in the Hebrew Bible, allows us to conclude that some, if not all, of the other members of the group apart from the author of the Book of the Watchers were also scribes. Why would the author have designated a hero, a revealer of heavenly mysteries, from the past, *as a scribe* if that did not correspond to the self-designation of the members of his group? The likelihood of this view is strengthened as we push deeper into the evidence.

As noted above, in social identity theory the cognitive dimension of group belonging embraces both the sense of belonging to a group and the characteristic beliefs held by the group. The original beliefs of the group in view related to astronomical knowledge. Their views on this subject were very distinctive, especially because by the third century BCE they were very old fashioned compared to what was then known about the heavens. The only complete text of the Astronomical Book survives in an Ethiopic translation, which greatly abbreviates the lengthy original as now known from four Aramaic manuscripts found in Cave 4 at Qumran and discussed by J. T. Milik.[108] The material in the Aramaic original is highly schematic and prolix, as Milik's transcriptions and translations reveal.[109] Otto Neugebauer, the celebrated historian of ancient Near Eastern mathematical astronomy, described the book as representing "a primitive picture of the cosmic order" and noted that the treatment of the heavenly bodies is "always hemmed in by a rigid schematism unrelated to reality."[110] Although he considered that some aspects of the presentation suggested an early Babylonian background

---

108. Milik presents what he describes as a 'preliminary' treatment of the Astronomical Book (1976:273–97, at 273).

109. For example, see Milik 976:278–81.

110. In Black 1985:387 (part of Otto Neugebauer's Appendix A to this work, pp. 386–419, on the "astronomical" chapters of 1 Enoch, with additional comments on the Aramaic fragments by Matthew Black). VanderKam (1984:92) agrees that the Astronomical Book "reflects certain elements from a primitive level of Mesopotamian astronomy."

unlike the sophisticated Babylonian astronomy of the Persian or Seleucid-Parthian period, he took the view that the "whole Enochian astronomy is clearly an *ad hoc* construction and not the result of a common semitic tradition."[111] VanderKam also considers that the work "reflects certain elements from a primitive level of Mesopotamian astronomy."[112] Thus in the Astronomical Book the day is divided into eighteen parts and these are varied as the day lengthens or shortens across the year (so in mid summer the day is twelve eighteenths and the night six eighteenths, whereas in mid winter the day is twelve eighteenths and the night six eighteenths). While this computation does not accord with astronomical reality, "the same ratios of day to night are attested in some astronomical texts from Mesopotamia."[113] VanderKam also suggests that it "shares several traits with astrological divination," making the attractive proposal (by way of linking Enoch with the Sumerian king Enmeduranki) that the author "derived his schematic scientific data precisely from mantic contexts in which it would be likely that earlier levels of science survived."[114]

The revolutionary step taken by this group of scribes, most probably in the Astronomical Book but adopted in the Book of the Watchers, lay precisely in integrating a body of old Babylonian astronomy with Enoch. We have already noted above Yoram Cohen's observation that scribes working in cuneiform at the end of the Achaemenid and Seleucid periods traced their lineage back to famous authors from the past. The scribes with whom we are concerned here took a similar step, but went much further by turning the patriarch Enoch into a scribe when he was not so described in the biblical text and by making him a mouthpiece for their astronomical knowledge. Biblical warrant existed for this in the fact that Enoch lived to be 365 years old (Gen 5:23) and thus appeared to have a connection with the solar calendar (although in the Astronomical Book the solar year is 364 years long: 1 Enoch 72:32), which provided a warrant for a far wider familiarity with astronomical matters.

But these scribes went even further than this. Because Enoch "walked with God" (Gen 5:24) and thus must have been a suitable person to interact with God and the angels in heaven, he was an eminently suitable figure to pass on heavenly revelations, which dealt not only with astronomical matters but with central aspects of human experience, especially the existence

---

111. Black 1985:387.
112. VanderKam 1984:92.
113. Ibid.:93.
114. Ibid.:92.

of evil and how God would deal with it. The latter issue lies at the heart of the communicative purpose of 1 Enoch 1–36.[115]

Beliefs relating to astronomy and also to the exalted nature and scribal function of Enoch thus constitute the principal aspects of the cognitive dimension of belonging to the Enochic group. The evaluative and emotional dimensions may be dealt with more briefly. It goes without saying that a group that constituted itself around so illustrious a figure from the past as Enoch, his honour amplified beyond the picture of him in Genesis 5 in the manner just set out, must have evaluated themselves very highly vis-à-vis other groups who did not relate to him in this way. An unambiguous indicator of this high sense of worth can be seen in the fact that in some later works in the Enochic corpus (but not the Book of Parables or the Eschatological Admonition) Enoch is described as setting down his revelations for his "children." This phenomenon can be seen as early as 175–170 BCE, in the Apocalypse of Weeks, in which Enoch states that he "is making things known to you, my sons" (93:2). It appears in the Bridging Exhortation (91:3:"Hear, O sons of Enoch") and also at the start of the Epistle of Enoch (92:1: "Written by Enoch the scribe . . . to all my sons who will dwell on the earth"). The Enochic scribal group thus saw in Enoch an ancestor. He was fictive rather than actual kin perhaps, but they were nevertheless tied closely to him and enjoyed the honour that came from him, just as Israelites rejoiced in their actual descent from Abraham. As for the emotional dimension, to possess such a view would have entailed that the members of the Enochic group entertained positive feelings about belonging to it.

The data already discussed indicate the comparability of ideas concerning exemplars and prototypes from social identity to the relationship between the figure of Enoch and the members of the Enochic scribal group. As noted above, the process of self-categorization encapsulates how a group forms, in that two or more people in a certain setting begin to view themselves in terms of similarities and differences that they shared as opposed to other people. They accept they belong to this group as opposed to other groups. This was what happened to the Enochic scribal group. By internalizing information relating to the group, including its possession of old-fashioned yet distinctive astronomical learning and the modification of the Genesis picture of Enoch to make him a scribe and recipient of heavenly mysteries, they engaged in self-stereotyping as they began to see themselves as representatives of this group. This inevitably involved depersonalization as explained above, as differences they had as individuals with other individuals became less salient when membership of the Enochic scribal

---

115. On evil and the divine response to it in 1 Enoch 1–36, see Esler 2017b.

group was valorized. All this assisted them in conforming to shared ingroup prototypes and led to their manifesting ingroup normative attitudes and behavior. Enoch provided them with the foundational model that they needed to emulate in order to accept and internalize group beliefs and norms. The closer they aligned themselves to Enoch, the more positively were they viewed by other group members. All this was conducive to group cohesion. Their astronomical knowledge and preservation of revelations allegedly made to Enoch constituted the primary group beliefs, while notions of righteousness were probably the dominant area of normative behavior. It is not at all surprising, therefore, to find that the description of Enoch as a scribe of righteousness in an early Enochic text like the Book of the Watchers (12:4) is matched by later references to the ingroup as 'the sons of righteousness" (93:2) or equivalent expressions (91:19: "my children . . . walk in the paths of righteousness"; 107:1: "until there arise generations of righteousness"), or "the righteous" (84:6; 108:14). Nor are we surprised to see the description of Enoch as truthful (15:1) find a resonance later in the Epistle of Enoch (1 Enoch 92–105) that is addressed to "to the last generations who will observe truth and peace" (92:1).

THE ENOCHIC SCRIBES' LACK OF CONNECTION WITH THE TEMPLE

Earlier chapters of this volume contain an argument that heaven in 1 Enoch 1–36 was modeled not on the Jerusalem temple but on the court of Achaemenid or Seleucid kings, with the angels not fashioned after priests but after the courtiers of such a court, some of whom would have held military commands. The final part of this chapter brings this argument to its conclusion by arguing that the Enochic scribe or scribes responsible for 1 Enoch 1–36 were not connected with the temple. There are two phases to this argument: firstly, to show that there were scribes in Judea who were not associated with the temple and, secondly, to provide grounds for assigning the Enochic scribal group to those non-temple scribes.

Non-Temple Scribes in Judea

Historical evidence exists for the existence in Judea of a recognized category of temple scribe during the period under consideration. The formal recognition of such a category implies the existence of scribes who were not included within it.

An edict of Artaxerxes I (reigned 465–424 BCE) reported in 1 Esdras 8 describes a number of benefits for the Judeans who had returned to Judea from Babylon. Among them there is a tax exemption for temple personnel: "You are also informed that no tribute or any other tax is to be laid on any of the priests or Levites or temple singers or gatekeepers or temple servants or persons employed in this temple, and that no one has authority to impose any tax upon them (8:22; RSV)." The parallel passage in the Aramaic of Ezra (7:24) has "servants of this house of God" instead of "persons employed in this temple." Although the word "scribe" is not used, since there certainly were scribes working in the temple, they would have been exempted from tax.

The point becomes clearer, however, in two passages from Josephus. Book 11 of the *Judean Antiquities* reports a decree of Xerxes I (reigned 486–465 BCE) issued for the benefit of the Judeans who had returned from Babylon that contains the following: "And I enjoin you not to lay any treacherous imposition, or any tributes, upon their priests or Levites, or sacred singers, or porters, or sacred servants, and scribes of the temple" (*JA* 11.120–138 at 128). The second Josephus passage comes much closer in time to the writing of 1 Enoch. According to Josephus, because the Judeans sided with the Seleucid king Antiochus III in his conflict with Ptolemy for possession of Palestine (202–195 BCE), he rewarded them afterwards, as set out in a letter he sent known as the Seleucid Charter (*JA* 12.138–44). One of the benefits mentioned in the letter was a tax exemption for certain temple personnel, namely, "the priests and scribes of the temple" (οἱ ἱερεῖς καὶ γραμματεῖς τοῦ ἱεροῦ) and the temple-singers (12:142)."[116] Schams (who omits mention of the similar passage in *JA* 11.128) has suggested that this indicates either that "a class of scribes existed in association with the temple, or at least that Antiochus III thought that such a class existed."[117] She considers, on the basis of some other (unspecified, but perhaps including *JA* 11.128) evidence from the Persian period that scribes functioned in the temple, that the former alternative is more likely. She also argues that since the detail of temple scribes does not enhance the literary aims of Josephus it is unlikely he would have invented it.[118] Yet she suggests that the scribes may have "fulfilled a variety of functions in the temple without being recognized as a class."

While Schams' broad acceptance of temple scribes as historical is reasonable, her use of the word "class" here is confusing and unnecessary. It is enough to say that the statement quoted from the Seleucid Charter indicates

---

116. Josephus, *JA* 12:142.
117. Schams 1998:90.
118. Ibid.

(a) that there were some scribes who did work in the temple, that they were, in effect "licensed" for this purpose, whether they did other work or not, and (b) that they received a tax exemption. It follows from the way in which the Charter focuses on these particular scribes, however, that there were some scribes who did not work in or for the temple. Of the total number of scribes in Jerusalem and the rest of Judea, this means that there was an important distinction between those who had a relationship with the temple and those who did not. Here we encounter a text-book in-group/out-group dichotomy of the sort that lies at the heart of social identity theory.

According to Karel van der Toorn, the Hebrew Bible was the product of a literate, scribal elite and the scribes who manufactured it "were professional writers affiliated to the temple in Jerusalem."[119] Given the division just observed between scribes working for the temple and those who were not, however, there is really no basis for asserting such an affiliation of all scribes responsible for biblical texts, or extra-biblical texts like 1 Enoch 1–36, with the temple. In Emar, during a period of about 140 years, the surviving evidence indicates that there were about forty scribes who drafted everyday legal documents, together with more than a dozen scholarly scribes and their students. The bulk of the surviving tablets come from one scribal family. When one remembers the very wide range of transactions that were recorded in writing, it is obvious that there was a very large amount of work available for scribes in the private sector and therefore no need for them to be employed in temple contexts. This pattern was repeated among Judeans between about 800 and 500 years later, as evident in the legal papyri that have been unearthed at the Judean mercenary settlement in Elephantine (fifth century BCE), in the Samaria papyri (c. 375 BCE) and in the papyri from the Dead Sea area (roughly 50–200 CE), the Babatha archive above all (94–132 CE). If a provincial center like Emar needed at least fifty scribes and scholars (and there could well have been more) over a century and a half to perform the necessary writing tasks, we should regard Jerusalem as also requiring a considerable number of scribes. The fact that at Emar a scribal school was located in a private house as opposed to a temple and that scribes worked on a variety of documents, with the great majority focusing on general commercial and legal transactions, provides a further caution against assuming an affiliation of all Israelite scribes to the temple in Jerusalem.

It is worth noting that a potentially huge source of public work for Judean scribes in Judea, in Jerusalem especially, apart from the temple, was provided during this period by the Seleucid administration.[120] As G. G.

---

119. Van der Toorn 2007:1.
120. On Ptolemaic administration, see Bagnall 1976.

Aperghis has shown,[121] the Seleucid kings were very efficient in extracting tribute, rent, and taxes from subject peoples. Some of this money was deployed on city-building and the maintenance of armies, and involved minting of coins and sophisticated financial administration. The Seleucid presence in Jerusalem through most of the relevant period would have meant that large numbers of documents of a wide variety of types would have required drafting. More work could have come from officers and soldiers of the Seleucid army in Judea, including Jerusalem.

The Enochic Scribal Group as Non-Temple Scribes

The second phase of the argument for the non-temple nature of the Enochic scribal group involves proffering evidence that they were included within the larger number of non-temple scribes we now may be confident existed in Judea. First of all, there is evidence external to 1 Enoch 1–36 already mentioned. Sirach, as noted above, was penned by a pro-temple and pro-temple cult author (whom we should regard as associated with a group of like-minded persons) who attacks what are probably Enochic works. It is unlikely, although not (admittedly) impossible, that such a confrontation would occur if the Enochic scribes were temple scribes. The most likely explanation is that there we have an example of an author bringing to the surface an underlying inter-group conflict, between one group of scribes that is associated with the temple and another that is not.

The second area of evidence comes from the Enochic corpus, in particular from the Apocalypse of Weeks, which was the Enochic work written after the Astronomical Book and the Book of the Watchers and is to be dated to 175–170 BCE. In this work the sixth week concludes with events in 587 BCE: the burning of the temple and the exile of the people (93:8). The seventh week covers the next period, which we know involved the return of some of the people to Judea and the re-building of the temple. If the Enochic scribal group was associated with the temple, this week would include these events, which were found so stirring by other Judean authors (see Ezra and Nehemiah). But this is not at all what we find. Here is how the author of the Apocalypse of Weeks describes the seventh week:

> After this, in the seventh week, there will arise a perverse generation,
> and many will be its deeds,
> and all its deeds will be perverse.
> And at its conclusion, the chosen will be chosen,

---

121. Aperghis 2004.

> as witnesses of righteousness from the everlasting plant of righteousness. to whom will be given sevenfold wisdom and knowledge. (93:9-10)[122]

It is hard to credit that a temple scribe would have produced a picture like this, in which the temple is not even mentioned and where everything to do with the period is portrayed as buried in perversity. Instead, all of the Judeans are treated as a wicked outgroup, with the ingroup (the Enochic scribal group) arising at the end of this period as witnesses of righteousness. This text renders it unlikely in the extreme that the Enochic scribes were associated with the temple.

CONCLUSION

From this discussion I conclude that some time in the third century BCE (or earlier) a group of scribes formed whose core beliefs encompassed some old Babylonian astronomical learning and also the role of Enoch as acquainted with such knowledge and as a revealer of heavenly mysteries by virtue of his being with God. They saw in Enoch an exemplar of their group and aligned their identity with his, both in relation to their being scribes but also as proponents of righteousness and truth. These were not temple scribes, but rather scribes who were active in drafting documents for other clients, either private persons or possibly agents of the Seleucid (and, perhaps from the mid second century BCE onwards, the Hasmonean) administration. Work for the political authorities in Judea may have taken some of them to the Seleucid capital and royal court in Antioch-on-the-Orontes prior to the 160s BCE, and after that they would have had first hand experience of the Hasmonean court in Jerusalem until 63 BCE, when the Romans intervened.

This group persisted for some 300 years, periodically producing new works that responded to the changing context in Judea, while preserving the earlier texts their predecessors had composed. To revert to the discussion of ethnic identity in Chapter 1 of this volume, these scribes were ethnic Judeans who would have been caught up in the various indicators of Judean ethnic identity discussed there, only one of which included matters to do with the temple and its cult. Since they were not temple scribes and since there is evidence of tension between their group and the pro-temple group represented by Sirach in the early second century BCE, while the early Apocalypse of Weeks exhibits a profoundly negative attitude to the temple, it is highly unlikely that they would have reached for the model of the Jerusalem temple and its priests in portraying heaven in 1 Enoch 1-36.

---

122. ET Nickelsburg and VanderKam 2012:140.

Instead, the person or persons responsible for 1 Enoch 1–36 utilized a model from the politics of their day, although one with which Judeans had been familiar for centuries, from the time of the exile in the sixth century BCE. This was the royal courts of the Achaemenid and Seleucid kings. The Enochic scribes portrayed God like a Persian king, as an aloof monarch in the throne-room of his palace,[123] separated from but accompanied and watched over by courtiers in the form of angels, some of whom had very senior portfolios and also military responsibilities.

The artist of the thirteenth century painting of Raphael in the monastic church in Gorgora on Lake Tana, shown on the cover of this volume and discussed in the Prologue, understood this. His Raphael is no priest but a sword-bearing military leader and senior servant of his king, poised in the very moment of executing his master's will by ensuring that righteousness will prevail in this particular place on earth. Thus the tradition of Ethiopian Christianity, here expressed in overwhelming visual form, accurately captured the meaning of heaven in 1 Enoch 1–36 in a manner that has hitherto eluded modern scholarly discussion.

---

123. For a new artistic representation of this scene (in 1 Enoch 14), see the painting by Angus Pryor on the cover of Esler 2017a.

8

CONCLUSION
God's Court and Courtiers in the Book of the Watchers

Some time in the third century BCE (or maybe earlier) a Judean scribe from among a scribal group not attached to the Jerusalem temple produced, in the name of Enoch, an Aramaic text now called the Book of the Watchers or, with respect to the larger Enochic corpus that eventually developed, 1 Enoch 1–36. Chapter 1 in this volume addresses a number of issues that help establish the broad framework within which the presentation of heaven in the text can be usefully examined.

First Enoch 1–36 was probably written a little later than another text by an Enochic scribe: the Astronomical Book, or 1 Enoch 72–82. In writing the Book of the Watchers, and in particular the cosmic journeying of Enoch in its second half, the scribe presupposed a body of astronomical lore of the sort that is set out in an orderly and detailed way in the Astronomical Book. The scribal group responsible for these texts were drawing upon, and obviously very proud of possessing, this astronomical tradition. This is in spite of, or perhaps because of, its representing astronomical knowledge from Babylon that was already out of date in the third century BCE.

The fundamental interest of the scribe responsible for 1 Enoch 1–36 was the co-existence of God and the evil that beset human beings and the earth itself. This was a situation demanding divine action to reward the righteous and punish the wicked. Not only was this a theological interest, but it arguably remains the central problem for theology. The existence of evil was so pressing for the author and for his audience that the first substantive section of the book contains an elaborate description of how and why God will deal with it (1:2—5:9). This passage itself begins with a prediction of God's appearance at the end-time leading a war-band of myriads of angels to achieve his righteous purpose (1:4-9). The author seems to have wished to reassure his audience that all would turn out for the good eventually, in spite of the horrors in the meantime that he was about to relate.

As the vehicle for writing about this concern the author took a giant leap of theological and literary imagination, not least entailing the invention of the apocalyptic genre. Amalgamating the figure of Enoch in Gen 5:18-24 (probably developed in light of the Babylonian king Enmeduranki), a modified version of Gen 6:1-4 (embellished with some version of the Prometheus myth), and a body of astronomical learning, he composed a narrative of the fall of the Watchers, the consequences for humanity and the earth, and God's response. He also made Enoch an active agent in that response (1 Enoch 1-16). With Enoch firmly in the frame, the author completed the text with an account of Enoch being taken on a tour of the cosmos accompanied by archangels as guides (1 Enoch 17-36).

A central interest of 1 Enoch 1-36 is the role of heaven in the work. Heaven includes the place itself (with its architecture), the characters to be found there and the role of the place and these characters in the narrative. Plausible interpretation of the text as a whole benefits from close scrutiny of its presentation of heaven. Existing scholarship, however, in seeking to interpret heaven in the text, almost universally proceeds on the basis that the relevant entity within which to frame the discussion is "Judaism," by and large meaning a religion whose adherents were "Jews," which is how the *Ioudaioi* of our sources are usually (although decreasingly) translated. The arrival of a widespread and social-science informed interest in group identities on our social and intellectual scene in the last few decades has established the case for regarding "Judaism" as a category error in relation to the *Ioudaioi* of the ancient Mediterranean. Fusing the social identity theory of Henri Tajfel with insights into ethnic identity originating with Fredrik Barth has delivered powerful theoretical resources for probing ancient identities. Within this new approach the *Ioudaioi* were the members of an ethnic group, not the adherents of a religion. Even the concept of "religion" has come under sustained attack as inappropriate for this setting by writers such as Carlin Barton, Daniel Boyarin, Steve Mason, Brent Nongbri, and myself.

As an ethnic group, the *Ioudaioi* were similar in many respects to numerous other such groups in their world, like the Romans, Greeks ("Hellenes"), Egyptians, Parthians, Scythians, and so on. This is central to the argument Josephus maintains in his *Contra Apionem*. All these groups were identified by a common proper name (in every case based on the name of their homeland), possessed shared myths of ancestry and a shared history, enjoyed a common culture (covering language, customs and religious phenomena, especially in the form of a state-sponsored cult), were linked to a homeland whether they lived there or in diaspora communities, and felt a sense of communal solidarity.

The appropriate translation for *Ioudaioi* is "Judeans" since this word preserves the link to the homeland, Judea, from which the name derived. But—to correct a common misconception—this is an ethnic designation not a geographic one; that is, it refers to a person's land of origin, whether he or she currently resides there or not. Translating *Ioudaioi* as "Jews" severs this connection with the homeland that was central to their sense of identity (as it was for all other ethnic groups) and leaves one with a designation for this kind of group unlike any other in the ancient Mediterranean. Such exceptionalism constitutes a warning sign that later issues concerning this people are being anachronistically retrojected back onto them in a manner that makes it harder to understand them with historical accuracy in their own setting. In saying this, however, I acknowledge that today's Jews are the cultural, religious and in many cases biological descendants of the ancient Judeans and form one group with them.

The currently dominant stream in the interpretation of heaven in 1 Enoch 1–36 is that it reflects the Jerusalem temple, especially to the extent that the angels and even Enoch are viewed as priests. Taking this kind of interpretative step, by explaining one area of experience in terms of another, can be understood using the theory of metaphor developed by George Lakoff and Mark Johnson. Insisting that metaphors are not just rhetorical ornamentation but crucial to the functioning of our conceptual system, Lakoff and Johnson distinguish the "source domain" from the "target domain." The target domain is typically less concrete and more abstract than its source. This approach is applicable not merely to common metaphors in everyday speech, but to imaginative structures such as fables and other literary structures. On the current view just mentioned, heaven would be the target domain and the Jerusalem temple would the source domain—I say "would be" because the proponents of this view do not use this framework in their research. While Lakoff and Johnson's theory of metaphor is adopted in this book, the notion of the Jerusalem temple as the source domain proves repeatedly and fatally problematic. The main problem with this view (especially relevant to the defection of the Watchers considered below) is that attempts to find in the text signs that angels are like priests, with the Watchers representing priests who have married the wrong women, rest on very strained interpretations of the textual data. They also presuppose the

Conclusion 191

erroneous idea that the relevant social entity is the "religion" of "Judaism" when it is really the Judean ethnic group.

Further weakening the likelihood of the heaven-as-temple view is that, when ancient Israelite authors reasonably close in time to the composition of 1 Enoch 1–36 did wish to present heaven as a temple, they left the reader in no doubt of their intentions. Thus in the *Songs of the Sabbath Sacrifice* and the *Testament of Levi* there is express mention of heaven as a temple, of God in the holy of holies, and of the angels as priests, who offer sacrifice that produces a fragrant smell. That the author of the *Testament of Levi* has used 1 Enoch 1–36 and yet needed to add such features to his own narrative—because they were not to be found there—speaks volumes.

When one seeks to identify a likely source domain for the depiction of heaven in 1 Enoch 1–36, one possible candidate that suggests itself is the divine council known especially from the mythological texts from Ugarit, which has echoes in arguably similar phenomena attributed to Yahweh in the Hebrew Bible. Obstacles to finding a source for the Enochic heaven in the Ugaritic divine council, however, subsist in the fact that God is far above the angels in status and that the discussions that characterize a council are not really to be found in the Book of the Watchers. Lowell Handy has suggested a way forward by proposing that the council of Ugarit was itself modeled on the "bureaucracy" of Ugarit and other cities in its setting. He has pointed to the differentiated and hierarchical arrangement of gods in the Ugaritic pantheon that reflects a "bureaucratic" organisation. Although the notion of bureaucracy is a form of administrative arrangement that developed in the modern period and is not really at home in the ancient world, Handy's insight in suggesting that a form of ancient political organization might have provided the source domain for a representation of heaven is very helpful. But we need to find the right one.

The thesis argued for in this volume is that the source domain relied upon by the author of the Book the Watchers, when it came to understanding heaven, was that of a king in his royal court surrounded by his courtiers. There are occasional references in the scholarship to the Enochic heaven as a court, but the idea is never developed nor taken with the seriousness that it deserves. This neglect reflects the prevalence of "Judaism" as the broad interpretative framework, when we should rather be thinking of the Judean ethnic group. Moreover, the likelihood that the Enochic author employed the ancient royal court as a source domain for his portrayal of God in heaven, and thus had a positive view of such an institution, provides further reason to doubt current scholarly views that in apocalyptic texts like 1 Enoch 1–36 we have discourses "against empire" or against imperial oppression.

Recent years have witnessed the emergence of a new area of historical investigation that focuses on the courts and courtiers of absolute monarchs, ancient and modern. Chapter 2 provides an overview of this research that sets out a social-scientific model applied in the interpretation of particular features of the 1 Enoch 1–36 in later chapters. Interest in royal courts was inspired by the publication of Norbert Elias' *Court Society*, a sociological study of the courts of the *ancien régime* (especially that of Louis XIV). This work advocated close attention to the court as a system of power relations structured by unwritten rules governing the relationships between king and courtiers. Extant information on the workings of Persian and Hellenistic monarchies reveals numerous examples of all the phenomena Elias investigated.

For Elias the court served as the household of the royal family and also provided the central organ for the administration of the state. It was a mixture of spatial framework and social figuration. Within the court were taken decisions that affected the whole kingdom. The members of the court were the king and his family, senior officials or "courtiers" with specific responsibilities who were often arranged in hierarchical order (above all in the distinction between an "inner" and an "outer" court), and lower-status people, servants, bodyguards and so on. Often also to be found there were visitors in the form of sages (either as tutors to the king's children or as recipients of his patronage so that learning might flourish) or envoys of foreign powers. Senior courtiers had access to the king, in particular to provide him with information and advice and to receive his instructions. Since the ultimate basis of the king's power to rule lay in his possessing an army loyal to him, some of his senior courtiers were often given military commands. Fundamental to the whole system was the high status that accrued to courtiers by virtue of their membership of the court. This status subsisted in large part in the social distance that existed between those who were members of the court and the others in the kingdom who were not.

Although the court could persist for generations or even centuries, it was not static. The position of courtiers was constantly changing and sometimes the court experienced major convulsions. Nevertheless, persist it usually did, mainly because of the inter-dependence of king and courtiers. The courtiers needed the king to maintain their positions, but he needed them to carry out his instructions. The king's dependence on his courtiers was greater the more isolated he kept himself from his people (the Achaemenid kings offering an extreme example of this). In particular, the greater a king's isolation the more he needed to obtain accurate intelligence on what was happening in his kingdom. While much of this was provided by courtiers, another prominent means of obtaining information took the form of written memoranda, petitions, provided to courtiers by the king's subjects for submission to the king and action if he thought fit. Courtiers thus fulfilled a central role in operating as mediators between the king and his subjects.

These phenomena of the court were accompanied by a major emphasis on representation and display, on "image-management." This took various forms, especially costumes, ceremonies (including those controlling access to the king's person) and architecture. The palace of the king, with its throne-room and throne, and the large apartments of senior courtiers constituted a vital *locus* for such display.

Norbert Elias' sociological approach to courts and courtiers finds abundant comparative material in 1 Enoch 1–36, and this material is considered in Chapter 3 of this volume. God is explicitly presented as a king, indeed as king of kings and as an absolute monarch, capable of ruling without help from anyone. Many other titles are attributed to him in the text, including "lord," a designation often used of other ancient kings. Although God has no family, he still needs somewhere to live, and the text speaks of his "dwelling" and "house" in heaven. We should not, however, regard the emphasis on the kingship of God as self-evident, when other types of political rule were known in this world.

As with other kings, in God's abode decisions were made that shaped the destiny of his kingdom. These decisions extended to heaven and earth and revealed God's kingship over both, even though the expression "kingdom of God" does not appear. Heaven is the center of the administration of the kingdom. Like every king, God needs and has an army. This is starkly announced at the beginning of the text in the mighty army of angels God will lead to earth at the End to conquer evil permanently. Although there are several portrayals in the Hebrew Bible of God acting as a warrior, none of them matches the clarity and force of God leading his army in the Book of the Watchers.

The prominent designation for the angelic beings in heaven is "Watchers." The primary reference in the word is their function of "watching," meaning to perform their duty as guards in heaven, on station on its walls, to survey creation, including the earth, for problems which may arise. Heaven is also where the angels live, permanently, a factor that distinguishes them from the Jerusalem priests who came up to the temple during their courses or for the big festivals and then returned home. The angels are differentiated in three main ways: between (a) those who abandoned heaven and those who stayed; (b) those named and those unnamed; and (c) those with specific responsibilities (especially the archangels) and those without. Named angels with important roles appear to have had privileged access to God, just like the "inner court" in other absolute monarchies, ancient and early modern. None of the responsibilities allocated to the major angels in 1 Enoch 20 has anything to do with cultic activity. This feature is inconsistent with the author's understanding of heaven as a temple.

The other member of the heavenly court is Enoch himself. The text elaborates on Enoch's being taken by God in Gen 5:24 in a manner that homologates his position to that of the sages who were often to be found in ancient courts. An ancient audience would probably have understood him to have been a righteous scribe before his translation to heaven. While he was there, however, he received instruction in the secrets of the cosmos from angelic guides, secrets that he was most curious to learn and some of which he wrote down. Such a picture of Enoch has no connection with the functions of a priest. On the other hand, it certainly does serve to legitimate the distinctive astronomical knowledge of the Enochic scribal group.

As with the courtiers in Louis XIV's Versailles, the angels in heaven acquired identity and status from their position. In heaven they had an eternal station, which the Watchers who departed from heaven abandoned. They were eternal spiritual beings who improperly joined with mortal physical ones in the form of human women. This transgression of boundaries, as explained by Mary Douglas in *Purity and Danger,* represents "impurity" and "defilement" of the sort frequently attributed to them in the text. The court model explains their predicament in way that the temple-and-priests model does not.

Like other courts, the Enochic heaven persisted over time. Equally like them, however, it was subject to change, of which the defection of the Watchers from heaven and the action that had to be taken from heaven as a result would prove to be the most dramatic example. This change occurred in a social context where the angels were not anonymous. Many of them are named and are differentiated by responsibility or action. Elias' notion of a "social figuration" is appropriate for the angels because it encompasses relationships that are cordial on the one hand, and tense and difficult on the other.

Just as kings, like the Persian monarchs, could exist in splendid isolation from their subjects, so too did God. Unlike other kings, God needed no counsellor, but he had them anyway. There were even angels stationed on the ramparts of heaven gazing, at least in part, on earth and reporting to him what they saw. Thus in 1 Enoch 9 the archangels offer God advice on the dire events on earth, even though they concede he knew this anyway. So the form of a typical royal court is preserved, even if God has more knowledge than any other king. Some angels, the archangels most certainly, did have privileged access to him, although there is no justification for discovering any cultic dimensions to this. This was simply the way an ancient court worked, where members of the inner court had personal contact with the king and members of the outer court did not.

A notable feature of the Book of the Watchers is the phenomenon of appeals being made to heaven. This happens either directly and orally, as in the case of the earth and its inhabitants in thrall to the murderous Giants (and the spirit of Abel complaining about Cain), or in writing and through the services of a mediator, as when the Watchers ask Enoch to write a petition to God that he forgive them, a petition God denies. Current explanations view this phenomenon as based on Israelites asking priests to intercede with God on their behalf. But priests in the Jerusalem temple did not act in this way and the idea of a priest penning a written petition to God has no basis in evidence. Yet if we resort to the source domain of court and courtiers a highly probable explanation emerges. Ancient monarchs (and lesser administrative figures) regularly received petitions from their subjects via mediators. It was, indeed, a regular function of courtiers to act as mediators (on behalf of cities, for example) bringing such petitions to the attention of the king. The language used of both informal and oral, and formal and written, petitions in 1 Enoch 1–36 closely matches the language used of these petitions in ancient Greek literature and papyri. If any feature of 1 Enoch 1–36 provides an unanswerable objection to the temple and priests model being operative in the text, it is this.

The subject of Chapter 4 is the narrative of the most dramatic events in 1 Enoch 1–36. This concerns the secession of the Watchers from heaven to marry human women on earth and the consequences of this action, as the giant progeny that result ravage the earth and its inhabitants, and the secrets the Watchers reveal to human beings cause other problems. Existing attempts to explain this (by scholars such as George Nickelsburg, David Suter, and Martha Himmelfarb) find in it a reflection of the actions of priests in the temple in Jerusalem who have married the wrong type of women, either the wrong Israelite women or foreigners. On examination, the various arguments put forward to maintain this position prove lacking. That the Watchers defiled themselves by taking on human wives does not connect to cultic issues. It relates to the illicit crossing of social boundaries. Focusing on the defilement suffered by the angels also leaves far too much of the text unaccounted for. In addition, language that refers to heaven as holy is tortured into references to a "sanctuary" or "temple." Equally problematic are attempts to impute cultic features to 1 Enoch 1–36 because these features are to be found in other Israelite texts roughly contemporaneous with that work, which appear to hold it in high regard.

A more promising line of investigation into the secession of the Watchers fixes upon its relationship to the social realities of royal courts.

A king's control of his kingdom was subject to external threats, through invasion by foreign powers, and internal threats, in the form of rebellion. The French court was ultimately swept away by the Revolution at the end of the eighteenth century. But "rebellion" does not just mean organised, armed resistance to the government ("the first sense"), but also open and determined defiance of or resistance to any authority ("the second sense"). In the latter sense it extends to defiance to rules and accepted ways of behaving, as well as to people in authority. Although it has been suggested that the context for the action of the Watchers and the Giants they fathered lies in the wars among Alexander's successors at the end of the fourth century BCE, a more likely explanation is to be found in the phenomenon of revolt by courtiers for which there is abundant evidence amongst Persian and Hellenistic monarchies.

The Behistun Inscription of Darius the Great provides examples of revolts by courtiers (with gruesome punishments meted out upon the rebels), as do the Hellenistic kingdoms in the third century BCE. Darius sometimes makes clear that the rebellions involved a breach of loyalty owed to him. Some of the Hellenistic instances were rebellions in the second sense, resistance to a king's authority and his rules rather than an organised armed attempt to topple him.

The idea that the source domain for the secession of the Watchers was the phenomenon of rebellion against Persian and Hellenistic monarchs, but in the second sense (determined resistance to authority), is a very plausible one, not least because of the structural similarity between the two situations. The narrative of the Watchers, on its face, looks like a rebellion by courtiers against their king's rules. The oath the Watchers swear locates the narrative in the wider eddies of ancient politics. Examination reveals that the "great sin" that the Watchers openly acknowledge they will be committing (1 Enoch 6:3) subsists precisely in this act of rebellion. It is concerned solely with their initial action in leaving heaven. They have breached the divine order of things, in that heaven is for immortal and spiritual beings such as the angels and the earth for mortal and physical human beings (1 Enoch 15:3–7). Just as with the courtiers of Louis XIV, remaining at court was necessary for the identity, status and, ultimately, the salvation of the Watchers. One feature that differentiates God's response to this rebellion from those that Darius the Great confronted is that there is no sign of any personal investment in what the Watchers have done. The question of whether they have been disloyal does not arise, presumably because God is so far above them that he cannot be personally engaged by such behavior. There are actually two aspects to their rebellion. Firstly, that they have gone absent without leave and have abandoned their post. In addition, this means that they have left the place where they should be living. Like Louis XIV, God wanted his courtiers to share his residence and he is aggrieved that they have left it. Secondly, they have incurred impurity and defilement. This is not a matter connected with the cult. Rather, as Mary Douglas has pointed out, impurity consists of the breach of social boundaries and occurs when a person or thing is in the wrong place. The Watchers breached a fundamental boundary—one erected by God—when, as spiritual and eternal beings, they coupled with physical and mortal ones.

The consequences of the Watchers' rebellion fall within two categories: firstly, the actions of the Giants and, secondly, the actions of human beings in consequence of the knowledge revealed to them by the Watchers.

Evidence for or relevant to ancient rebellions in Persian and Hellenistic kingdoms does include data reasonably similar to the first category. Women were left pregnant when raped by the soldiers in armies that captured the cities and towns in which they lived. Invading armies consumed the food supplies and other goods of the territories they moved across. Rebels confiscated lands, murdered people who blocked their path to success or exiled them to other lands.

In relation to the second category of consequences, the Watchers' revelation of secrets also finds a close ancient parallel—in the Promethean myth. Prometheus also engaged in rebellion in the second sense (determined resistance to authority and rules) against his king, Zeus, by disregarding the latter's instruction not to help human beings in that he gave them the precious gift of fire that allowed human civilisation to advance. Like Prometheus, Asael revealed mysteries that should have remained in heaven (1 Enoch 9:6).

God's response to the rebellion of the Watchers closely parallels the behavior of ancient Persian and Hellenistic kings in putting down revolts. The Watchers were courtiers who had entirely fallen out of favor with their king. The savage punishment and death that Darius heaped upon the rebel Tritantaechmes finds strong echoes in how God orders the archangels to deal with the Watchers and the Giants (1 Enoch 10). Asael is to be bound, buried in the earth and eventually killed. Shemihazah and the others with him are to see their "beloved sons," the Giants, perishing and they too are to be bound, tortured and killed. The few differences between God and Darius are to be explained by the fact that God is God. The author of 1 Enoch 1–36 is working with his eye to the broad political world of ancient kingdoms and the rebellions that sometimes convulsed them, not to the far narrower setting of the temple and its cult.

One aspect of the model of the royal court covered in Chapter 2 was the importance of image-management by the king. Central to this process were the spatial and architectural arrangements of the palace. Chapter 5 is occupied with a consideration of this issue. The starting-point is the extremely common view in current Enochic scholarship that the architectural structure of heaven is modeled on that of the Jerusalem temple. From the outset it seems that the whole enterprise of arguing that heaven replicates a terrestial temple inverts the true position. Ancient Near Eastern peoples believed that the gods lived in heaven and that temples on earth were copies of that reality. This suggests the need to interpret the Enochic heaven on its own terms rather than too easily regarding it as modeled on the temple in Jerusalem. It is also necessary to remember that a king's palace was often to be found close to a temple and that the former was often larger than the latter. Such a situation reflected the social and political superiority of the monarch, vis-à-vis temple priests and his own courtiers.

Textual analysis of 1 Enoch 14:8–23 brings out both the nature of the architecture of heaven and also the character of God's presentation in that context. Integral to understanding the text is the recognition that the narrative has a clearly expressed and realistic sequential logic. By this is meant that, following Enoch's translation to heaven in 1 Enoch 14:8, he moves in an orderly way—that corresponds to the spatial and architectural realities—from heaven's outer reaches to a room in a building from which he observes God in the next room. This is the case even though he encounters paradoxical and extraordinary architectural features during his progression. The realistic sequential logic of 1 Enoch 14 stands in sharp contrast to another Israelite text descriptive of heaven, the *Songs of the Sabbath Sacrifice*, which instead highlights the number seven in its arrangement of the features of heaven.

Following Enoch's remarkable transportation to heaven courtesy of clouds, mists, shooting stars, lightning flashes, and winds (1 Enoch 14:8), he goes in (meaning he crosses space) until he comes to a structure that is best interpreted as the perimeter wall of heaven. It is built of hailstones encircled with tongues of fire. This conclusion involves sorting out some textual problems in the Greek version (here from the Akhmim manuscript) in relation to another Greek version that underlies the Ethiopic reading. Even in the Akhmim Greek version, however, the wall that Enoch encounters is called a τεῖχος, which meant the wall of a town, not of a house or building. Enoch is to be understood as passing through one of the gates of the outer wall of heaven, with the gates (that necessarily imply a wall) mentioned elsewhere in the Book of the Watchers. This conclusion excludes the suggestion that Enoch has encountered a structure that is modeled on the vestibule of the Jerusalem temple, one of the three contiguous rooms of which it was composed: vestibule-nave-holy of holies.

Enoch then approaches a "great house" which he describes from the outside (before he enters it). This means he has crossed open space between the wall and the house, which provides further evidence that the first structure he came to was not a vestibule of a temple-shaped edifice. Since Enoch does not enter the "great house" until v. 13, the translation of features of the building should reflect the fact that he is observing it from outside. Hence he sees its "groundworks" (not "floor") and its "upper storeys" (not "ceiling"). The cherubim on the outside of this building are probably actual (protective) angels and not just decorative paintings or reliefs. The source for such an idea is more likely to lie in the large carved genies that protected palaces in Mesopotamia (such as that found at the palace of Sargon II of Assyria at Khorsabad [Figure 5.1]) than in Ezek 41:18–20.

When Enoch enters this "great house" he discovers it also paradoxically integrates fire and snow. He has an experience of the numinous, as fear and trembling seize him. Through another door in this "house" he sees a larger "house" or room, contiguous to the one he is in (he will soon report that God sits in that room on his throne). By taking into account the spatial and architectural details provided to this point in the narrative, it is possible to draw the arrangement of the wall and the building that Enoch comes across. This drawing is Figure 5.2.

Royal image-maintenance, but in a manner appropriate to a divine king, is very evident in the room in which God sits on a throne. This room is naturally interpreted as the throne-room of a royal palace, with Enoch located in an antechamber to it. Unlike the temple in Jerusalem, there is no veil that separates the two rooms. This is yet another sign that it is not modeled on the holy of holies in the Jerusalem temple.

An important aspect of God's throne and his apparel is their representation in terms of the sun. The divine throne has the "roundness" of the sun; it does not have "wheels," an error found in many translations, and is not dependent on the divine *kābôd*-conveyance in Ezekiel. Furthermore, God's apparel is like the appearance of the sun. This solar imagery is to be explained as deriving from the interest of the Enochic tradition in Mesopotamian astronomy by scribes who also utilised the report in Gen 5:23–24 that Enoch lived for 365 years before he was taken by God. This is of course the same number of days as in a solar year (although, based on Enoch 72:32, the Enochic scribes may have thought it was 364 days).

The aim of Chapter 6 is to conclude the project of differentiating the architecture of heaven in 1 Enoch 1–36 from that of the temple in Jerusalem and to propose that a more likely source domain is to be found in the palaces of Achaemenid and Hellenistic kings, with "Palace S" in the capital of Cyrus the Great at Pasargadae offering a particularly instructive comparator. The temple in Jerusalem, with which the scribe or scribes who produced 1 Enoch 1–36 would have been familiar, was that erected by Zerubabbel at the end of Exile (and later substantially remodeled by Herod the Great). Although there is little, if any, physical evidence remaining of this building, on the basis of the surviving literary evidence it is reasonable to assume that it was similar to that built by Solomon. This would mean that it was a structure of three contiguous rooms: the vestibule, the nave and the holy of holies. God's dwelling as described in 1 Enoch 14 differs from this in five important respects. Whereas the Jerusalem temple had three rooms, the Enochic structure had two. Although in the temple the holy of holies was smaller than the nave, in the Enochic structure the second "room" was larger than the first. In the Enochic building there was no veil at the entrance between the two rooms. In the Enochic structure, unlike the Jerusalem temple, there was an actual throne on which God sat. Finally, the Enochic structure lacked an altar. There are two areas of similarity, in that both structures had a wall around them and cherubim appeared on their walls, but both are explicable and do not detract from the fundamental differences between the two buildings. The fact that the author did not represent God's dwelling in terms of the temple in Jerusalem, when he could so easily have done so, is positive evidence against his having any interest in portraying other aspects of heaven (such as the angels being priests) as modeled on the temple.

Achaemenid and Hellenistic royal palaces were an expression of kingship, royal power and political control. They tended to be in a walled precinct for security reasons and they also contained a throne-room. We have the same arrangement in 1 Enoch 14. An instructive possible source domain for the representation of the Enochic architecture of heaven is to be found in Pasargadae, the capital that Cyrus the Great commenced building in about 546 BCE. Its central area was a walled precinct, entered through a massive gate structure ("Gate R"), containing two palaces, one with a large central room ("Palace S") and the other, a larger structure ("Palace P"), where the king and his family lived. This capital could have been known to Judeans from personal experience or report. Even if it is not the actual source of inspiration for the Enochic heaven, it is a fine example of how our imaginations can be liberated from the temple paradigm as soon as we turn our gaze in the direction of more plausible structures associated with royal courts.

Palace S, which is best regarded as an audience-hall or a palace of audience, consisted of a high, central hypostyle hall, surrounded by a building of lower height (Figure 6.7). It would have contained a throne when the king was using it.

God's dwelling in 1 Enoch 14 exhibits marked similarities to Palace S. In both cases one must first pass through a wall to gain access to the building where the king is to be found. The structures both have two rooms (not three) and the first room one enters is smaller than the second. The throne in the larger room would have been visible to people in the first room of the structure. Apart from a wall and a gate, there were no buildings adjacent to Palace S, just as God's dwelling in 1 Enoch 14 existed without neighboring edifices. A large carved genie that survives from Gate R indicates a possible source for the idea of cherubim on the walls of God's dwelling in 1 Enoch 14. While both Palace S and 1 Enoch 14 represent audacious efforts at royal image-management, the paradoxical combination of fire and ice attributed to the structures of the Enochic heaven produces an effect that transcends even the impressive architecture of Cyrus the Great.

In Chapter 7 I develop the detailed consideration of 1 Enoch 1–36 offered in previous chapters by addressing an issue that relates to the reason *why* in this text heaven is presented as a royal court. The answer lies in the nature of the scribe or scribes who produced this text and the other works in the Enochic corpus. It consists of the argument that 1 Enoch was composed over a long period of time by a group of scribes who, within a social identity perspective, regarded Enoch as an exemplar of their identity, but who were not connected to the temple in Jerusalem.

This first entails explaining the generation of the texts comprising 1 Enoch in their order of composition from the third century BCE (or earlier) to the first century CE. This was a tradition that evolved over approximately 300 years and was connected to Enoch from the very outset. But it was a tradition that also represented Enoch as a scribe, either expressly or by reference to his performance of scribal functions. The Hebrew Bible was not the source of the notion that Enoch was a scribe. Most probably, the authors were scribes who were possessed of a body of distinctive astronomical learning and who selected a venerable figure from the past, Enoch, to become their revered spokesperson.

Such a long tradition focused on Enoch raises the question of whether there was a collection of people who passed that tradition on over three centuries. While scholarship has been alive to this issue, the reliance on folk psychology in probing it, rather than seeking assistance in relevant social-scientific perspectives, has hampered its elucidation. Taking up the notion of the "group" as it is understood in that area of social psychology known as social identity theory, developed by Henri Tajfel and John Turner, offers an illuminating way forward. This approach requires that a group should be defined in terms of people's self-categorizations, although in many cases it will also be necessary that the group be known to other persons. In this theory "social identity" refers not to the nature of the group but to the identity each individual member derives from belonging to it. Thus understood, social identity has cognitive, evaluative and emotional dimensions. A group can exist for a long period, even if it changes the cultural features that differentiate it from other groups over time. From this perspective, group prototypes and exemplars are very significant. They describe how group norms are embodied in real or imagined members of the group. They are models that members must emulate in order to manifest in-group beliefs and behavior. Within the framework of social identity theory, Enoch was a scribe who possessed angelically revealed knowledge of the heavens and human history and who served as an exemplar for a particular group of scribes. By aligning themselves with Enoch so understood they distinguished themselves from other scribes and scribal groups.

Further support for the likelihood of a scribal group lying behind 1 Enoch exists in the group dimension of the book production in the ancient world. Modern views of the individual author, often construed as some form of "genius," are deeply anachronistic when projected back onto the ancient Mediterranean. There were pronounced communal and interactive dimensions to the authorship of ancient works. This consideration encourages us to think in terms of a plurality of people being involved in the production of each section of 1 Enoch over the centuries of its composition. In addition, that various parts appeared over some three centuries, and were redacted into a whole, supports the existence of people who took responsibility for this tradition across a considerable period of time.

The richly documented existence and practices of the scribes from Emar in northern Syria during the fourteenth to twelfth centuries BCE provide invaluable comparable material for understanding what a group of Enochic scribes might have been like. At Emar a large number of scribes, many from one family, were active in the production of a wide range of commercial and legal documents on the one hand, and cultic and scholarly texts on the other. Some of these scribes were not associated exclusively with either the palace or the temple. More generally, across Mesopotamia, scribes often traced their lineage back to famous authors who, though long dead, were still alive within scribal memory. It makes good sense to regard a group of scribes in an ancient city as forming a group in the social identity sense, with scribal families having a significant role in, or at times constituting, such a group.

Specific evidence for an Enochic scribal group exists. External to 1 Enoch is the evidence to be derived from Sirach. This is a text strongly aligned with the Jerusalem temple and the temple cult. Yet at several points it makes statements that seem direct contradictions of views expressed in 1 Enoch. Whereas in 1 Enoch, for example, the great wisdom represented by the Tree in the garden Enoch encounters on his journey is inaccessible to ordinary mortals, in Sirach Wisdom spreads out from Jerusalem to all mankind though the activity of sages like Ben Sira. As another example, 1 Enoch favors a solar calendar, but Sirach a lunisolar one. This kind of material is best explained on the basis that Ben Sira represented one group of (pro-temple) scribes, and the scribes handing on the Enochic tradition another. Evidence for an Enochic scribal group internal to 1 Enoch occurs in 1 Enoch 104:9–13. Here we encounter the phenomenon of rivals who refute the words of Enochic texts and write works in their own names (as opposed to the pseudepigraphic practice of the Enochic scribes). This indicates that there were outgroups in tension with the Enochic ingroup, so that the situation was one of fraught intergroup relationships upon which social identity theory focuses.

The manner in which Enoch is presented across the various parts of 1 Enoch, especially in relation to the theme of books and writing and his explicitly scribal role, strengthens the argument for the work's composition by a scribal group. That the tradition has designated a hero, a revealer of heavenly mysteries from the past, as a scribe suggests he corresponds to the self-designation of the members of this group.

The special nature of the astronomy in 1 Enoch, especially its rather ancient nature, and the fact that the patriarch Enoch has become a scribe even though he is not so described in Genesis, represent the principal aspects of the cognitive dimension of belonging to the Enochic group. Positive evaluative and emotional dimensions of belonging to the group were likely to have existed because of the elevated view the Enochic scribes took of themselves vis-à-vis other groups who did not have this relationship with Enoch. The fact that in later parts of the corpus Enoch mentions his sons and children means that this scribal group regarded Enoch as an ancestor, to whom they were closely tied, enjoying the honour that came from him just as all Israelites rejoiced in their descent from Abraham. Similarly, the designation of Enoch as righteous forms the basis for the group regarding itself as righteous. He was exemplary of the righteousness of the group as well as of its scribal character.

The final, and yet, in relation to the thesis of this volume, perhaps the most fundamental aspect of the Enochic scribal group was its lack of connection with the temple in Jerusalem. To make this case first involves demonstrating that there were scribes in Israel who were not attached to the temple. Although this is what we are led to expect from the activities of the scribes of Emar, primary evidence for it exists in literary evidence for a group of scribes who were associated with the temple. Temple scribes were recognizable as such so unmistakably that during certain periods this status exempted them from Seleucid taxation. This was the case under Antiochus

III at the beginning of the second century BCE, quite close to the time of the composition of 1 Enoch 1–36. The existence of one group of scribes who worked in the temple and were thus exempt from tax necessarily implies the existence of others who were not attached to or licensed by the temple. We know from the large amount of general commercial and legal documentation that needed to be drafted in a culture like this that there was plenty of work for scribes apart from whatever the temple provided. In addition, the administrative activity of the Seleucid administration ("the palace") would have provided a major source of public funding for scribes, including members of the Enochic group, apart from the temple. No doubt individual soldiers in the Seleucid army would also often have needed the assistance of scribes. Compelling evidence internal to 1 Enoch exists that the scribal group responsible for its composition and transmission were not temple scribes. This evidence emerges in how the Apocalypse of Weeks describes, in the Seventh Week, the period after the return from Exile when the temple was rebuilt. In this section of the text the temple is not even mentioned and everything related to the period is portrayed as immersed in perversity. All of the Judeans are treated as a wicked outgroup, with the exception of the ingroup (the Enochic scribal group) who emerge at the end of this period as witnesses of righteousness.

It is to this non-temple, Enochic scribal group then, that our thanks are due for the composition of 1 Enoch 1–36. That its author or authors depicted heaven not in terms of the temple in Jerusalem, but as a court with its king and courtiers, is an inevitable reflection of their lack of connection with the temple, indeed of their conflict with the scribes who were so connected. Yet the Enochic scribes were still Judeans and still familiar with Israelite tradition. Probably through work carried out for the Seleucid and then Hasmonean administrations, they were actively part of the wider world of Judean and other ethnic groups. Accordingly, when describing God in his heaven they naturally looked to the kings, courts and courtiers with whom they were familiar. The thirteenth century Ethiopian artist responsible for the painting of the archangel Raphael, in heavy military guise, reproduced on the cover of this volume, also had that world in mind when he created the image. It now deserves the close attention of Enochic scholarship.

BIBLIOGRAPHY

Albertz, Rainer. 1994. *A History of Israelite Religion in the Old Testament Period.* Vol. 2: *From the Exile to the Maccabees.* Translated by John Bowden. Old Testament Library. Louisville: Westminster John Knox.

Antohin, Alexandra Sellassie. 2014. "Expressions of Sacred Promise: Ritual and Devotion in Ethiopian Orthodox Praxis." PhD diss., University College London.

Aperghis, G. G. 2004. *The Seleukid Royal Economy: The Finances and Financial Administration of the Seleukid Empire.* Cambridge: Cambridge University Press.

Argall, Randal A. 1995. *1 Enoch and Sirach: A Comparative Literary and Conceptual Analysis of the Themes of Revelation, Creation, and Judgment.* SBL Early Judaism and Its Literature 8. Atlanta: Scholars.

———. 2002. "Competing Wisdoms: 1 Enoch and Sirach." In Boccaccini 2002:169–78.

Arnal, William E. 2001. *Jesus and the Village Scribes: Galilean Conflicts and the Setting of Q.* Minneapolis: Fortress.

Arnaud, D. 1985–1987. *Recherches au pays d'Astata: Emar VI: Les textes suměriens et accadiens.* 4 vols. Paris: ERC.

Aster, Shawn Zelig. 2006. "The Phenomenon of Divine and Human Radiance in the Hebrew Bible and in Northwest Semitic and Mesopotamian Literature: A Philological and Comparative Study." PhD diss., University of Pennsylvania.

Atzmon, Gil et al. 2010. "Abraham's Children in the Genome Era: Major Jewish Diaspora Populations Comprise Distinct Genetic Clusters with Shared Middle Eastern Ancestry." *American Journal of Human Genetics* 86:850–59.

Austin, William G., and Stephen Worchel, eds. 1979. *The Social Psychology of Intergroup Relations.* Monterey, CA: Brooks/Cole.

Avigad, Nahman. 1983. *Discovering Jerusalem.* Nashville: Abingdon.

Bagnall, Roger S. 1976. *The Administration of the Ptolemaic Possessions Outside Egypt.* Columbia Studies in the Classical Tradition 4. Leiden: Brill.

———, ed. 2009 *The Oxford Handbook of Papyrology.* Oxford: Oxford University Press.

Balcer, Jack Martin. 1977. "The Athenian Episkopos and the Achaemenid 'King's Eye.'" *American Journal of Philology* 98:252–63.

Barclay, John M. G. 2011. *Pauline Churches and Diaspora Jews.* WUNT 275. Tübingen: Mohr/Siebeck.

Barnard, Alan, and Jonathan Spencer, eds. 1996. *Encyclopedia of Social and Cultural Anthropology.* London: Routledge.

Bar-Tal, Daniel. 1990. *Group Beliefs: A Conception for Analyzing Group Structure, Processes, and Behavior.* Springer Series in Social Psychology. New York: Springer.

———. 1998. "Group Beliefs as an Expression of Social Identity." In Worcher et al., eds. 1998:93–113.
Barth, Fredrik, ed. 1969a. *Ethnic Groups and Boundaries: The Social Organization of Culture Difference*. Edited by Fredrik Barth. London: George Allen & Unwin.
———. 1969b. "Introduction." In Barth 1969a:9–38.
Barton, Carlin A., and Daniel Boyarin. 2016. *Imagine No Religion: How Modern Abstractions Hide Ancient Realities*. New York: Fordham University Press.
Barton, John, and John Muddiman, eds. 2001. *The Oxford Bible Commentary*. Oxford: Oxford University Press.
Berger, Peter. 1969. *The Social Reality of Religion*. London: Faber & Faber (published in the U.S. under the title *The Sacred Canopy*).
Black, Matthew, ed. 1970. *Apocalypsis Henochi Graece*. Pseudepigrapha Veteris Testamenti Graece 3. Leiden: Brill.
———. 1985. *The Book of Enoch or I Enoch. A New English Edition*. In consultation with James C. VanderKam. Studia in Veteris Testamenti Pseudepigrapha 7. Leiden: Brill, 1985.
Black, Max. 1962. *Models and Metaphors: Studies in Language and Philosophy*. Ithaca, NY: Cornell University Press.
Boccaccini, Gabriele, ed. 2002a. *The Origins of Enochic Judaism: Proceedings of the First Enoch Seminar*. Turin: Zamorani.
———. 2002b. *Roots of Rabbinic Judaism: An Intellectual History, from Ezekiel to Daniel*. Grand Rapids: Eerdmans.
———, ed. 2005. *Enoch and Qumran Origins: New Light on a Forgotten Connection*. Grand Rapids: Eerdmans.
———, ed. 2007. *Enoch and the Messiah Son of Man: Revisiting the Book of Parables*. Grand Rapids: Eerdmans.
Boccaccini, Gabriele, and John J. Collins, eds. 2007. *The Early Enoch Literature*. JSJSup 121. Leiden: Brill.
Bonner, C., and H. C. Youtie. 1937. *The Last Chapters of Enoch in Greek*. Studies and Documents 8. London: Christophers.
Botha, Pieter J. J. 2012. *Orality and Literacy in Early Christianity*. Biblical Performance Criticism Series 5. Eugene, OR: Cascade Books.
Boucharlat, Rémy. 2001. "The Palaces and the Royal Achmaenid City: Two Case Studies—Pasagardae and Susa, in Nielsen 2001:113–23.
Bourriaud, Nicolas. 2002. *Relational Aesthetics*. Dijon: Les presses du réel.
Brands, Gunnar, and Wolfram Hoepfner, eds. 1996. *Basileia: Die Paläste der hellenistischen Könige*. Mainz: von Zabern.
Brosius, Maria. 2007. "New Out of Old? Court and Court Ceremonies in Achmaenid Persia." In Spawforth 2007a:17–57.
Brown, Rupert. 2000. *Group Processes*. 2nd ed. Oxford: Blackwell.
Butz, Reinhardt, and Lars-Arne Dannenberg. 2004. "Theoriebildungen des Hofes." In Butz et al., eds. 2004:1–41.
Butz, Reinhardt, Jan Hirschbiegel, and Dietmar Willoweit, eds. 2004. *Hof und Theorie: Annäherungen an ein historisches Phänomen*. Norm und Struktur: Studien zum sozialen Wandel in Mittelalter und Früher Neuzeit 22. Cologne: Böhlau.
Byron, Reginald. 1996. "Identity." In Barnard and Spencer, eds. 1996:292.

Cartledge, Paul, Peter Garnsey, and Erich S. Gruen, eds. 1997. *Hellenistic Constructs: Essays in Culture, History, and Historiography*. Hellenistic Culture and Society 26. Berkeley: University of California Press.

Charles, R. H. 1906. *The Ethiopic Version of the Book of Enoch: Edited from Twenty-Three MSS, Together with the Fragmentary Greek and Latin Versions*. Oxford: Clarendon.

———. 1908. *The Greek Versions of the Testaments of the Twelve Patriarchs. Edited from Nine Mss. Together with the Variants of the Armenian and Slavonic Versions and Some Hebrew Fragments*. Oxford: Clarendon.

———, ed. 1913. "Book of Enoch." In *The Apocrypha and Pseudepigrapha of the Old Testament in English*. Vol. 2: *Pseudepigrapha*, 163–77. Oxford: Clarendon.

Charlesworth, James H., ed. 1983. *The Old Testament Pseudepigrapha*. Vol. 1: *Apocalyptic Literature and Testaments*. Garden City, NY: Doubleday.

———, ed. 1985. *The Old Testament Pseudepigrapha*. Vol. 2. Garden City, NY: Doubleday.

Charlesworth, James H., and Darrell J. Bock, eds. 2013. *Parables of Enoch: A Paradigm Shift*. T. & T. Clark Early Jewish and Christian Texts Series 11. London: Bloomsbury.

Charlesworth, James H., and Ephraim Isaac. 2015. *O Livro de Enoque Etíope ou 1 Enoque*. Translated by Orlando Iannuzzi Filho. Sao Paulo: Entre os Tempos.

Charlesworth, James H., and Carol A. Newsom, eds. 1999. *The Dead Sea Scrolls: Hebrew, Aramaic, and Greek Texts with English Translations*. Vol. 4B, *Angelic Liturgy: Songs of the Sabbath Sacrifice*. Princeton Theological Seminary Dead Sea Scrolls Project. Tübingen: Mohr/Siebeck.

Clifford, Richard J. 1972. *The Cosmic Mountain in Canaan and the Old Testament*. Harvard Semitic Monographs 4. Cambridge: Harvard University Press.

Cohen, Yoram. 2005. "A Family Plot: The Zu-Bala Family of Diviners and Hittite Administration in the Land of Astata." In Hazirlayan and Süel 2005:213–24.

———. 2009. *The Scribes and Scholars of the City of Emar in the Late Bronze Age*. Harvard Semitic Studies 59. Winona Lake, IN: Eisenbrauns.

———. 2012. "The Historical and Social Background of the Scribal School at the City of Emar in the Late Bronze Age." In van Egmond and van Soldt 2012:115–27.

Collins, John J. 1978. "Methodological Issues in the Study of 1 Enoch: Reflections on the Articles of P. D. Hanson and G. W. Nickelsburg." In *SBL Seminar Papers, 1978*, edited by Paul J. Achtemeier, 315–22. Missoula, MT: Scholars.

———, ed. 1979a. *Apocalypse: The Morphology of a Genre*. Semeia 14. Missoula, MT: Scholars.

———. 1979b. "Introduction: The Morphology of a Genre." In Collins 1979a:1–20.

———. 2005. "Response: The Apocalyptic Worldview of Daniel." In Boccaccini 2005:59–66.

———. 2007a. "Enoch and the Son of Man: A Response to Sabion Chialà and Helge Kvanvig." In Boccaccini 2007:216–27.

———, ed. (2014) *The Oxford Handbook of Apocalyptic Literature*. Oxford: Oxford University Press.

———. 2016. *The Apocalyptic Imagination. An Introduction to Jewish Apocalyptic Literature*. 3rd ed. Grand Rapids: Eerdmans.

Czajkowski, Kimberley. 2017. *Localised Law: The Babatha and Salome Archives*. Oxford: Oxford University Press.

Day, John. 1994. *Yahweh and the Gods and Goddesses of Canaan*. JSOTSup 265. Sheffield: Sheffield Academic.

Deignan, Alice. 2005. *Metaphor and Corpus Linguistics*. Amsterdam: Benjamins.
Dexinger, F. 1977. *Henochs Zehnwochenapokalypse und offene Probleme der Apokalyptic-forschung*. Studia Post-Biblica 29. Leiden: Brill.
Dillmann, August. 1955 (1865). *Lexicon Linguae Aethiopicae*. Reprint, New York: Ungar.
———. 2005 (1851). *The Ethiopic Text of 1 Enoch*. Reprint, Ancient Texts and Translations. Eugene, OR: Wipf & Stock. [Original pub.: *Liber Henoch Aithiopice*. Leipzig: Vogel.]
Dillmann, August, and Bezold, Carl. 2003 (1923). *Ethiopic Grammar*. 2nd ed. Translated by James A. Crichton. Reprinted, edited by K. C. Hanson. Ancient Language Resources. Eugene, OR: Wipf & Stock, 2003.
Douglas, Mary. 1966. *Purity and Danger: An Analysis of the Concepts of Pollution and Taboo*. London: Routeldge & Kegan Paul.
Dubovsky, Peter. 2006. *Hezekiah and the Assyrian Spies: Reconstruction of the Neo-Assyrian Intelligence Services and its Significance for 2 Kings 18–19*. Biblica et Orientalia 49. Rome: Pontificio Istituto Biblico.
Duindam, Jeroen, Tulay Artan, and Metin Kunt, eds., 2011. *Royal Courts in Dynastic States and Empires: A Global Perspective*. Rulers & Elites: Comparative Studies in Governance 1. Leiden: Brill.
Dunn, James D. G., ed. 1999. *Jews and Christians: The Parting of the Ways A.D. 70 to 135*. Grand Rapids: Eerdmans.
———. 2011. *The Partings of the Ways: Between Christianity and Judaism and Their Significance for the Character of Christianity*. 2nd ed. London: SCM.
Dvornik, Francis. 1974. *Origins of Intelligence Services: The Ancient Near East, Persia, Greece, Rome, Byzantium, the Arab Muslim Empires, the Mongol Empire, China, Muscovy*. New Brunswick, NJ: Rutgers University Press.
Egmond, W. S. van, and W. H. van Soldt. 2012. *Theory and Practice of Knowledge Transfer: Studies in School Education in the Ancient Near East and Beyond: Papers Read at a Symposium in Leiden, 17–19 December 2008*. Pihans: Uitgaven van het Nederlands Instituut voor het Nabije Oosten te Leiden 121. Leiden: Nederlands Instituut voor het Nabije Oosten.
Elias, Norbert. 1974. *La societé de cours*. Paris: Calmann-Lévy (German original 1969).
———. 1983. *The Court Society*. Translated by Edmund Jephcott. Oxford: Blackwell (German original 1969).
Erho, Ted M., and Loren Stuckenbruck. 2013. "A Manuscript History of Ethiopic Enoch." *JSP* 3:87–133.
Erikson, Erik H. 1959. *Identity and the Life-Cycle*. New York: Norton.
Esler, Philip F. 1987. *Community and Gospel in Luke-Acts: The Social and Political Motivations of Lucan Theology*. SNTS Monograph Series 57. Cambridge: Cambridge University Press.
———. 1996. 'Group Boundaries and Intergroup Conflict in Galatians: A New Reading of Gal. 5:13–6:10." In *Ethnicity and the Bible*, edited by Mark Brett 215–40. Biblical Interpretation Series 19. Leiden: Brill.
———. 1998. *Galatians*. New Testament Readings. London: Routledge.
———. 2003. *Conflict and Identity in Romans: The Social Setting of Paul's Letter*. Minneapolis: Fortress.
———. 2006. "Paul's Contestation of Israel's (Ethnic) Memory of Abraham in Galatians 3." *BTB* 36:23–34.

———. 2007. "From *Ioudaioi* to Children of God: The Development of a Non-Ethnic Group Identity in the Gospel of John." In Hagedorn et al., eds. 2007:106–37.

———. 2009. "Judean Ethnic Identity in Josephus' *Against Apion*." In Rodgers et al., eds. 2009:73–91.

———. 2011. "Judean Ethnic Identity and the Purpose of Hebrews." In McGowan and Richards 2011:469–89.

———. 2013. "Judean Ethnic Identity and the Matthean Jesus." In von Gemünden et al., eds. 2013:193–210.

———. 2014a. "Social-Scientific Approaches to Apocalyptic Literature." In Collins, ed. 2014:123–44.

———. 2014b. "An Outline of Social Identity Theory." In Tucker and Baker, eds. 2014:13–40.

———. 2015a. "Intergroup Conflict and Matthew 23: Towards Responsible Historical Interpretation of a Challenging Text." *Biblical Theology Bulletin* 45:38–59.

———. 2015b. "Rival Group Identities in the Matthean Gospel: Evidence from Matthew 1–2 and 23." In McConville and Pietersen, eds. 2015:19–35.

———. 2016. "Giving the Kingdom to an *Ethnos* that Will Bear Its Fruit: Ethnic and Christ-Movement Identities in Matthew." In Gurtner et al., eds. 2016:19–35.

———, ed. 2017a. *The Blessing of Enoch: I Enoch and Contemporary Theology*. Eugene, OR: Cascade Books.

———. 2017b. "*Deus Victor*: The Nature and Defeat of Evil in the Book of the Watchers (1 Enoch 1–36)." In Esler, ed. 2017a:166–90.

———. 2017c. *Babatha's Orchard: The Yadin Papyri and An Ancient Jewish Family Tale Retold*. Oxford: Oxford University Press.

Falk, Daniel K. 1998. *Daily, Sabbath, and Festival Prayers in the Dead Sea Scrolls*. Studies on the Texts of the Desert of Judah 27. Leiden: Brill.

Fischer, Ronald, and Crysta Derham. 2016. "Is In-Group Bias Culture Dependent? A Meta-Analysis across 18 Societies." *Springerplus* 5:70. https://www.ncbi.nlm.nih.gov/pmc/articles/PMC4723375.

Fitzmyer, Joseph A. 2001. "Tobit." In Barton and Muddiman, eds. 2001:626–32.

———. 2003. *Tobit*. Commentaries on Early Jewish Literature. Berlin: de Gruyter.

Flemming, Johann. 1902. *Das Buch Henoch: Aethiopischer Text*. Leipzig: Hinrichs.

Fletcher-Louis, Crispin H. T. 2002. *All the Glory of Adam: Liturgical Anthropology in the Dead Sea Scrolls*. Studies on the Texts of the Desert of Judah 42. Leiden: Brill.

Gammie, John G. 1990. "The Sage in Hellenistic Royal Courts." In Gammie and Perdue, eds. 1990:147–53.

Gammie, John G., and Leo G. Perdue, eds. 1990. *The Sage in Israel and the Ancient Near East*. Winona Lake, IN: Eisenbrauns.

García Martínez, Florentino. 1994. *The Dead Sea Scrolls Translated: The Qumran Texts in English*. Translated by Wilfred G. E. Watson. Leiden: Brill.

Gemünden, Petra von, David G. Horrell, and Max Küchler, eds. 2013. *Jesus-Gestalt und Gestaltungen: Rezeptionen des Galiläers in Wissenschaft, Kirche un Gesellschaft: Festschrift für Gerd Theissen*. NTOA 100. Göttingen: Vandenhoeck & Ruprecht.

Gershevitch, Ilya, ed. 1985. *The Cambridge History of Iran*. Vol. 2, *The Median and Achaemenian Periods*. Cambridge: Cambridge University Press.

Gerth, H. H. and C. Wright Mills, eds. and trans. 1991 (1948). *From Max Weber: Essays in Sociology*. Rev. ed. by Bryan S. Turner. London: Routledge.

Gibson, J. C. L. 1978. *Canaanite Myths and Legends*. 2nd ed. Edinburgh: T. & T. Clark.

Grainger, John D. 2017. *Great Power Diplomacy in the Hellenistic World*. New York: Routledge.

Gurtner, Daniel M., Grant Macaskill, and Jonathan T. Pennington, eds. 2016. *In the Fullness of Time: Essays on Christology, Creation, and Eschatology in Honor of Richard Bauckham*. Grand Rapids: Eerdmans.

Hagedorn, Anselm C., Zeba A. Crook, and Eric Stewart, eds. 2007. *In Other Words: Essays on Social Science Methods and the New Testament in Honor of Jerome H. Neyrey*. Social World of Biblical Antiquity 2/1. Sheffield: Sheffield Phoenix.

Halperin, David J. 1988. *The Faces of the Chariot: Development of Rabbinic Early Jewish Responses to Ezekiel's Vision*. Texte und Studien zum Antiken Judentum 16. Tübingen: Mohr/Siebeck.

Handy, Lowell K. 1994. *Among the Host of Heaven: The Syro-Palestinian Pantheon as Bureaucracy*. Winona Lake, IN: Eisenbrauns.

Hanson, Paul D. 1977. "Rebellion in Heaven, Azazel and Euhemeristic Heroes in 1 Enoch 6–22." *JBL* 96:195–223.

Haran, Menahem. 1978. *Temples and Temple-Service in Ancient Israel: An Enquiry into the Character of Cult Phenomena and the Historical Setting of the Priestly School*. Oxford: Clarendon.

Harkins, Angela Kim, Kelley Coblentz Bautch, and John C. Endres, eds. 2014. *The Watchers in Jewish and Christian Traditions*. Minneapolis: Fortress.

Harland, Philip A. 2013. *Associations, Synagogues and Congregations: Claiming a Place in Ancient Mediterranean Society*. 2nd (online) ed. Kitchener, ON: Philip A. Harland. http://philipharland.com/associations/

Hazirlayan, Yayma, and Aygül Süel, 2005. *V. Uluslararasi Hititoloji Kongresi Bildirileri, Çorum 02–08 Eylül 2002: Acts of the Vth International Congresks (sic) of Hititology, Çorum 02–08 Eylül 2002*. Ankara: Nokta Ofset.

Heermann, Vera. 1986. *Studien zur makedonischen Palastarchitektur*. Nürnberg: Philosophischen Fakultät I der Friedrich–Alexander–Universität Erlangen–Nürnberg.

Herman, Gabriel. 1987. *Ritualised Friendship and the Greek City*. Cambridge: Cambridge University Press.

———. 1997. "The Court Society of the Hellenistic Age." In Cartledge, Garnsey, and Gruen, eds. 1997:199–224.

Himmelfarb, Martha. 1993. *Ascent to Heaven in Jewish and Christian Apocalypses*. New York: Oxford University Press.

———. 2006. *A Kingdom of Priests: Ancestry and Merit in Ancient Judaism*. Philadelphia: University of Pennsylvania Press.

———. 2007. "Temple and Priests in the Book of the Watchers, the Animal Apocalypse, and the Apocalypse of Weeks." In Boccaccini and Collins, eds. 2007:219–35.

Hogg, Michael A., and Dominic Abrams. 1988. *Social Identifications: A Social Psychology of Intergroup Relations and Group Processes*. London: Routledge.

Hogg, Michael A., and Scott A. Reid. 2006. "Social Identity, Self-Categorization, and the Communication of Group Norms." *Communication Theory* 16:7–30.

Hollander, H. W., and M. de Jonge. 1985. *The Testaments of the Twelve Patriarchs: A Commentary*. Studia in Veteris Testamenti Pseudepigrapha 8. Leiden: Brill.

Horrell, D. G. 2016. "Ethnicisation, Marriage, and Early Christian Identity: Critical Reflections on 1 Corinthians 7, 1 Peter 3 and Modern New Testament Scholarship." *NTS* 62:439–60.

Horsley, Richard A. 2010. *Revolt of the Scribes: Resistance and Apocalyptic Origins.* Minneapolis: Fortress.

Horsley, Richard A., and Patrick A. Tiller. 2012. *After Apocalyptic & Wisdom: Rethinking Texts in Context.* Eugene, OR: Cascade Books.

Hundley, Michael B. 2013. *Gods in Dwellings: Temples and Divine Presence in the Ancient Near East.* Writings from the Ancient World Supplement Series. Atlanta: Society of Biblical Literature.

Hunt, A. S. 1934. *Select Papyri.* Vol. 2. Loeb Classical Library. Cambridge: Harvard University Press.

Hutchinson, John, and Anthony Smith, eds. 1996a. *Ethnicity.* Oxford: Oxford University Press.

———. 1996b. "Introduction." In Hutchinson and Smith, eds. 1996a:3–14.

Isaac, E. 1983. "1 (Ethiopic Apocalypse of) Enoch: Second Century B.C.—First Century A.D.: A New Translation and Introduction." In Charlesworth, ed. 1983:5–89.

Jonge, Marinus de. 1991. "The Main Issues in the Study of the Testaments of the Twelve Patriarchs." In *Jewish Eschatology, Early Christian Christology and the Testaments of the Twelve Patriarchs: Collected Essays of Marinus de Jonge,* 147–63. Novum Testamentum Supplements 63. Leiden: Brill.

Joyce, Paul M., and Dalit Rom-Shiloni, eds. 2015. *The God Ezekiel Creates.* Library of Hebrew Bible/Old Testament Studies 607. London: Bloomsbury.

Kampen, John. 2007. "The Books of the Maccabees and Sectarianism in Second Temple Judaism." In Xeravits and Zsengellér, eds. 2007:11–30.

Kee, Howard Clark. 1983. "The Testaments of the Twelve Patriarchs." In Charlesworth, ed. 1983:775–828.

Kee, Min Suc. 2007. "The Heavenly Council and Its Type-Scene." *JSOT* 31:259–73.

Keel, Othmar. 1997. *The Symbolism of the Biblical World: Ancient Near Eastern Iconography and the Book of Psalms.* Translated by Timothy J. Hallett. Winona Lake, IN: Eisenbrauns.

King, L. W., and R. C. Thompson. 1907. *The Sculptures and Inscription of Darius the Great on the Rock of Behistun in Persia: A New Collation of the Persian, Susian, and Babylonian Texts, with English Translations.* London: British Museum. http://en.wikipedia.org/wiki/Full_translation_of_the_Behistun_Inscription.

Klauck, Hans-Josef et al., eds. 2009. *Encyclopedia of the Bible and Its Reception.* Vol. 2, *Anim–Atheism.* Berlin: de Gruyter.

Klingbeil, Martin. 1999. *Yahweh Fighting from Heaven: God as Warrior and as God of Heaven in the Hebrew Psalter and Ancient Near Eastern Iconography.* Orbis Biblicus et Orientalis 169. Göttingen: Vandenhoeck & Ruprecht.

Kloppenborg, John S. 2006. "Associations in the Ancient World." In Levine et al., eds. 2006:323–38.

———. 2009. "Associations, Voluntary." In Klauck et al., eds. 2009:1062–69.

Kövecses, Zoltán. 2005. *Metaphor in Culture: Universality and Variation.* Cambridge: Cambridge University Press.

Kugler, Robert A. 1996. *From Patriarch to Priest: The Levi-Priestly Tradition from Aramaic Levi to Testament of Levi.* SBL Early Judaism and Its Literature 9. Atlanta: Scholars.

———. 2001. *The Testaments of the Twelve Patriarchs.* Guides to Apocrypha and Pseudepigrapha. Sheffield: Sheffield Academic.

Kuhrt, Amélie. 2007. *The Persian Empire: A Corpus of Sources from the Achaemenid Period*. London: Routledge.

Kutbay, Boney Lea. 1998. *Palaces and Large Residences of the Hellenistic Age*. Studies in Classics 8. Lewiston, NY: Mellen.

Kvanvig, Helge S. 1988. *Roots of Apocalyptic: The Mesopotamian Background of the Enoch Figure and the Son of Man*. Wissenschaftliche Monographien zum Alten und Neuen Testament 61. Neukirchen-Vluyn: Neukirchener.

———. 2005. "Jubilees—Read as a Narrative." In Boccaccini, ed. 2005:75–83.

———. 2007. "The Son of Man in the Parables of Enoch." In Boccaccini 2007:179–215.

Ladd, George E. 1952a. "The Kingdom of God in the Jewish Apocryphal Literature: Part 3." *Bibliotheca Sacra* 109: 318–31.

———. 1952b. The Kingdom of God in the Jewish Apocryphal Literature: Part 4." *Bibliotheca Sacra* 110:32–49.

Lakoff, George, and Mark Johnson. 2003 (1980). *Metaphors We Live By*. Chicago: Chicago University Press. (This is the 1980 edition with an afterword from 2003.)

Laurence, Richard. 1821. *The Book of Enoch, The Prophet: An Apocryphal Production, Supposed to Have Been Lost for Ages; But Discovered at the Close of The Last Century in Abyssinia; Now First Translated from an Ethiopic Ms. in the Bodleian Library*. Oxford: Parker. (Revised editions appeared in 1833, 1838, and 1842.)

———. 1838. *Libri Enoch Prophetae Versio Aethiopica*. Oxford: Parke.

———. 1883. *The Book of Enoch the Prophet: Translated from an Ethiopic Ms. in the Bodleian Library by the Late Richard Laurence, DD.L, Archbishop of Cashel*. London: Kegan Paul, Trench.

Leslau, Wolf. 1987. *Comparative Dictionary of Ge'ez: Ge'ez–English/English–Ge'ez*. Wiesbaden: Harrassowitz.

Levine, Amy Jill, Dale C. Allison, and John Dominic Crossan, eds. 2006. *The Historical Jesus in Context*. Princeton Readings in Religion. Princeton: Princeton University Press.

Lisowsky, Gerhard. 1993. *Konkordanz zum hebräischen Alten Testament: nach dem von Paul Kahle in der Biblia hebraica edidit Rudolf Kittel: besorgten Masoretischen Text / unter verantwortlicher Mitwirkung von Leonhard Rost*. Stuttgart: Württembergische Bibelanstalt.

Lods, Adolphe. 1892. *Le livre d'Hénoch: fragments grecs découverts à Akhmïm (Haute-Egypte): publiés avec les variantes du texte éthiopien*. Paris: Leroux.

Lynn, John A. 1997. *Giant of the Grand Siècle: The French Army, 1610–1715*. Cambridge: Cambridge University Press.

Malina, Bruce J. 1996. "Mediterranean Sacrifice: Dimensions of Domestic and Political Religion." *BTB* 26:26–44.

Mason, Steve. 2007. "Jews, Judaeans, Judaizing, Judaism: Problems of Categorization in Ancient History." *JSJ* 38:457–512.

———. 2016. *Orientation to the History of Roman Judaea*. Eugene, OR: Cascade Books.

Mason, Steve, and Philip F. Esler. 2017. "Judaean and Christ-Follower Identities: Grounds for a Distinction." *NTS* 63:493–515.

McConville, J. Gordon, and Lloyd K. Pietersen, eds. 2015. *Conception, Reception and the Spirit: Essays in Honor of Andrew T. Lincoln*. Eugene, OR: Cascade Books.

McGowan, Andrew B., and Kent Harold Richards, eds. 2011. *Method and Meaning: Essays on New Testament Interpretation in Honor of Harold A. Attridge*. Resources for Biblical Study 67. Atlanta: Society of Biblical Literature.

Meissner, Burkhard. 2000. "Hofmann und Herrscher: Was es für Griechen hiess, Freund eines Königs zu sein." *Archiv für Kulturgeschichte* 82:1–36.
Meyer, Leon de, and Ernie Haerinck, eds. 1989. *Archaeologia Iranica et Orientalis: Miscellanea in Honorem Louis Vanden Berghe*. 2 vols. Ghent: Peeters.
Michalak, Aleksander R. 2012. *Angels as Warriors in Late Second Temple Jewish Literature*. WUNT 2/330. Tübingen: Mohr/Siebeck.
Milik, J. T. 1976. *The Books of Enoch: Aramaic Fragments of Qumran Cave 4*. With the collaboration of Matthew Black. Oxford: Clarendon.
Milligan, George, ed. 1927. *Selections from the Greek Papyri*. Cambridge: Cambridge University Press.
Mullen, E. Theodore, Jr. 1980. *The Divine Council in Canaanite and Early Hebrew Literature*. Harvard Semitic Monographs 24. Chico, CA: Scholars.
Netzer, Ehud. 1999. *Die Paläste der Hasmonäer und Herodes' des Grossen*. Sonderhefte der Antiken Welt. Mainz: Zabern.
Newsom, Carol. 1980. "The Development of 1 Enoch 6–19." *CBQ* 42:310–29.
———. 1985. *Songs of the Sabbath Sacrifice: A Critical Edition*. Harvard Semitic Studies 27. Atlanta: Scholars.
Newsom, Carol A., and James H. Charlesworth, with Brent A. Strawn and Henry M. Rietz. 1999. "Angelic Liturgy: Songs of the Sabbath Sacrifice." In Charlesworth and Newsom 1999:1–189.
Nickelsburg, George W. E. 1977. "Apocalyptic and Myth in 1 Enoch 6–11." *JBL* 6:383–405.
———. 1981. "Enoch, Levi, and Peter: Recipients of Revelation in Upper Galilee." *JBL* 100:575–600.
———. 2001. *1 Enoch 1: A Critical Edition on the Book of 1 Enoch, Chapters 1–36; 81–108*. Hermeneia. Minneapolis: Fortress.
Nickelsburg, George W. E., and James C. VanderKam. 2012. *1 Enoch: The Hermeneia Translation*. Minneapolis: Fortress.
Nielsen, Inge. 1994. *Hellenistic Palaces: Tradition and Renewal*. Studies in Hellenistic Civilization 5. Aarhus: Aarhus University Press.
———. 1998. *Hellenistic Palaces: Tradition and Renewal*. 2nd ed. Studies in Hellenistic Civilization 5. Aarhus: Aarhus University Press.
———, ed. 2001. *The Royal Palace Institution in the First Millennium BC: Regional Development and Interchange between East and West*. Monographs of the Danish Institute at Athens 4. Aarhus: Aarhus University Press.
Nongbri, Brent. 2015. *Before Religion: A History of a Modern Concept*. New Haven: Yale University Press.
Orton, David E. 1989.*The Understanding Scribe: Matthew and the Apocalyptic Ideal*. JSNT Supplement Series 25. Sheffield: JSOT Press.
Orlov, Andrei A. 2005. *The Enoch–Metatron Tradition*. Texts and Studies in Ancient Judaism 107. Tübingen: Mohr/Siebeck.
Otto, Rudolf. 1923. *The Idea of the Holy: An Inquiry into the Non-Rational Factor in the Idea of the Divine and Its Relation to the Rational*. Translated by John W. Harvey. London: Oxford University Press.
Palme, Bernhard. 2009. "The Range of Documentary Texts: Types and Categories." In Bagnall, ed. 2009:358–94.
Parker, Bradley J. 2011. "The Construction and Performance of Kingship in the Neo-Assyrian Empire." *Journal of Anthropological Research* 67:357–86.

Parpola, Simo. 1970–1983. *Letters from Assyrian Scholars to the Kings Esarhaddon and Assurbanipal*. 2 vols. Alter Orient und Altes Testament 5. Neukirchen-Vluyn: Neukirchener.

Pearce, Laurie E., and Cornelia Wunsch. 2014. *Documents of Judean Exiles and West Semites in Babylonia in the Collection of David Sofer*. Cornell University Studies in Assyriology and Sumerology 28. Bethesda, MD: CDL.

Plöger, Otto. 1968. *Theocracy and Eschatology*. Translated by S. Rudman. Oxford: Blackwell.

Portier-Young, Anathea. 2011. *Apocalypse against Empire: Theologies of Resistance in Early Judaism*. Grand Rapids: Eerdmans.

———. 2014. "Symbolic Resistance in the Book of the Watchers." In Harkins et al., eds. 2014:39–49.

Raphael, Melissa. 2003. *The Female Face of Auschwitz: A Jewish Feminist Theology of the Holocaust*. Religion and Gender. London: Routledge.

Reicher, Stephen, and Nick Hopkins. 2001. *Self and Nation: Categorization, Contestation and Mobilization*. London: Sage.

Rodgers, Zuleika, with Margaret Daly-Denton and Anne Fitzpatrick McKinley, eds. 2009. *A Wandering Galilean: Essays in Honour of Sean Freyne*. JSJSup 132. Leiden: Brill.

Rowlands, Guy. 2002. *The Dynastic State and the Army under Louis XIV: Royal Service and Private Interest, 1661–1701*. Cambridge Studies in Early Modern History. Cambridge: Cambridge University Press.

Russell, James R. 1990. "Sages and Scribes at the Courts of Ancient Iran." In Gammie and Perdue, eds. 1990:141–46.

Savalli-Lestrade, Ivana. 1998. *Les philoi royaux dans l'Asie hellénistique*. Hautes études du monde gréco-romain 25. Geneva: Droz.

Schäfer, Peter. 2009. *The Origins of Jewish Mysticism*. Tübingen: Mohr/Siebeck.

Schubert, Paul. 2009. "Editing a Papyrus." In Bagnall, ed. 2009:197–215.

Schams, Christine.1998. *Jewish Scribes in the Second-Temple Period*. JSOTSup 291. Sheffield: Sheffield Academic.

Selincourt, Aubrey de. 1954. *Herodotus: The Histories*. Harmondsworth, UK: Penguin.

Smith, Dennis. 2001. *Norbert Elias and Modern Social Theory*. Theory, Culture & Society. London: Sage.

———. 2009. "Norbert Elias and *The Court Society*: From Gallapagos to Versailles via Quai des Orfèvres." Court Studies Forum. http://homepages.lboro.ac.uk/~ssds3/d.smith/Norbert%20Elias%20and%20The%20Court%20Society.pdf.

Smith, Eliot R., and Michael A. Zarate. 1990. "Exemplar and Prototype Use in Social Categorization." *Social Cognition* 8:243–62.

Smith, Mark S. 2001. *The Origins of Biblical Monotheism: Israel's Polytheistic Background and the Ugaritic Texts*. Oxford: Oxford University Press.

———. 2002. *The Early History of God: Yahweh and Other Deities in Ancient Israel*. 2nd ed. Grand Rapids: Eerdmans.

Smith, William Cantwell. 1991 (1962). *The Meaning and End of Religion*. Minneapolis: Fortress.

Sokoloff, Michael. 1990. *A Dictionary of Jewish Palestinian Aramaic of the Byzantine Period*. Tel Aviv: Bar Ilan University Press.

———. 2003. *A Dictionary of Judean Aramaic*. Tel Aviv: Bar Ilan University Press.

Sommerstein, Alan H., and Torrance, Isabelle C. 2014. *Oaths and Swearing in Ancient Greece*. Beiträge zur Altertumskunde 307. Berlin: de Gruyter.
Soskice, Janet Martin. 1985. *Metaphor and Religious Language*. Oxford: Clarendon.
Spawforth, A. J. S., ed. 2007a. *The Court and Court Society in Ancient Monarchies*. Cambridge: Cambridge University Press.
———. 2007b. "Introduction." In Spawforth, ed. 2007a:1–16.
———. 2007c. "The Court of Alexander the Great between Europe and Asia." In Spawforth, ed. 2007a:82–120.
Stone, Michael. 1988. "Enoch, Aramaic Levi and Sectarian Origins." *JSJ* 19:159–70.
Stronach, David 1978. *Pasargadae*. Oxford: Clarendon.
———. 1985. "Pasargadae." In Gershevitch 1985:838–55.
———. 1989. "The Royal Garden at Pasargadae: Evolution and Legacy." In de Meyer and Haerinck, eds. 1989:475–502.
Strong, John T. 2015. "The God that Ezekiel Inherited." In Joyce and Rom-Shiloni, ed. 2015:24–54.
Strootman, Rolf. 2007. "The Hellenistic Royal Court: Court Culture, Ceremonial and Ideology in Greece, Egypt and the Near East." Ph.D. diss., University of Utrecht.
———. 2011. "Hellenistic Court Society: The Seleukid Imperial Court Under Antiochos the Great, 223–187 BCE." In Duindam et al., eds. 2011:63–89.
———. 2014. *Courts and Elites in the Hellenistic Empires: The Near East after the Achaemenids, c. 330—30 BCE*. Edinburgh Studies in Ancient Persia. Edinburgh: Edinburgh University Press.
Stuckenbruck, Loren T. 2007. *1 Enoch 91–108*. Commentaries on Early Jewish Literature. Berlin: de Gruyter.
———. 2013a. "The Book of Enoch: Its Reception in Second Temple Jewish and in Christian Tradition." *Early Christianity* 4:7–40.
———. 2013b. "The Parables of Enoch as the Son of Man in the Early Enoch Tradition." In Charlesworth and Bock, eds. 2013:315–28.
Stuckenbruck, Loren T., and Gabriele Boccaccini, eds. 2016. *Enoch and the Synoptic Gospels: Reminiscences, Allusions, Intertextuality*. Early Judaism and Its Literature 44. Atlanta: Scholars.
Suter, David W. 1979. "Fallen Angel, Fallen Priest: The Problem of Family Purity in 1 Enoch 6–16." *HUCA* 50:115–35.
———. 2002. "Revisiting 'Fallen Angel, Fallen Priest.'" In Boccaccini, ed. 2002a:137–42.
———. 2007. "Temples and the Temple in the Early Enoch Tradition: Memory, Vision, and Expectation." In Boccaccini and Collins, eds. 2007:196–218.
Sweet, Ronald F. G. 1990. "The Sage in Mesopotamian Palaces and Royal Courts." In Gammie and Perdue, eds. 1990:90–107.
Tajfel, Henri, ed. 1978a. *Differentiation between Social Groups: Studies in the Social Psychology of Intergroup Relations*. European Monographs in Social Psychology 14. London: Academic Press.
———. 1978b. "Introduction." In Tajfel, ed. 1978a:1–23.
———. 1981. *Human Groups and Social Categories: Studies in Social Psychology*. Cambridge: Cambridge University Press.
———, ed. 1982. *Social Identity and Intergroup Relations*. European Studies in Social Psychology. Cambridge: Cambridge University Press.
Tajfel, Henri, and John Turner. 1979. "An Integrative Theory of Intergroup Conflict." In Austin and Worchel, eds. 1979:33–47.

Theissen, Gerd, and Dagmar Winter. 2002. *The Quest for the Plausible Jesus: The Question of Criteria*. Translated by M. Eugene Boring. Louisville: Westminster John Knox.

Tiller, Patrick A. 2005. "The Sociological Context of the Dream Visions of Daniel and 1 Enoch." In Boccaccini, ed. 2005:23–26.

———. 2012. "The Social Settings of the Components of *1 Enoch*." In Horsley and Tiller 2012:81–99.

Toorn, Karel van der. 2007. *Scribal Culture and the Making of the Hebrew Bible*. Cambridge: Harvard University Press.

Tov, Emanuel. 2009. *Scribal Practices and Approaches Reflected in the Texts Found in the Judean Desert*. Studies on the Texts of the Desert of Judah 54. Atlanta: Society of Biblical Literature.

Tucker, Brian, and Coleman A. Baker, eds. 2014. *T & T Clark Handbook to Social Identity in the New Testament*. London: Bloomsbury.

Turner, John C. 1982. "Towards a Cognitive Re-Definition of the Social Group." In Tajfel, ed. 1982:15–40.

Turner, John C. et al. 1987. *Rediscovering the Social Group: A Self-Categorization Theory*. Oxford: Blackwell.

Turner, Mark. 1987. *Death Is the Mother of Beauty: Mind, Metaphor, Criticism*. Chicago: University of Chicago Press.

———. 1996. *The Literary Mind*. New York: Oxford University Press.

VanderKam, James C. 1984. *Enoch and the Growth of an Apocalyptic Tradition*. Catholic Biblical Quarterly Monograph Series 16. Washington, DC: Catholic Biblical Association of America.

———. 2007. "Mapping Second Temple Judaism." In Boccaccini and Collins, ed. 2007: 1–20.

Vikman, Elisabeth. 2010. "Ancient Origins: Sexual Violence in Warfare, Part 1." *Anthropology and Medicine* 12:21–31.

Waterfield, Robin. 2010. *Polybius: The Histories*. Translated by Robin Waterfield with an introduction and notes by Brian McGing. Oxford World's Classics. Oxford: Oxford University Press.

———. 2012. *Dividing the Spoils: The War for Alexander the Great's Empire*. New York: Oxford University Press.

Weber, Max. 1991. "The Social Psychology of World Religions." In Gerth and Mills, ed. 1991:267–301.

Williams, Ronald J. 1990. "The Functions of the Sage in the Egyptian Royal Court." In Gammie and Perdue, eds. 1990:95–98.

Wills, Lawrence M. 1990. *The Jew in the Court of the Foreign King: Ancient Jewish Court Legends*. Minneapolis: Fortress.

Winterling, Aloys, ed. 1997. *Zwischen 'Haus' und 'Stadt': antike Höfe im Vergleich*. Historische Zeitschrift Beiheft 23. Munich: Oldenbourg.

Wintermute, O. S. 1985. "Jubilees." In Charlesworth, ed. 1985:35–142.

Worchel, Stephen J., Francisco Morales, Darío Páez, and Jean-Claude Deschamps, eds. 1998. *Social Identity: International Perspectives*. London: Sage.

Wright, Archie T. 2013. *The Origin of Evil Spirits: The Reception of Genesis 6:1–4 in Early Jewish Literature*. 2nd ed. WUNT 2/198. Tübingen: Mohr/Siebeck.

Wright, Benjamin G. III. 2002. "Sirach and 1 Enoch: Some Further Considerations." In Boccaccini, ed. 2002a:179–87.

Xeravits, Géza G., and József Zsengellér, eds. 2007. *The Books of the Maccabees: History, Theology, Ideology: Papers of the Second International Conference on the Deuterocanonical Works, Papa, Hungary, 9-11 June 2005*. JSJSup 155. Leiden: Brill.

Yadin, Yigael, Jonas C. Greenfield, Ada Yardeni, and Baruch A. Levine, eds. 2002. *The Documents from the Bar Kochba Period in the Cave of Letters: Hebrew, Aramaic and Nabatean-Aramaic Papyri*. Jerusalem: Israel Exploration Society, Institute of Archaeology, Hebrew University and Shrine of the Book, Israel Museum.

INDEX OF ANCIENT DOCUMENTS

OLD TESTAMENT

Genesis

5	181
5:18–24	189
5:21–24	156
5:23–24	199
5:23	135, 180
5:24	7, 63, 180, 194
6:1–4	9, 189
8:13	123
10:30	55
18:23–35	73
19:8	123
27:39	55

Exodus

12:40	55
15:1–2	73
15:17	84
26:31–35	130
30:9–10	70

Leviticus

16	70
19:33–34	16

Numbers

5:17	122
6:24–26	74
15:2	55

Deuteronomy

28:65	84

Joshua

10:13	84
15:33	121
14:43	121

Judges

5:18	122
9:6	84
11:30–32	73
16:5	122

1 Samuel

1:9–18	73

2 Samuel

9:12	55
22:7	32
30:21 (LXX)	75

1 Kings

6:2–3	115
6:2	137
6:3	115, 138
6:5–6	138
6:15	122
6:16	122
6:20	137
6:21	137

1 Kings (continued)

6:28–35	124
6:29	138
6:30	122
6:31	137
7:7	122
7:23–26	126, 138
7:38–39	126
8:22–29	73
8:30	55
8:64	138
10:5	85
22:19–23	28, 29

2 Kings

2:19	55

1 Chronicles

9:25	60
24	60
28:2	84
28:18	137

2 Chronicles

3:4–7	138
3:7	124
3:14	130, 137
6:21	55
9:4	85
23:13	85
24:13	84
29:25–30	63
29:27–28	63
30:16	84
35:10	84
35:15	84
36:22–34	137
36:22–33	143

Ezra

1	143
1:1–8	143
1:1–4	137
3:2–7	138
4	170
4:3	143
4:5	143
5:13–17	143
6:2	77
6:3	143
6:14	143
6:15–18	137
7:6	170
7:11	170
7:12	170
7:24	183
10	83
10:18	83
10:23	83

Nehemiah

2:2	48
8:1	170
8:7	85
8:13	170
9:3	85
13:13	170

Tobit

8:3	2
11:10–15	2
12:12	77
12:15	3

Esther

1:13–15	41
1:16–20	41
1:21–22	41

1 Maccabees

4:51	139
10:72	84

Job

1:6–12	28
2:1–6	28
9:8	122

Psalms

18:6	32
18:7–15	58
18:9	58
18:10	124

18:11	58	**Ezekiel**	
18:14	58	1	124, 134
29:3-9	58	1:4	124
29:9	32	1:5-23	134
46:6-11	58	1:12	124
46:7	58	1:26	134
46:9	58	1:27	133
46:11	58	10	134
46:15	58	10:1	133
46:17	58	10:2	134
65:10-14	58	10:6	134
68:14-21	58	10:9	134
77:54	84	10:11	134
82	28	40-48	82, 124
83:13-15	58	40:43	123
83:13-17	58	41:15-16	124
89:6-7	28	41:16	122
118:25	122	41:18-20	124, 199
144:4-7	58	41:20	122
144:5-6	58	44:13	69
		44:15	69
Sirach		45:4	69
3:21-23	173		
7:29-31	172	**Daniel**	
11:5	122	1:21	143
11:6	122	6:24 (Theodotion)	122
20:18	122	6:28	143
24	173	7-12	134
24:4-5	173	7	134
34:1-8	173	7:9	131, 134
35:1-11	173	8:17	85
36:10	122	10:1	143
43:6-8	173		
45:6-22	173	**Amos**	
50:1-21	173	9:3	122
50:27	175		
		Micah	
Isaiah		1:2	32
25:12	122		
26:5	122	**Habbakuk**	
29:4	122	2:20	32
44:28	143		
45:1	143	**Haggai**	
45:13	143	2:3	137
Jeremiah			
38:37	122		

Zechariah

4:10	3

Malachi

2:6–7	81
3:16	77

1 Enoch[1]

1–36	2, 3, 4, 6, 7, 8, 9, 10, 11, 12, 19, 21, 22, 26, 27, 28, 29, 30, 31, 32, 33, 34, 37, 53, 54, 55, 58, 62, 63, 65, 68, 71, 72, 73, 74, 75, 79, 82, 87, 89, 90, 95, 96, 98, 104, 107, 110, 111, 112, 113, 116, 121, 131, 132, 134, 136, 139, 151, 153, 155, 157, 164, 170, 171, 176, 178, 179, 181, 182, 188, 189, 190, 191, 193, 195, 197, 199, 200, 201
1:1—32:6a	7, 155
1–5	176
1:2—5:9	189
1:2	54, 65, 176
1:3–4	56, 57, 134
1:3	11, 54, 55, 60
1:4–9	3, 4, 11, 25, 56, 189
1:5	60
1:8	159
1:9	7, 57, 70, 113
6–19	10
6–16	10, 72
6–11	31, 86, 89, 176
6:1—9:4	7
6–8	22, 34, 79
6:1—7:5	89
6:1–7	11
6:1	95
6:2	59, 60
6:3	61, 95, 97, 98, 196
6:4–5	79, 96
6:5	60
6:7–8	61
6:7	61, 68
7:1—9:2	104
7–8	11
7:1	79, 100, 101
7:2–5	79
7:2	100
7:3–5	100
7:3	102
7:4	102
7:6	67, 72, 75, 80, 100, 102
8	67
8:1–3	80, 100, 101
8:1–2	80
8:1	101
8:2	101
8:3–4	80
8:4—10:14	7
8:4	67, 72, 80, 101
9–10	73
9	11, 28, 67, 69, 194
9:1–11	29, 89
9:1	59, 71, 72, 84
9:2	54, 59, 72, 116
9:3	75
9:4	53, 54
9:4–11	70
9:5	71
9:6	103, 197
9:9–10	104
9:10	72, 75, 116
9:11	71
10–11	11, 67
10:1—11:2	29
10	28, 61, 64, 197
10:1	54
10:4–6	105, 107
10:4–5	3, 57
10:7	60
10:8	176
10:9	59, 60
10:10	75, 76
10:11–13	105, 107
10:12	57
10:15	60
12–16	31, 67, 73, 82, 86, 89
12:1—13:3	11
12	177

---

1. 1 Enoch and Jubilees are included in the Old Testament references out of respect to the Orthodox Tewahedo Churches of Ethiopia and Eritrea among whom they are regarded as Old Testament scripture.

12:1-2	64	14:17	121, 123, 130
12:2	61	14:18-22	132
12:3-4	156, 177	14:18-20	25
12:3	54, 61, 64, 177	14:18-19	131
12:4—13:4	103	14:18	132, 133
12:4—13:2	177	14:20-23	131
12:4	54, 60, 65, 75, 83, 85, 96, 98, 103, 177, 182	14:20	11, 25, 54
		14:21-23	63, 68
12:6	76	14:21	28, 55, 61
13	73, 77	14:22	69, 133
13:1-2	76	14:23	61, 69, 83, 84
13:2	72	14:24—16:4	6
13:3	177	14:24	54, 128
13:4-5	76	14:25	128
13:4	72, 75, 77, 177	15-16	31
13:6	72, 75, 76, 77, 177	15:1—16:4	25, 104
13:7	72, 75, 76, 77, 178	15:1	156, 178, 182
13:8-10	178	15:2-4	76
13:8	174	15:2	61, 72, 73, 75, 76, 77, 178
13:10	61	15:3-7	97, 100, 104, 196
14-16	11, 82	15:3-4	83
14	6, 11, 25, 34, 55, 82, 111, 113, 116, 135, 139, 140, 141, 142, 151, 198, 200, 201	15:3	66, 98
		15:4	66, 82
		15:6-7	66
14:1-7	178	15:4-7	86, 87
14:1	54	15:7	60, 99
14:2	54	15:8—16:1	7
14:3	61, 8	15:8-12	67
14:4	72, 75, 76, 177	15:9	61
14:7	72, 78, 178	15:10	60
14:8-23	6, 110, 198	16:1	67
14:8	113, 198	16:2	61, 72, 75, 76, 178
14:9	11, 25, 114, 116, 117, 118, 119	17-36	11, 65, 107, 189
14:10-19	11	17-19	10
14:10-13	116	18:4	132
14:10-12	116, 118, 119, 126	18:14	54
14:10-11	130	19:1-2	107
14:10	55, 114, 118, 121, 122	19:3	65
14:11	124, 126	20	61, 62
14:12	124, 126	20:1-8	3, 30
14:13-14	127	20:1	3, 4, 59
14:13	55, 116, 118, 119, 127, 128, 199	20:3	3
		20:7	3
14:14-15	127	21:6	54
14:14	127, 128	21:10	107
14:15	55, 114, 117, 118, 127	22:5-7	72, 75
14:16-23	130	22:5	75
14:16	130	22:6	75

1 Enoch (continued)

22:7	75
22:14	54
24:1	121
24:3	54
25:2	65
25:3–4	107
25:3	53, 135
25:5	53
25:7	54
27:3	54
27:5	54
32	173
32:3	174
33	178
33:2–3	178
33:3	65
33:4	178
34:1—36:2	59, 116
35:1	116
36:1	116
36:2–3	107
36:4	54
37–71	154, 155, 156
37:1	155
39:2	156
68:1	156
69:8–10	156
72–82	7, 8, 154, 155, 173, 177, 188
72:1	155, 156, 178
72:2–37	135
72:32	180, 199
72:4	133
73:2	133
74:2	156
80:1	155
81:6	156
81:7	159
82:1	156
82:2	159, 174
82:3b	173
82:10	58
83–90	154
83–84	154, 155
83:2	156
83:10	156
84:6	182
84:2	53
85–90	154
85:1–2	155
89:39	25
89:50	25
89:54	25
89:66	25
89:72	25
89:76	156
90:14	156
90:17	156
90:22	156
91:1–10	154, 155, 156
91:3	155, 181
91:11–17	154, 155
91:18–19	154, 155, 156
91:19	182
92–105	154, 155, 182
92:1	155, 156, 182
93:1–10	154, 155
93:1	155
93:2	181, 182
93:3	155
93:8	185
93:9–10	186
102:3	25
103:2a	174
104:9–13	174, 176, 203
104:9	174
104:10	175
104:10a	175
104:11	175
104:12	175
104:12a	174
104:13	175
106–107	154, 155
106:13	155
106:19	156
107:1	156, 182
108	154, 155
108:1	155, 156
108:14	182

Jubilees

4:15	81
4:16–26	25
4:17	156

NEW TESTAMENT

Matthew
8:8	123
21:43	18
25:24	75

Mark
2:4	123

Luke
7:6	123
7:36	75
8:37	123
19:44	121

John
16:26	75

Acts
9:25	114

2 Corinthians
11:33	114

Galatians
3	18

Jude
14–15	7

JUDEAN APOCRYPHA

1 Esdras
1:21	55
2	143
6:4	123
8	183
8:22	183

3 Maccabees
1:29	122
2:22	122
6:37	75

4 Maccabees
6:7	122
17:3	123

JUDEAN PSEUDEPIGRAPHA

Testament of Levi
2.5–7	25
2.6–5.4	4
2.7–8	25
3	112
3.1–8	25
3.4	25, 26
3.5–6	26
5.1	25, 26
5.2	25, 26
8.2–10	26
9.7	26
9.10	26
10.5	25
14.1	25
18.6	25

JOSEPHUS

Judean Antiquities
7.14.7 §367	70
8.3 §§61–98	137
11.120–138	183
11.128	183
12.138–144	183
12.142	183
13.372–383	106

Judean War
5.5.4—5.5.5 §§211–219	139
5.5.5 §221	130
5.207	115
5.207–219	115

MISHNAH

Middot
4:5	130
4:7	115

PHILO

De virtutibus
51–174	16
65	17
102–103	16–17

QUMRAN

Songs of the Sabbath Sacrifice
1QapGen 19.24–8	156
1QSb 4.24–27	81
4Q203.8	156
4Q400 frag.1, col. 1	23
4Q403 I, 40–45	24
4Q403, frags. 14–15	24
4Q405, frags. 20–22	24, 124
4Q405, frag. 23, col. 1	24
4Q405, col. 4	24

BABYLONIAN TALMUD

Hagigah
12b	112

GREEK AUTHORS

Aeschylus

Prometheus Bound
4	102
10	102
10–11	103
40	103
96	102
120–122	103
122	103
149	103
153–159	107
170	102
202–203	102
216–218	103
221	102
305	102
310	102
389	103
403	103
542–544	103
756	102
956	102
969	102
996	102

Aristotle

De Mundo
398a	47

Diodorus Siculus

Bibliotheca historica
1.55.7	54

Herodotus

Histories
1.99	47
1.100	48
3.31	40
3.119.2	45
8.137	121

Plutarch

Agesilaus
24	78

Life of Artaxerxes
3.1	142

Polybius

The Histories
4.76	94
4.76.9	75
5.2	94
5.26	45, 94

5.28	94	**BEHISTUN INSCRIPTION**	
5.34–39	94	**OF DARIUS I**	
5.39	93		
5.40	94	Line 1	53
5.40–41	93	11	92
5.54	94	13	41, 91, 102
5.57	95	14	102
5.72–78	95	16–20	91
6.3–10	54	16	92
		19	56

Strabo

Geography

		21–25	91
		22	92
		24–25	41
15.3.8	142	24	91, 92
		26–30	92

Xenophon

Cyropaedia

		31–32	92
		33–34	92
		33	91, 92, 104
8.4.3–5	40	35	92
		38–39	92

The Education of Cyrus

		38	41–42, 92
7.5.37–41	47	40	91, 92
		49–50	41
		49	92
		68	41

INDEX OF AUTHORS

Abrams, Dominic, 161, 205
Albertz, Rainer, 90, 205
Allison, Dale C., 212
Antohin, Alexandra Sellassie, 1, 205
Aperghis, G. G., 185, 205
Argall, Randal A., 73, 164, 172, 173, 174, 205
Arnal, William E., 167, 205
Arnaud, D., 168, 205
Artan, Tulay, 208
Aster, Shawn Zelig, 133, 205
Atzmon, Gil, 18, 205
Austin, William G., 205
Avigad, N., 60, 205

Bagnall, Roger S., 184, 205
Baker, Coleman A., 216
Balcer, Jack Martin, 49, 205
Barclay, John M. G. 161, 205
Barnard, Alan, 205
Bar-Tal, Daniel, 161, 206
Barth, Fredrik, 13, 14, 206
Barton, Carlin A., 15, 206
Barton, John, 206
Bautch, Kelley Coblentz, 210
Berger, Peter, 30, 206
Bezold, Carl, 208
Black, Matthew, 22, 53, 64, 69, 84, 118, 119, 124, 127, 128, 130, 132, 179, 180, 206
Black, Max, 19, 32, 206
Boccaccini, Gabriele, 7, 73, 206
Bock, Darrell J., 207
Bonner, C., 8, 205
Botha, Pieter J. J., 165, 166, 206

Boucharlat, Rémy, 142, 145, 206
Bourriaud, Nicolas, 2, 206
Boyarin, Daniel, 15, 206
Brands, Gunnar, 36, 206
Brosius, Maria, 40, 45, 46, 47, 48, 52, 92, 93, 141, 144, 145, 146, 147, 148, 149, 150, 206
Brown, Rupert, 160, 161, 162, 206
Butz, Reinhardt, 38, 206
Byron, Reginald, 13, 206

Cartledge, Paul, 207
Charles, R. H., 24, 26, 68, 118, 122, 123, 128, 131, 132, 207
Charlesworth, James H., 8, 23, 207
Clifford, Richard J., 28, 126, 207
Cohen, Yoram, 167, 168, 169, 170, 171, 180, 207
Collins, John J., 7, 9, 10, 22, 158, 207
Crook, Zeba A., 210
Crossan, John Dominic
Czajkowski, Kimberley, 167, 207

Daly-Denton, Margaret, 214
Dannenberg, L.-A., 38, 206
Day, John, 28, 208
Deignan, Alice, 20, 208
Derham, Crysta, 209
Deschamps, Jean-Claude, 216
Dexinger, F. 1977, 208
Dillmann, August, 208
Douglas, Mary, 82, 100, 194, 197, 208
Dubovsky, Peter, 49, 208
Duindam, J., 208
Dunn, James D., 12, 208

Dvornik, Francis, 49, 208

Egmond, W. S. van, 208
Elias, Norbert, 36, 37, 38, 39, 44, 45, 46, 48, 49, 51, 52, 68, 88, 92, 98, 99, 104, 192, 193, 208
Endres, John C., 210
Erho, Ted M., 8, 208
Erikson, E. H., 13, 208
Esler, Philip F., 8, 10, 16, 33, 160, 167, 181, 208–9

Falk, Daniel K., 23, 209
Fischer, Ronald, 209
Fitzmyer, Joseph A., 3, 209
Flemming, Johann, 7, 8, 209
Fletcher-Louis, Crispin H. T., 22, 80, 115, 209

Gammie, John G., 42, 43, 209
García Martínez, Florentino, 23, 24, 209
Garnsey, Peter, 207
Gemünden, Petra von, 209
Gershevitch, Ilya, 209
Gerth, H. H., 30, 209
Gibson, J. C. L., 28, 209
Grainger, John D., 209
Greenfield, Jonas C., 217
Gruen, Eric, 207, 210
Gurtner, Daniel M., 210

Haerinck, Ernie, 213
Hagedorn, Anselm C., 210
Halperin, David J., 22, 210
Handy, Lowell K., 27, 28, 30, 31, 191, 210
Hanson, Paul D., 9, 10, 210
Haran, Menahem, 138, 210
Harkins, Angela Kim, 210
Harland, Philip A., 18, 210
Hazirlayan, Yayma, 210
Heermann, Vera, 36, 210
Herman, Gabriel, 36, 37, 38, 50, 51, 93, 210
Himmelfarb, Martha, 10, 22, 24, 31, 32, 73, 80, 85, 86, 87, 88, 114, 115, 116, 117, 195, 210

Hoepfner, Wolfram, 36, 206
Hogg, Michael A., 161, 163, 210
Hollander, H. W., 210
Hopkins, Nick, 163, 214
Horrell, D. G., 18, 210
Horsley, Richard A., 33, 167, 174, 210
Hundley, Michael B., 61, 110, 111, 115, 211
Hunt, A. S., 77, 78, 211
Hutchinson, John, 14, 211

Isaac, E., 8, 123, 131, 177, 211

Johnson, Mark, 19, 20, 21, 190, 212
Jonge, Marinus de, 23, 210
Joyce, Paul M., 211

Kampen, John, 22, 211
Kee, Howard Clark, 24, 26, 211
Kee, Min Suc, 27, 211
Keel, Othmar, 126, 211
King, L. W., 15, 41, 42, 53, 56, 91, 102, 105, 211
Klauck, Hans-Josef, 211
Klingbeil, Martin, 58, 211
Kloppenborg, John S., 18, 211
Kövecses, Zoltán, 20, 211
Küchler, Max, 209
Kugler, Robert A., 4, 24, 25, 211
Kuhrt, Amélie, 47, 211
Kunt, Metin, 208
Kutbay, Boney Lea, 36, 141, 212
Kvanvig, Helge S., 22, 73, 115, 157, 159, 212

Ladd, George A., 54, 212
Lakoff, George, 19, 20, 21, 190, 212
Laurence, Richard, 131, 212
Leslau, Wolf, 122, 123, 132, 133, 212
Levine, Amy-Jill, 212
Levine, Baruch A., 217
Lisowsky, Gerhard, 122, 212
Lods, Adolphe, 124, 212
Lynn, J., 41, 212

Macaskill, Grant, 210
Malina, Bruce J., 14, 212
Mason, Steve, 12, 16, 18, 212

Index of Authors

McConville, J. Gordon, 212
McGowan, Andrew B., 212
McKinley, Anne Fitzpatrick, 214
Meissner, Burkhard, 50, 213
Meyer, Leon de, 213
Michalak, Aleksander, 2, 213
Milik, J. T., 7, 8, 55, 57, 101, 104, 113, 114, 119, 121, 131, 179, 213
Milligan, George, 213
Mills, C. Wright, 30, 209, 213
Morales, Francisco, 216
Muddiman, John, 206
Mullen, E. Theodore, Jr., 28, 31, 213

Netzer, Ehud, 36, 213
Neugebauer, Otto, 179
Newsom, Carol A., 9, 23, 62, 63, 112, 113, 114, 124, 130, 134, 213
Nickelsburg, George W. E., 7, 9, 10, 22, 25, 31, 53, 54, 55, 56, 57, 59, 61, 62, 64, 65, 66, 68, 69, 70, 71, 73, 77, 80, 82, 83, 84, 85, 86, 88, 89, 90, 98, 101, 114, 118, 119, 123, 126, 127, 128, 130, 131, 133, 135, 154, 157, 158, 174, 175, 176, 177, 178, 186, 195, 213
Nielsen, Inge, 36, 141, 149, 213
Nongbri, Brent, 15, 213

Orton, David E., 213
Orlov, Andrei A., 22, 115, 213
Otto, Rudolf, 127, 213

Páez, Darío, 216
Palme, Bernhard, 77, 213
Parker, Bradley J., 37, 49, 54, 213
Parpola, Simo, 42, 214
Pearce, Laurie E., 143, 214
Pennington, Jonathan T., 210
Perdue, Leo G., 42, 209
Pietersen, Lloyd K., 212
Plöger, Otto, 158, 214
Portier-Young, Anathea, 33, 90, 214

Raphael, Melissa, 127, 214
Reicher, Stephen, 163, 214
Reid, Scott A., 161, 163, 210
Richards, Kent Harold, 212

Rietz, Henry M., 213
Rodgers, Zuleika, 214
Rom-Shiloni, Dalit, 211
Rowlands, Guy, 41, 214
Russell, James R., 42, 214

Savalli-Lestrade, Ivana, 50, 214
Schäfer, Peter, 109, 115, 214
Schubert, Paul, 77, 214
Schams, Christine, 167, 170, 183, 184, 214
Selincourt, Aubrey de, 48, 214
Smith, Anthony, 14, 211
Smith, Dennis, 36, 214
Smith, Eliot R., 162, 214
Smith, Mark S., 27, 28, 214
Smith, William Cantwell, 14, 15, 214
Sokoloff, Michael, 59, 214
Soldt, W. H. van, 208
Soskice, Janet Martin, 19, 214
Sommerstein, Alan H., 214
Spawforth, A. J. S., 36, 38, 39, 40, 46, 93, 215
Spencer, Jonathan, 205
Stewart, Eric C., 210
Stone, Michael E., 157, 215
Strawn, Brent A., 213
Stronach, David, 142, 145, 146, 147, 148, 149, 150, 151, 215
Strong, John T., 126, 134, 215
Strootman, Rolf, 35, 36, 37, 43, 50, 51, 93, 94, 215
Stuckenbruck, Loren T., 2, 7, 8, 131, 154, 155, 156, 177, 208, 215
Süel, Aygül, 210
Suter, David W., 10, 22, 72, 73, 80, 81, 82, 83, 84, 85, 86, 87, 88, 118, 195, 215
Sweet, Ronald F. G., 42, 215

Tajfel, Henri, 13, 160, 161, 162, 201, 215
Theissen, Gerd, 165, 216
Thompson, R. C., 15, 41, 42, 53, 56, 91, 102, 105, 211
Tiller, Patrick A., 158, 159, 174, 216
Toorn, Karel van der, 166, 171, 184, 215

Index of Authors

Torrance, Isabelle C., 214
Tov, Emanuel, 167, 216
Tucker, Brian, 216
Turner, John C., 13, 160, 161, 162, 163, 201, 216
Turner, Mark, 21, 216

VanderKam, James C., 8, 62, 66, 101, 123, 131, 133, 153, 154, 156, 158, 159, 165, 179 180, 186, 216
Vikman, Elisabeth, 101, 216

Waterfield, Robin, 45, 90, 216
Weber, Max, 30, 216
Williams, Ronald J., 42, 216
Wills, Lawrence M., 43, 44, 216

Winter, Dagmar, 165, 216
Winterling, Aloys, 36, 216
Wintermute, O. S., 25, 216
Worchel, Stephen J., 216
Wright, Archie T., 9, 82, 216
Wright, Benjamin G. III, 173, 174, 216
Wunsch, Cornelia, 143, 214, 216

Xeravits, Géza G., 217

Yadin, Yigael, 167, 217
Yardeni, Ada, 217
Youtie, H. C., 8, 206

Zarate, Michael A., 162, 214
Zsengellér, József, 217

www.ingramcontent.com/pod-product-compliance
Lightning Source LLC
Chambersburg PA
CBHW032057230426
43662CB00035B/583